Reasoning about Rational Agents

Reasoning about Rational Agents

Michael Wooldridge

The MIT Press
Cambridge, Massachusetts
London, England

This book was set in Times Roman by the author using the LaTeX document preparation system and printed and bound in the United States of America.

Library of Congress Cataloging-in-Publication Data

Wooldridge, Michael J., 1966–
  Reasoning about rational agents / Michael Wooldridge.
    p. cm.—(Intelligent robots and autonomous agents)
  Includes bibliographical references and index.
  ISBN 0–262–23213–8 (hc: alk. paper)
  1. Intelligent agents (Computer software). I. Title. II. Series.
QA76.76I58W66   2000
006.3—dc21   00-035474
                                              CIP

10 9 8 7 6 5 4 3

To Janine

Contents

Preface

This book is about a certain class of computer systems that are known as *agents*, and more specifically, *rational agents*. We call these computer systems *agents* because they are capable of *independent, autonomous action* in order to meet their design objectives: put crudely, they are capable of *deciding for themselves* what to do in any given situation. We call them *rational* agents because they make *good* decisions about what to do.

Engineering rational agents may at first sight appear to be a somewhat abstract, even fanciful endeavor, divorced from the everyday reality of computer science and software engineering. This is not the case. Rational agents are finding a wide range of applications. A famous example is NASA's Deep Space 1 (DS1) mission. Launched from Cape Canaveral on 24 October 1998, DS1 was the first space probe to have an autonomous, agent-based control system [165]. Before DS1, space missions required a ground crew of up to 300 staff to continually monitor progress. This ground crew made all necessary control decisions on behalf of the probe, and painstakingly transmitted these decisions to the probe for subsequent execution. Given the length of typical planetary exploration missions, such a procedure was expensive and, if the decisions were ever required *quickly*, it was simply not practical. The autonomous control system in DS1 was capable of making many important decisions itself. This made the mission more robust, particularly against sudden unexpected problems, and also had the very desirable side effect of reducing overall mission costs. The DS1 example may seem somewhat extreme: after all, spacecraft control systems are hardly an everyday software engineering problem. But the same technology is finding applications in much more commonplace domains. For example, such agents are increasingly being used for Internet-based electronic commerce applications, where they autonomously buy and sell goods on behalf of a user [168].

As it turns out, for all but the simplest of applications, it is very difficult to build computer systems that can autonomously make good decisions about what to do. For sure, there are a number of very powerful mathematical frameworks available, which can help us to understand and analyze many decision-making scenarios. *Decision theory* is an obvious example. Decision theory tells us that a rational agent is one that chooses an action which maximizes expected utility, where expected utility is defined in terms of the actions available to the agent, the probability of certain outcomes, and the preferences the agent has with respect to these outcomes. In multiagent scenarios, where an agent is required to interact with other agents, *game theory* has proved to be a powerful predictive and analytic tool. However, valuable and important though tools such as decision theory and game theory are, they give us few clues with respect to *implementing* rational agents.

This book focuses on a model of rational decision making as *practical reasoning*, of the kind that humans engage in every day. The model is called the *belief-desire-intention* (BDI) model, because it acknowledges the primacy of beliefs, desires, and, crucially, intentions, in the practical reasoning process. The BDI model is particularly interesting because it combines three distinct components:

- A *philosophical* component.

The BDI model is based on a widely respected theory of rational action in humans, developed by the philosopher Michael Bratman [20].

- A *software architecture* component.

The BDI model of agency does not prescribe a specific implementation. The model may be realized in many different ways, and indeed a number of different implementations of it have been developed. However, the fact that the BDI model *has* been implemented successfully is a significant point in its favor. Moreover, the BDI model has been used to build a number of significant real-world applications, including such demanding problems as fault diagnosis on the space shuttle.

- A *logical* component.

The third component of the BDI model is a family of logics. These logics capture the key aspects of the BDI model as a set of logical axioms. There are many candidates for a formal theory of rational agency, but BDI logics in various forms have proved to be among the most useful, longest-lived, and widely accepted.

The emphasis in this book is primarily on the logical foundations of BDI systems. BDI logics were developed by Anand Rao and Michael Georgeff, in order to give an abstract, idealized semantics to the BDI agents they were building throughout the early 1990s at the Australian AI Institute [80]. Building on the work of researchers in both theoretical computer science and artificial intelligence, they were able to demonstrate how a particular type of *multi-modal* logic could be used to capture many aspects of Bratman's BDI theory.

In this book, I build upon and significantly extend the basic logical framework of Rao and Georgeff. I begin by introducing the concept of an agent, and give some basic background both to the philosophical foundations and software design of BDI agents. After introducing the basic BDI model, I present

$\mathcal{LORA}$, the formal framework that will be used throughout the remainder of the book. $\mathcal{LORA}$ — which stands for "$\mathcal{L}$ogic $\mathcal{O}$f $\mathcal{R}$ational $\mathcal{A}$gents" — is a BDI logic, which extends Rao and Georgeff's original formalism. $\mathcal{LORA}$ allows us to represent and reason about the beliefs, desires, intentions, and actions of agents within a system, and how these beliefs, desires, intentions, and actions change over time.

Once the basic logical framework is introduced, the remainder of the book is taken up largely with an investigation of how it can be used to capture a range of important aspects of rational agency. These aspects can be divided into those that relate to *individual agents* and those that relate to *multiple* agents. With respect to individual agents, I show how $\mathcal{LORA}$ can be used to capture many of our intuitions about the relationships among beliefs, desires, and intentions, as well as other concepts such as ability. The major contribution of the book comes from the focus on multiagent aspects. Specifically, I show how $\mathcal{LORA}$ can be used to capture:

- mutual mental states and the closely related notion of teamwork;
- communication between agents, in the form of speech acts; and
- cooperative problem solving, whereby a group of agents collaborate to achieve some task.

There is some tension between the desire to write a book that is rigorous from the perspective of mathematical logic, and the desire to write a book that is readable. Logical rigor all too often seems to preclude readability: the level of detail required to pass muster with logicians can be daunting to the uninitiated. In the event, I have done my best to compromise. Thus, as well as giving formal definitions and complete proofs of all results, I have tried wherever possible to explain at length the intuition behind the formalism, and to give extensive pointers to further reading. Those sections that contain a significant proportion of abstract mathematical material are separated out from the main text, and indicated in the relevant section header by means of an asterisk ("*").

BDI is probably the most-implemented framework for building rational agents. I hope that after reading this book, you will understand why so many researchers believe it represents a powerful framework through which to understand, implement, and reason about rational agency.

Acknowledgments

First, thanks to my colleagues from London, Manchester, Liverpool, and elsewhere, who have provided me with a friendly and supportive environment in which to work over the years. In particular, I would like to thank Innes Ferguson, Michael Fisher, Afsaneh Haddadi, Nick Jennings, Alessio Lomuscio, Jörg Müller, and Simon Parsons, all of whom I have had the pleasure of working with closely.

Mike Georgeff and Anand Rao have both been generous in their encouragement of my research over the years. As well as owing an obvious intellectual debt to them, this book has also therefore benefited from their experience in less obvious, but no less important ways.

Many other colleagues from the international academic community have helped to shape my ideas both about multiagent systems and about the academic profession in general. I should at least thank Cristiano Castelfranchi, Keith Decker, Ed Durfee, Dov Gabbay, Wiebe van der Hoek, Michael Huhns, Mark d'Inverno, Sarit Kraus, Yves Lespérance, Mike Luck, John-Jules Meyer, Carles Sierra, Munindar Singh, Katia Sycara, Milind Tambe, and Gerhard Weiß. (If I missed anyone . . . you know who you are!)

I started work on this book while on a short sabbatical at the University of Melbourne in Australia. I would like to thank Leon Sterling for the opportunity to visit his Department, and for the warm reception and hospitality I received throughout my stay. Thanks also to Liz Sonenberg and David Kinny for their support — David in particular for showing me around and making me welcome.

When I first conceived this book, I was employed at Queen Mary and Westfield College, University of London; thanks to David Olver and Laurie Cuthbert for their support while at QMW.

Bob Prior at MIT Press has been a source of encouragement and good humor throughout the writing of this book, for which I am very grateful. In addition to Bob, I would like to thank Katherine Innis and Deborah Cantor-Adams from MITP for their help and feedback.

Thanks to all those who read and commented on drafts of this book, sometimes when those drafts should perhaps not have seen the light of day: Trevor Bench-Capon, Rogier van Eijk, Peter McBurney, Simon Parsons, and Martijn Schut.

Finally, to my wife Janine, who means everything to me: thank you.

Michael Wooldridge
Liverpool, Spring 2000

Reasoning about Rational Agents

1 Rational Agents

The world we inhabit is full of agents. We encounter them every day, as we go about our lives. By the term "agent," I mean an entity that acts upon the environment it inhabits. Agents are not merely observers of their environment, nor are they the passive recipients of actions performed by other entities. Rather, agents are the active, purposeful originators of action. These actions are performed in order to modify and shape the environment inhabited by the agent. People like you and I are the most obvious examples of agents in the real world, but there are many others, such as legal entities like governments, companies, and corporations.

In our dealings with the world, we often make a distinction between agents that are *rational* and those that are not, in the following sense. An agent is said to be rational if it chooses to perform actions that are in its own best interests, given the beliefs it has about the world. For example, if I have a goal of staying dry, and I believe it is raining, then it is rational of me to take an umbrella when I leave my house. Taking the umbrella will enable me to satisfy my goal of staying dry, and in this sense, it is in my best interest. You would still be inclined to refer to my behavior as rational even if I was mistaken in my belief that it was raining: the point is that I made a decision that, if my beliefs were correct, would have achieved one of my goals.

In one sense, human agents are notoriously *irrational* when they make decisions. From time to time, we all make decisions that, with the benefit of hindsight, are self-evidently poor. When evaluated against strict metrics of rationality, humans rarely perform well. But this paints a misleading picture. The fact is that, overall, humans are very *good* decision makers. We inhabit a continuously changing physical world of extraordinary richness, complexity, and diversity. Our plans are constantly thwarted, both by random quirks of nature and, occasionally, by the deliberately malicious intervention of our peers. We are forced to make decisions for which we are ill prepared, both in terms of prior experience and in terms of the information upon which to base decisions. And yet, despite all this, we prosper. As decision makers, we seem to be quite robust to the vagaries of our environment. We successfully interact with our peers even when they are in conflict with us, and we cope with uncertainty about the world, failed actions and plans, and the complexity of our environment.

One goal of the artificial intelligence (AI) community is to engineer computer programs that can act as autonomous, rational agents. We wish to build computer programs that can *independently* make good decisions about what actions to perform. But it is not enough to have programs that *think* of a good action to perform — we wish to have them actually *execute* these actions. In other words, we want to create rational agents that are *embodied* in some environment — that inhabit and act upon some environment in the same way that we inhabit and act upon ours.

Ideally, we would like to engineer agents that are as good at making decisions and acting upon them as we are. Of course, this goal is a long way from being achieved. Unfortunately, like so many other problems encountered throughout the history of AI, it has proven extraordinarily difficult to engineer agents that can select and execute good decisions for moderately complex environments. Nor is the problem likely to be solved in any meaningful sense for some time yet.

1.1 Properties of Rational Agents

In order to understand why it is hard to engineer a rational agent, let us consider what sorts of properties we expect a rational agent to exhibit. First, it is important to understand that we usually consider agents to be systems that are *situated* or *embodied* in some environment — agents are not *disembodied* systems. By this, I mean that agents are capable of *sensing* their environment and have a repertoire of possible *actions* that they can perform in order to modify the environment. This leads to the view of an agent as shown in Figure 1.1. The requirement that agents must be embodied implies that many of the systems that have been developed to date within AI do not count as agents. Examples include most theorem provers and expert systems.

The environment that an agent occupies may be physical (in the case of robots inhabiting the physical world) or a software environment (in the case of a software agent inhabiting a computer operating system or network). In the case of a physically embodied agent, actions will be physical, such as moving objects around. The sensor input received by the agent will be comprised of video feeds and the like. In the case of a software agent, actions will be software commands (such as the UNIX rm command, which removes a file), and sensor input will be obtained by performing commands such as ls (which obtains a directory listing) [53].

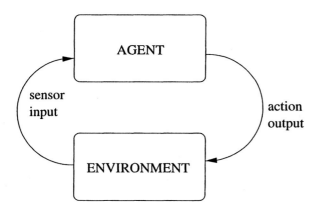

Figure 1.1
Agents and their environments. The agent takes sensory input from the environment, and produces as output actions that affect it.

Note that in almost all realistic applications, agents have at best *partial* control over their environment. Thus, while they can perform actions that change their environment, they cannot in general *completely* control it. It therefore makes sense to divide the environment, conceptually at least, into those parts that the agent *controls*, those parts it *partially controls*, and those parts over which it has *no control*. (If we regard an agent's internal state as being part of the environment, then this would be controlled by the agent.)

Apart from being situated in an environment, what other properties do we expect a rational agent to have? Wooldridge and Jennings [249] argue that agents should have the following properties:

- autonomy;
- proactiveness;
- reactivity; and
- social ability.

At its simplest, autonomy means nothing more than being able to operate independently. Thus, at the very least, an autonomous agent makes independent decisions — its decisions (and hence its actions) are under its own control, and are not driven by others. Autonomous agents are therefore the loci of decision making. However, autonomy is usually taken to have a slightly stronger meaning than this. We generally assume that an autonomous agent is one that has its own beliefs, desires, and intentions, which are not subservient to those of other agents. This is not to say that these beliefs, desires, and intentions are necessarily *represented* within an agent — the point is that we regard a rational agent as "having its own agenda," which may or may not concur with that of other agents.

Proactiveness means being able to exhibit goal-directed behavior. If an agent has a particular goal or intention, then we expect the agent to try to *achieve* this intention. For example, if I have an intention to write a book, then it is rational of me to actually *act towards* this intention, by eventually putting pen to paper. Moreover, proactiveness means *exploiting serendipity*. For example, if I have a desire to become rich, and an opportunity to make a fortune arises, then it is only rational of me to try to exploit this opportunity, perhaps by generating a new goal. Proactiveness rules out entirely passive agents, who never try to do anything.

Being reactive means being responsive to changes in the environment. As I noted above, in everyday life, our plans rarely run smoothly. They are frequently thwarted, both by the vagaries of nature and by other agents fouling them up. When we become aware that our plans have gone awry, we do not ignore this fact. We respond, by choosing an alternative course of action. Responses may be of the "stimulus → response" style, or they may involve further deliberation. For example, if I am driving my car and I realize I am about to crash into something, I will swerve to avoid it. It is unlikely that this kind of response involves much deliberation on my part; the behavior seems to be "hardwired." In contrast, if I am traveling to Heathrow Airport for a 9.30 AM flight, and I discover that the train I was about to catch is not running, I will actively deliberate in order to fix upon a course of action that will still enable me to catch my flight. This deliberation typically involves at least some reasoning about the alternatives available (catching a taxi or bus, for example). Crucially, however, I fix upon an alternative sufficiently quickly that it will deliver me to the airport in time — I will not deliberate for so long that it becomes impossible to catch the flight.

Designing a *purely* reactive system, which simply responds to environmental stimuli, is not hard. We can implement such a system as a lookup table, which simply maps environment states directly to actions. Similarly, developing a purely goal-driven system is not hard. (After all, this is ultimately what conventional computer programs are.) However, implementing a system that achieves an effective *balance* between goal-directed and reactive behavior turns out to be very hard. We elaborate on this problem in the next chapter.

Finally, let us say something about *social ability*. In one sense, social ability is trivial. After all, every day, millions of computers across the world routinely exchange information with both humans and other computers. But the ability to exchange bit streams is not really social ability. Consider that, in the human world, comparatively few of our goals can be achieved without interaction with other people and organizations, who cannot be assumed to share our goals. These agents are themselves autonomous, with their own agendas to pursue. To achieve our goals in such situations, we must *negotiate* and *cooperate* with these agents. We may be required to understand and reason about their beliefs and goals, and to perform actions (such as paying them money) that we would not otherwise choose to perform, in order to get them to cooperate with us, and achieve our goals. This type of social ability — the ability to interact (through negotiation and cooperation) with other self-interested agents — is much more complex and much less understood than simply the ability to exchange bit streams. In the later chapters of this book, I focus on such interactions in detail.

1.2   A Software Engineering Perspective

It is important to understand that the engineering of rational agents is not simply an abstract intellectual pursuit. It arises as a result of problems faced by software engineers across the world at the start of the new millennium.

Originally, software engineering concerned itself primarily with what are known as "functional" systems. A functional system is one that simply takes some input, performs some computation over this input, and eventually produces some output. Such systems may formally be viewed as functions f : $I \rightarrow O$ from a set I of inputs to a set O of outputs. The classic example of such a system is a compiler, which can be viewed as a mapping from a set I of legal source programs to a set O of corresponding object or machine code programs. Although the internal complexity of a functional system may be great (e.g., in the case of a compiler for a complex programming language such as ADA), functional programs are, in general, comparatively simple to engineer correctly and efficiently. Unfortunately, many of the computer systems that we desire to build are not functional in the sense we describe here. Rather than simply computing a function of some input and then terminating, such systems are *reactive*, in the following sense:[1]

---

1 There are at least three current usages of the term "reactive system" in computer science. The

Reactive systems are systems that cannot adequately be described by the *relational* or *functional* view. The relational view regards programs as functions ... from an initial state to a terminal state. Typically, the main role of reactive systems is to maintain an interaction with their environment, and therefore must be described (and specified) in terms of their on-going behavior ... [E]very concurrent system ... must be studied by behavioral means. This is because each individual module in a concurrent system is a reactive subsystem, interacting with its own environment which consists of the other modules. [177]

Pnuelian reactive systems have long been recognized to be harder to engineer correctly and efficiently than functional systems. Indeed, Pnuelian reactive systems form a major research theme in their own right within mainstream computer science [11, 144, 145].

It should be clear that all agents (in the sense that I describe them) are Pnuelian reactive systems, although of course not all Pnuelian reactive systems are agents. Researchers and developers throughout many subfields of computer science are beginning to recognize that agents represent an important new way of thinking about and designing Pnuelian reactive systems in particular, and distributed computer systems in general. There are several reasons for this. First, we delegate increasingly sophisticated and complex activities to computers, where we require them to act independently on our behalf. Agents are a very natural metaphor for thinking about such systems. Second, agents reflect an important ongoing trend in computer science toward the understanding that interacting systems are the norm, rather than the exception. The rapid growth of the Internet is the most obvious public sign of the change in emphasis towards interacting, distributed systems. Interaction is a fundamental research issue in the agent community. Of particular interest are systems that can *cooperate* and *negotiate* with each other. As the Internet continues to grow in importance over the coming decades, the ability of computer systems to autonomously cooperate and negotiate will provide enormous opportunities in such areas as electronic commerce [168].

---

first, oldest usage is that by Pnueli and followers (see, e.g., [177], and the description above). Second, researchers in AI planning take a reactive system to be one that is capable of responding rapidly to changes in its environment — here the word "reactive" is taken to be synonymous with "responsive" (see, e.g., [112]). More recently, the term has been used to denote systems that respond directly to their environment, rather than reason explicitly about it (see, e.g., [40]). I use the adjective "Pnuelian" when referring to reactive systems in the sense that Pnueli describes.

1.3 Belief-Desire-Intention Agents

In this book, I focus on the *belief-desire-intention* (BDI) model of rational agency [22]. The BDI model gets its name from the fact that it recognizes the primacy of beliefs, desires, and intentions in rational action.

Intuitively, an agent's *beliefs* correspond to information the agent has about the world. These beliefs may be incomplete or incorrect. An agent's *desires* represent states of affairs that the agent would, in an ideal world, wish to be brought about. (Implemented BDI agents require that desires be *consistent* with one another, although *human* desires often fail in this respect.) Finally, an agent's *intentions* represent desires that it has *committed* to achieving. The intuition is that an agent will not, in general, be able to achieve *all* its desires, even if these desires *are* consistent. Ultimately, an agent must therefore fix upon some subset of its desires and commit resources to achieving them. These chosen desires, to which the agent has some commitment, are intentions [35].

What makes the BDI model particularly compelling is that it combines three important elements:

1. It is founded upon a well-known and highly respected theory of rational action in humans.

2. It has been implemented and successfully used in a number of complex fielded applications.

3. The theory has been rigorously formalized in a family of BDI *logics*.

The BDI theory of human rational action was originally developed by Michael Bratman [20]. It is a theory of *practical reasoning* — the process of reasoning that we all go through in our everyday lives, deciding moment by moment which action to perform next. Bratman's theory focuses in particular on the role that *intentions* play in practical reasoning. Bratman argues that intentions are important because they constrain the reasoning an agent is required to do in order to select an action to perform. For example, suppose I have an intention to write a book. Then while deciding what to do, I need not expend any effort considering actions that are incompatible with this intention (such as having a summer holiday, or enjoying a social life). This reduction in the number of possibilities I have to consider makes my decision making considerably simpler than would otherwise be the case. Since any real agent we might care to consider — and in particular, any agent that we can implement on a computer — must have resource bounds, an intention-based model of agency, which constrains decision-making in the manner described, seems attractive.

The BDI model has been implemented several times. Originally, it was realized in IRMA, the Intelligent Resource-bounded Machine Architecture [22]. IRMA was intended as a more or less direct realization of Bratman's theory of practical reasoning. However, the best-known implementation is the Procedural Reasoning System (PRS) [78] and its many descendants [61, 183, 46, 100]. In the PRS, an agent has data structures that explicitly correspond to beliefs, desires, and intentions. A PRS agent's beliefs are directly represented in the form of PROLOG-like facts [34, p.3]. Desires and intentions in PRS are realized through the use of a *plan library*.[2] A plan library, as its name suggests, is a collection of plans. Each plan is a recipe that can be used by the agent to achieve some particular state of affairs. A plan in the PRS is characterized by a *body* and an *invocation condition*. The body of a plan is a course of action that can be used by the agent to achieve some particular state of affairs. The invocation condition of a plan defines the circumstances under which the agent should "consider" the plan. Control in the PRS proceeds by the agent continually updating its internal beliefs, and then looking to see which plans have invocation conditions that correspond to these beliefs. The set of plans made active in this way correspond to the *desires* of the agent. Each desire defines a possible course of action that the agent may follow. On each control cycle, the PRS picks one of these desires, and pushes it onto an execution stack, for subsequent execution. The execution stack contains desires that have been chosen by the agent, and thus corresponds to the agent's *intentions*.

The third and final component of the BDI model is the logical component. This logical component provides a family of tools that allow us to reason about BDI agents.

1.4   Reasoning about Belief-Desire-Intention Agents

Computer science is, as much as it is about anything, about developing theories and formalisms that allow us to reason about the behavior of computational systems. The theory of a system can be understood as the *semantics* of that system. An obvious question, therefore, is: What sort of theory can we use to give a semantics to BDI systems? The answer presented by this book is to use BDI logics to *axiomatize* properties of agents.

---

2 In this description of the PRS, I have modified the original terminology somewhat, to be more in line with contemporary usage; I have also simplified the control cycle of the PRS slightly.

A fundamental problem in developing such a theory of rational agency is to give an account of the relationships that exist between an agent's mental states. In particular, a complete agent theory would explain how an agent's mental states lead it to select and perform rational actions, thus realizing the mapping from perception to action illustrated in Figure 1.1. To give a flavor of the issues involved in developing such a theory, consider the relationship between belief and intention. Suppose I intend to bring about some state of affairs φ. What does the fact that I intend φ imply about my beliefs with respect to φ? Well, clearly, it would make no sense for me to intend φ if I believe that φ is already true. If my book is written, then there is no point in me intending to write it. This property — that intending φ implies you do not already believe φ — is a *constraint* that should be satisfied by a rational agent. We can capture this constraint in a formula schema of $\mathcal{LORA}$, the logic I use throughout this book to represent the properties of agents.

$$(\text{Int } i\,\varphi) \Rightarrow \neg(\text{Bel } i\,\varphi) \tag{1.1}$$

Here, $(\text{Int } i\,\varphi)$ is a construction that means "agent i intends φ." It is not hard to guess that $(\text{Bel } i\,\varphi)$ means "agent i believes φ." A "complete" theory of rational agency would be comprised of a number of formula schemas such as (1.1), which would together axiomatize the properties of rational agency.

Unfortunately, giving anything like a complete account of the relationships between an agent's mental states is extremely difficult. Part of the problem is that the objects of study — beliefs, desires, and the like — are rather different to phenomena that we observe in the physical world. In attempting to develop formal theories of such notions, we are forced to rely very much on our intuitions about them. As a consequence, such theories are hard to validate (or invalidate) in the way that good scientific theories should be. Fortunately, we have powerful tools available to help in our investigation. Mathematical logic allows us to represent our theories in a transparent, readable form, and examine (through the medium of formal proof) the predictions that our theories make, in order to see whether or not their consequences make sense.

$\mathcal{LORA}$ stands for "$\mathcal{L}$ogic $\mathcal{O}$f $\mathcal{R}$ational $\mathcal{A}$gents." $\mathcal{LORA}$ is a BDI logic: originally developed by Anand Rao and Michael Georgeff [187, 186, 188, 189, 184, 185], BDI logics allow us to represent the beliefs, desires, and intentions of agents. In addition to the BDI component, $\mathcal{LORA}$ contains a *temporal* component, which allows us to represent the dynamics of agents and their environments — how they change over time. Finally, $\mathcal{LORA}$ contains an *action* component, which allows us to represent the actions that agents perform, and the effects that these actions have.

1.5 Frequently Asked Questions (FAQ)

Certain questions *are* frequently asked about the work presented in this book, and so it seems only appropriate that I should include a FAQ.

Why Not Decision Theory?

Decision theory is a mathematical theory of rational decision making. Decision theory defines a rational agent as one that *maximizes expected utility*. The basic ideas of decision theory are very simple. Assume we have some agent, and that Ac is the set of all possible actions available to it. The performance of an action by the agent may result in a number of possible outcomes, where the set of all outcomes is $\Omega = \{\omega, \omega', \ldots\}$. Let the probability of outcome $\omega \in \Omega$ given that the agent performs action $\alpha \in Ac$ be denoted by $P(\omega \mid \alpha)$, and finally, let the *utility* of an outcome $\omega \in \Omega$ for the agent be given by a function $U : \Omega \to \mathbb{R}$. If $U(\omega) > U(\omega')$, then the agent prefers outcome ω over outcome ω'.

The *expected utility* of an action $\alpha \in Ac$ is denoted $EU(\alpha)$. Thus $EU(\alpha)$ represents the utility that an agent could expect to obtain by performing action α.

$$EU(\alpha) = \sum_{\omega \in \Omega} U(\omega)P(\omega \mid \alpha) \tag{1.2}$$

A rational agent is then one that chooses to perform an action α that maximizes $EU(\ldots)$. It is straightforward to define the behavior of such an agent. Let the function f_{opt} take as input a set of possible actions, a set of outcomes, a probability distribution over possible outcomes given the performance of actions, and a utility function, and let this function return an action. Then we can define the desired behavior of f_{opt} as follows.

$$f_{opt}(Ac, \Omega, P, U) = \arg\max_{\alpha \in Ac} \sum_{\omega \in \Omega} U(\omega)P(\omega \mid \alpha) \tag{1.3}$$

As Russell and Norvig point out, equations (1.2) and (1.3) could be seen in one sense as defining the whole of artificial intelligence [198, p.472]. It seems that in order to build a rational agent, all we need to do is implement the function f_{opt}. But while decision theory is a *normative* theory of rational action (it tells us what an agent *should in principle do*) it has nothing to say about how we might efficiently *implement* the function f_{opt}. The problem is that f_{opt} seems to require an unconstrained search over the space of all actions and their outcomes. Such a search is prohibitively expensive, particularly in the case where an agent needs to consider sequences of actions (i.e., plans).

Another problem is that it is hard in practice to obtain the probability distribution P or utility function U. If we consider a domain defined by m attributes, each of which may take n values, then the set Ω will contain m^n different outcomes. Simply enumerating these outcomes is likely to be impractical in many circumstances. Even if it is possible to enumerate the outcomes, actually obtaining the required probabilities and utilities for them is notoriously hard [198, pp.475–480]. See the "Notes and Further Reading" section at the end of this chapter for references to how decision theory is currently being used in artificial intelligence.

Why Not Game Theory?

Game theory is a close relative of decision theory, which studies interactions between agents where each agent is accorded a utility function as described above [14]. The tools and techniques of game theory have found many applications in computational multiagent systems research, particularly when applied to such problems as negotiation [195, 199]. Game theory shares with decision theory many concepts, in particular the concept of a rational agent as one that acts to maximize expected utility. However, game theory also shares many of the problems of decision theory. While it tells us what a rational agent should do in principle, it does not give us many clues as to how to implement such decision makers efficiently. In addition, like decision theory, game theory is *quantitative* in nature.

It is important to note that all this should not be taken to imply that game theory is in any sense wrong, or that it is of no use. On the contrary, game theory is an extremely powerful analytic tool, which will certainly be applied more widely in years to come. But it does have limitations.

Why Logic?

There are some in the AI research community who believe that logic is (to put it crudely) the work of the devil, and that the effort devoted to such problems as logical knowledge representation and theorem proving over the years has been, at best, a waste of time. At least a brief justification for the use of logic therefore seems necessary.

_Computational Cognitive Science will explain how memory is encoded saved/accessed/modified/frozen /d 1st impacted from fantasy and "Tagged" + used for (PTSD) + other behaviors (see _____) Neuroscience will only obscure This_

As we don't yet have the insight categories

First, by fixing on a structured, well-defined artificial language (as opposed to unstructured, ill-defined natural language), it is possible to investigate the question of *what* can be expressed in a rigorous, mathematical way (see, for example, Emerson and Halpern [50], where the expressive power of a number of temporal logics are compared formally). Another major advantage is that any ambiguity can be removed (see, e.g., proofs of the unique readability of propositional logic and first-order predicate logic [52, pp.39–43]).

Transparency is another advantage:

By expressing the properties of agents, and multiagent systems as logical axioms and theorems in a language with clear semantics, the focal points of [the theory] are explicit. The theory is transparent; properties, interrelationships, and inferences are open to examination. This contrasts with the use of computer code, which requires implementational and control aspects within which the issues to be tested can often become confused. [68, p.88]

Finally, by adopting a logic-based approach, one makes available all the results and techniques of what is arguably the oldest, richest, most fundamental, and best-established branch of mathematics.

The final chapter in the main text of this book, chapter 9, considers in detail the role of logic in the theory and practice of multiagent systems.

Why Not First-Order Logic?

Those active in the area of logic for AI can be divided broadly into two camps: those who make use of classical (usually first-order) logic, and those who use non-classical logics (in particular, modal and temporal logics of the kind used in this book) of some sort. This book makes use of a logic called $\mathcal{LORA}$. From a technical point of view, $\mathcal{LORA}$ is a first-order branching time logic, containing modal connectives for representing the beliefs, desires, and intentions of agents, as well as a dynamic logic-style apparatus for representing and reasoning about the actions that agents perform.

Strong opinions are held in both camps on the relative merits of classical versus non-classical logics. Those in favor of classical logic point to a number of general arguments against modal logics:

1. First-order logic is sufficiently expressive that it can be used to encode almost any form of knowledge required.

2. While the satisfiability problem for first-order logic is only semi-decidable (see, e.g., [73, p.58]) the corresponding problem for modal and temporal logics tends to be even worse. Some multimodal logics are undecidable even in the

propositional case [91]. This makes it doubtful that there will ever be practical theorem-proving methods for such logics.

There is certainly some strength to the first argument. With sufficient ingenuity, one can use first-order logic to encode anything that can be encoded using a modal or temporal logic. In this sense, first-order logic is a truly generic formalism. But this argument misses the point slightly. To see what I mean, consider the following English-language statement.

We are not friends until you apologize. (1.4)

We can encode (1.4) in first-order logic by translating it to the following statement: there is some time t such that you apologize at t and t is later than *now*, such that for all time points t' between now and t, we are not friends at t'. This corresponds to the following first-order logic formula.

$$\exists t \cdot Time(t) \wedge (t > now) \wedge Apologize(you, t) \wedge$$
$$(\forall t' \cdot Time(t') \wedge (now \leq t' < t) \Rightarrow \neg Friends(us, t')) \quad (1.5)$$

Note that we are explicitly using terms of first-order logic to denote time points. Using $\mathcal{LORA}$, we can translate (1.4) as follows.

$$(\neg Friends(us)) \, \mathcal{U} \, Apologize(you) \quad (1.6)$$

The "$\mathcal{U}$" is a temporal connective of $\mathcal{LORA}$, which is read as "until." The obvious comment to make is that (1.6) is a much more succinct representation of (1.4). But more importantly, (1.6) is much closer to the natural language (1.4) than the rather arcane first-order translation (1.5). Because (1.5) explicitly incorporates the technical apparatus to deal with time, it has lost the structure of the English language (1.4), rendering it much harder to read.[3]

More generally, modal and temporal logics can be understood as specialized languages for representing the properties of relational structures. In the case of temporal properties, the relational structure in question is the temporal structure of the world: nodes in the structure correspond to time points, and arcs between nodes correspond to the passing of time. If we do not use modal connectives to represent properties of the relational structure, then we seem obliged to introduce the relational structure into the representation language itself, as we did with time points in (1.5). As the above example illustrates, this leads to formulae that are, at the very least, hard to read. In later chapters, we

---

3 If at this point you do not buy into the argument that (1.6) is more user-friendly than (1.5), then you are not going to enjoy the rest of this book.

will see how an agent's beliefs, desires, and intentions can also be understood as relational structures.

With respect to the issue of theorem proving, it should be noted that first-order logic hardly lends itself to efficient theorem proving. After all, even for propositional logic the satisfiability problem is NP-complete. Nobody would argue that theorem proving for modal and temporal logics is computationally easy. But with time, we will perhaps come to gain a much better understanding of how to build theorem provers for such logics — just as we have with first-order logic.

I Am a Logic Guru — Should I Read This Book?

For the purposes of this book, logic is a means to an end and not an end in itself. In other words, this book is first and foremost about rational agents and multiagent systems. It is not intended to be a book about logic. So, although the book contains many formal results, comparatively few of these are specifically about logic itself. There are no complexity or completeness results, for example, and no results on the expressive power of the logic used. Although the book is not primarily about logic, I have nevertheless attempted to ensure that it is "respectable" from a logical standpoint.[4] Thus the syntax and semantics of $\mathcal{LORA}$ are defined in as much detail as all but the most fastidious would expect, and detailed proofs are given for all results.

Logics like $\mathcal{LORA}$, which combine multiple modalities into a single framework, are very much at the cutting edge of contemporary logic research [139]. I therefore hope that this book will provide a fertile source of ideas and problems for researchers more interested in pure logic than its applications to agent theory.

I Am a Logic Novice — Should I Read This Book?

If you open a page of this book at random, there is a good chance that you will be confronted with logical notation of some kind. If you are not familiar with logic or comfortable with discrete mathematics, then this formalism will no doubt be off-putting. In fact, the "entry level" for reading this book is actually quite low. I do not presuppose anything more than some familiarity with basic discrete math notation (sets, functions, and relations) and the ability to read formulae of first-order logic. Almost all undergraduate courses in computer

---

4 A colleague who read a draft of this book quipped that no book about logic in AI could be respectable these days. If you are inclined to agree, you should probably stop reading now.

science will cover these prerequisites. If you have such a background, then you should be able to read the book and gain an understanding of the main ideas without delving into the formal details. Ultimately, all you need to know to understand most of the book is how to read formulae of $\mathcal{LORA}$. Chapter 3 explains how to read formulae of $\mathcal{LORA}$ without going into the details of the logic at all. If you prefer not to read the mathematically oriented sections of the book, then you should avoid chapter 4 completely, and all sections marked with an asterisk ("*") in the section header. The appendices survey the logical preliminaries required to understand the book.

Do I Need to Read the Proofs?

I do not enjoy reading proofs, or indeed writing them, but they are "a necessary evil" in the words of my editor at MIT Press. If you feel the same as I feel, then my advice is as follows. If you simply want to become familiar with the techniques used and the results in the book, then there is no reason to read any of the proofs at all. However, if you want to *use* $\mathcal{LORA}$ yourself, to build on any of the results presented in this book, or to gain a really deep understanding of the book, then you will simply have to bite the bullet. In fact, most of the proofs rely on a relatively small set of techniques, which will already be familiar to readers with a grounding in modal, temporal, and first-order logic.

How Do I Implement This Book?

$\mathcal{LORA}$ is *not* an executable logic, and there is currently no simple way of automating $\mathcal{LORA}$ so that it can be used directly as a knowledge representation formalism or a programming language. The possible roles that logics such as $\mathcal{LORA}$ might play in the engineering of agent systems are explored in detail in chapter 9.

Where Can I Find Out More?

I have done my best to make the material in this book as self-contained as possible, in that while it presupposes some basic knowledge of discrete maths and logic, all definitions and such are included in their entirety. There should therefore be no need to refer directly to other texts in order to understand the book. However, to help the reader find out more, every chapter (including this one) concludes with a section entitled "Notes and Further Reading," which gives historical notes, pointers to further reading, and open problems. The appendices also contain background material.

1.6   The Structure of This Book

The remainder of this book can be broadly divided into three parts:

• The first part (chapters 2 and 3) is background material. This part sets the scene, by introducing the basic concepts and formalism used throughout the book.
• The second part (chapters 4 and 5) develops the formal model that is used throughout the book, and shows how this framework can be used to capture some properties of individual rational agents.
• The third part (chapters 6, 7, and 8) shows how agents can be used to capture properties of multiagent, social systems.

In more detail:

• Chapter 2 ("The Belief-Desire-Intention Model") gives a detailed introduction to the BDI model. It begins by introducing Bratman's intention-based theory of practical reasoning, the foundation upon which the BDI model rests. After introducing this theory, I turn to the question of how BDI agents might be implemented. I consider a number of pseudo-code agent control loops, and discuss the extent to which they can be considered as capturing our pre-theoretic intuitions about beliefs, desires, and intentions.
• Chapter 3 ("An Introduction to $\mathcal{LORA}$") informally introduces $\mathcal{LORA}$. This chapter is intended for readers who do not have a strong background in logic. After this chapter, readers should be able to understand formulae of $\mathcal{LORA}$.
• Chapter 4 ("$\mathcal{LORA}$ Defined") gives a complete definition of the syntax and semantics of $\mathcal{LORA}$, and investigates some of its properties. This chapter presupposes some familiarity with quantified modal, temporal, and dynamic logics, but is otherwise entirely self-contained.
• Chapter 5 ("Properties of Rational Agents") investigates how $\mathcal{LORA}$ can be used to capture properties of rational agents. Examples of such properties include the possible interrelationships among beliefs, desires, and intentions, and degrees of realism. This chapter focuses in particular on the properties of *individual* agents.
• Chapter 6 ("Collective Mental States") changes the focus of the book from individual agents to groups of agents. It shows how $\mathcal{LORA}$ can be used to formalize collective mental states such as mutual beliefs, desires, and intentions,

but in addition, such notions as joint commitment.

• Chapter 7 ("Communication") shows how $\mathcal{LORA}$ can be used to define communicative (speech) acts between agents. Following a discussion of the history of speech acts in multiagent systems, I show how "request" and "inform" actions can be defined in $\mathcal{LORA}$, building on the prior work of Cohen and Levesque [36]. Roughly speaking, an inform action takes place when one agent attempts to get another agent to believe something; a request action takes place when one agent gets another agent to intend something. Using these two speech acts as primitives, I show how a range of other speech acts may be defined using $\mathcal{LORA}$.

• Chapter 8 ("Cooperation") shows how $\mathcal{LORA}$ can be used to define a model of cooperative problem solving. This model is an adaptation of the theory of cooperation introduced in [247, 248, 250]. It treats cooperative problem solving as a four-stage process, beginning when one agent recognizes the potential for cooperation with respect to one of its actions, which is followed by the agent attempting to solicit assistance from a team of agents, which then attempt to agree to a plan of (joint) action to achieve the goal, which finally is executed by the group.

• Chapter 9 ("Logic and Agent Theory") attempts to put the book into perspective. It discusses the role that logical theories of agency can or should play in the development of agent systems. Adopting a software engineering perspective, where such theories are treated as *specifications* that an idealized agent would satisfy, it investigates the extent to which they can be used in the implementation or verification of practical agent systems.

In addition, the book contains two appendices:

• Appendix A contains a summary of the notation used in the main text of the book.

• Appendix B contains a short, self-contained introduction to modal and temporal logics, for readers unfamiliar with this material.

1.7 Notes and Further Reading

There are now many introductions to intelligent agents and multiagent systems. Ferber [56] is an undergraduate textbook, although as its name suggests, this volume focussed on multiagent aspects rather than on the theory and practice of individual agents. A first-rate collection of articles introducing agent and multiagent systems is Weiß [233]; in particular, chapters 1, 2, 3, and 8 would provide an excellent introduction to the current volume. Three collections of research articles provide a comprehensive introduction to the field of autonomous rational agents and multiagent systems: Bond and Gasser's 1988 collection, *Readings in Distributed Artificial Intelligence*, introduces almost all the basic problems in the multiagent systems field, and although some of the papers it contains are now rather dated, it remains essential reading [18]; the *Readings in Planning* collection, from Allen, Hendler, and Tate may not appear to be the most obvious place to start for an introduction to agents, but the basic issue it addresses — deciding what action to perform — is central to the study of agents [2]; finally, Huhns and Singh's more recent collection sets itself the ambitious goal of providing a survey of the whole of the agent field, and succeeds in this respect very well [102]. For a general introduction to the theory and practice of intelligent agents, see Wooldridge and Jennings [249], which focuses primarily on the theory of agents, but also contains an extensive review of agent architectures and programming languages. For a collection of articles on the applications of agent technology, see [109]. A comprehensive roadmap of agent technology was published as [108].

Some authors view the whole of the artificial intelligence endeavor as one of constructing rational agents: Russell and Norvig's enormously successful, encyclopedic introductory AI textbook is the best-known example [198].

This question of "what is an agent" is one that continues to generate some debate, particularly on unmoderated email lists and news forums. Unfortunately, much of the debate is not as informed as one might wish. For an interesting collection of answers to the question, see [164]. The notion of a *software agent*, which inhabits a software environment, was introduced by Oren Etzioni [53]. Another good discussion can be found in Kaelbling [112].

The relevance of decision theory and game or economic theory to artificial intelligence was recognized in the very earliest days of the discipline; the work of Herb Simon is perhaps best known in this regard (see, e.g., [208]). Decision theoretic approaches to the planning problem are currently the focus of considerable attention within the artificial intelligence community — see [16] for an overview. Rao and Georgeff, who developed the basic BDI logic framework upon which $\mathcal{LORA}$ is based, investigated the relationship between the BDI model and classical decision theory in [185, pp.297–200]. They showed how the "choice and chance" trees employed in decision theory could be mapped into semantic models for their BDI logics.

Following the seminal work of Jeffrey Rosenschein and colleagues on the application of game-theoretic techniques to negotiation [195], game theory is now widely applied in multiagent systems research. A comprehensive overview is provided in [199].

Finally, logic has been widely used in artificial intelligence since John McCarthy's early work on the "advice taker" system [149]; see [73, 198] for detailed introductions to the use of logic in artificial intelligence, and see [103] for a general discussion on the role of logic in artificial intelligence. See also [167] and Birnbaum's response to this for some more strident views [15]. For discussions on the relative merits of first-order logic versus the alternatives (modal or temporal logics), see [191] or [70].

Although he is a strong advocate of logic in artificial intelligence, John McCarthy has reservations about the utility of *modal* logic; a position paper on the topic, entitled *Modality, Si! Modal Logic, No!* appeared as [150]. Joseph Halpern responded to McCarthy's statement in the online journal *Electronic Transactions on Artificial Intelligence* in late 1999; at the time of writing, the online debate was continuing.

2 The Belief-Desire-Intention Model

In this chapter, I give a detailed introduction to the belief-desire-intention model of agency. As noted in chapter 1, the BDI model combines three distinct components: a *philosophical* component; a *software architecture* component; and a *logical* component. The purpose of this chapter is primarily to introduce the first and second components of the BDI model; the remainder of the book investigates the logical component in detail. I begin by introducing Bratman's theory of human practical reasoning.

2.1 Practical Reasoning

The BDI model has its roots in the philosophical tradition of understanding *practical reasoning* in humans. Put simply, practical reasoning is reasoning directed towards actions — the process of figuring out what to do:

Practical reasoning is a matter of weighing conflicting considerations for and against competing options, where the relevant considerations are provided by what the agent desires/values/cares about and what the agent believes. [21, p.17]

It is important to distinguish practical reasoning from *theoretical reasoning* [48]. Theoretical reasoning is directed towards beliefs. To use a rather tired example, if I believe that all men are mortal, and I believe that Socrates is a man, then I will usually conclude that Socrates is mortal. The process of concluding that Socrates is mortal is theoretical reasoning, since it affects only my beliefs about the world. The process of deciding to catch a bus instead of a train, however, is practical reasoning, since it is reasoning directed towards action.

Human practical reasoning appears to consist of at least two distinct activities. The first of these involves deciding *what* state of affairs we want to achieve; the second process involves deciding *how* we want to achieve these states of affairs. The former process — deciding what states of affairs to achieve — is known as *deliberation*. The latter process — deciding how to achieve these states of affairs — we call *means-ends reasoning*.

To better understand deliberation and means-ends reasoning, consider the following example. When a person graduates from university with a first degree, he or she is faced with some important choices. Typically, one proceeds in these choices by first deciding what sort of career to follow. For example, one might consider a career as an academic, or a career in industry. The process of deciding which career to aim for is deliberation. Once one has fixed upon a career, there are further choices to be made; in particular, how to bring about this career. Suppose that after deliberation, you choose to pursue a career as an academic. The next step is to decide *how to achieve* this state of affairs. This process is means-ends reasoning. The end result of means-ends reasoning is a *plan* or *recipe* of some kind for achieving the chosen state of affairs. For the career example, a plan might involve first applying to an appropriate university for a Ph.D. place, and so on. After obtaining a plan, an agent will typically then attempt to carry out (or *execute*) the plan, in order to bring about the chosen state of affairs. If all goes well (the plan is sound, and the agent's environment cooperates sufficiently), then after the plan has been executed, the chosen state of affairs will be achieved.

Thus described, practical reasoning seems a straightforward process, and in an ideal world, it would be. But there are several complications. The first is that deliberation and means-ends reasoning are *computational* processes. In all real agents (and in particular, artificial agents), such computational processes will take place under *resource bounds*. By this I mean that an agent will only have a fixed amount of memory and a fixed processor available to carry out its computations. Together, these resource bounds impose a limit on the size of computations that can be carried out in any given amount of time. No real agent will be able to carry out arbitrarily large computations in a finite amount of time. Since almost any real environment will also operate in the presence of *time constraints* of some kind, this means that means-ends reasoning and deliberation must be carried out in a fixed, finite number of processor cycles, with a fixed, finite amount of memory space. From this discussion, we can see that resource bounds have two important implications:

- Computation is a valuable resource for agents situated in real-time environments. The ability to perform well will be determined at least in part by the ability to make efficient use of available computational resources. In other words, an agent must *control* its reasoning effectively if it is to perform well.

- Agents cannot deliberate indefinitely. They must clearly *stop* deliberating at some point, having chosen some state of affairs, and commit to achieving this state of affairs. It may well be that the state of affairs it has fixed upon is not optimal — further deliberation may have led it to fix upon an another state of affairs.

We refer to the states of affairs that an agent has chosen and committed to as its *intentions*. The BDI model of agency is ultimately one that recognizes the primacy of intentions in practical reasoning, and it is therefore worth discussing the roles that they play in more detail.

2.2   Intentions in Practical Reasoning

First, notice that it is possible to distinguish several different types of intention. In ordinary speech, we use the term "intention" to characterize both *actions* and *states of mind*. To adapt an example from Bratman [20, p.1], I might intentionally push someone under a train, and push them with the intention of killing them. Intention is here used to characterize an action — the action of pushing someone under a train. Alternatively, I might have the intention this morning of pushing someone under a train this afternoon. Here, intention is used to characterize my state of mind. In this book, when I talk about intentions, I mean intentions as states of mind. In particular, I mean *future-directed intentions* — intentions that an agent has towards some future state of affairs.

The most obvious role of intentions is that they are *pro-attitudes* [21, p.23]. By this, I mean that they tend to lead to action. Suppose I have an intention to write a book. If I truly have such an intention, then you would expect me to make a *reasonable attempt* to achieve it. This would usually involve, at the very least, me initiating some plan of action that I believed would satisfy the intention. In this sense, intentions tend to play a primary role in the production of action. As time passes, and my intention about the future becomes my intention about the present, then it plays a direct role in the production of action. Of course, having an intention does not necessarily lead to action. For example, I can have an intention now to attend a conference later in the year. I can be utterly sincere in this intention, and yet if I learn of some event that must take precedence over the conference, I may never even get as far as considering travel arrangements.

Bratman notes that intentions play a much stronger role in influencing action than other pro-attitudes, such as mere desires:

My desire to play basketball this afternoon is merely a potential influencer of my conduct this afternoon. It must vie with my other relevant desires [...] before it is settled what I will do. In contrast, once I intend to play basketball this afternoon, the matter is settled: I normally need not continue to weigh the pros and cons. When the afternoon arrives, I will normally just proceed to execute my intentions. [21, p.22]

The second main property of intentions is that they *persist*. If I adopt an intention to become an academic, then I should persist with this intention and attempt to achieve it. For if I immediately drop my intentions without devoting any resources to achieving them, then I will not be acting rationally. Indeed, you might be inclined to say that I never really had intentions in the first place.

Of course, I should not persist with my intention for too long — if it becomes clear to me that I will never become an academic, then it is only rational to drop my intention to do so. Similarly, if the reason for having an intention goes away, then it would be rational for me to drop the intention. For example, if I adopted the intention to become an academic because I believed it would be an easy life, but then discover that this is not the case (e.g., I might be expected to actually teach!), then the justification for the intention is no longer present, and I should drop the intention.

If I initially fail to achieve an intention, then you would expect me to *try again* — you would not expect me to simply give up. For example, if my first application for a Ph.D. program is rejected, then you might expect me to apply to alternative universities.

The third main property of intentions is that once I have adopted an intention, the very fact of having this intention will constrain my future practical reasoning. For example, while I hold some particular intention, I will not subsequently entertain options that are *inconsistent* with that intention. Intending to write a book, for example, would preclude the option of partying every night: the two are mutually exclusive. This is in fact a highly desirable property from the point of view of implementing rational agents, because in providing a "filter of admissibility," intentions can be seen to constrain the space of possible intentions that an agent needs to consider.

Finally, intentions are closely related to beliefs about the future. For example, if I intend to become an academic, then I should believe that, assuming some certain background conditions are satisfied, I will indeed become an academic. For if I truly believe that I will never be an academic, it would be nonsensical of me to have an intention to become one. Thus if I intend to become an academic, I should at least believe that there is a good chance I will indeed become one. However, there is what appears at first sight to be a paradox here. While I might believe that I will indeed succeed in achieving my intention, if I am rational, then I must also recognize the possibility that I can *fail* to bring it about — that there is some circumstance under which my intention is not satisfied.

From this discussion, we can identify the following closely related situations:

- Having an intention to bring about φ, while believing that you will not bring about φ is called *intention-belief inconsistency*, and is not rational (see, e.g., [20, pp.37–38]).
- Having an intention to achieve φ without believing that φ will be the case is *intention-belief incompleteness*, and is an acceptable property of rational agents (see, e.g., [20, p.38]).

The distinction between these two cases is known as the *asymmetry thesis* [20, pp.37–41].

Summarizing, we can see that intentions play the following important roles in practical reasoning:

- *Intentions drive means-ends reasoning.*

If I have formed an intention, then I will attempt to achieve the intention, which involves, among other things, deciding *how* to achieve it. Moreover, if one particular course of action fails to achieve an intention, then I will typically attempt others.

- *Intentions persist.*

I will not usually give up on my intentions without good reason — they will persist, typically until I believe I have successfully achieved them, I believe I cannot achieve them, or I believe the reason for the intention is no longer present.

- *Intentions constrain future deliberation.*

I will not entertain options that are inconsistent with my current intentions.

- *Intentions influence beliefs upon which future practical reasoning is based.*

If I adopt an intention, then I can plan for the future on the assumption that I will achieve the intention. For if I intend to achieve some state of affairs while simultaneously believing that I will not achieve it, then I am being irrational.

Notice from this discussion that intentions *interact* with an agent's beliefs and other mental states. For example, having an intention to φ implies that I do not believe φ is impossible, and moreover that I believe given the right circumstances, φ will be achieved. However, satisfactorily capturing the interaction between intention and belief turns out to be surprisingly hard: the way in which intentions interact with other mental states is considered in chapter 5.

```
Algorithm: Agent Control Loop Version 1
1.   while true
2.       observe the world;
3.       update internal world model;
4.       deliberate about what intention to achieve next;
5.       use means-ends reasoning to get a plan for the intention;
6.       execute the plan
7.   end while
```

Figure 2.1
A basic agent control loop.

2.3   Implementing Rational Agents

Based on the discussion above, let us consider how we might go about building a BDI agent. The strategy I use is to introduce progressively more complex agent designs, and for each of these designs, to investigate the type of behavior that such an agent would exhibit, compared to the desired behavior of a rational agent as discussed above. This then motivates the introduction of a refined agent design, and so on.

The first agent design is shown in Figure 2.1. The agent continually executes a cycle of observing the world, deciding what intention to achieve next, determining a plan of some kind to achieve this intention, and then executing this plan.

The first point to note about this loop is that we will not be concerned with stages (2) or (3). Observing the world and updating an internal model of it are important processes, worthy of study in their own right; but they lie outside the scope of this volume. Instead, we are concerned primarily with stages (4) to (6). Readers interested in understanding the processes of observing and updating can find some key references in the "further reading" section at the end of this chapter.

One of the most important issues raised by this simple agent control loop follows from the fact that the deliberation and means-ends reasoning processes are not instantaneous. They have a *time cost* associated with them. Suppose that the agent starts deliberating at time t_0, begins means-ends reasoning at t_1, and subsequently begins executing the newly formed plan at time t_2. The time taken to deliberate is thus

$$t_{deliberate} = t_1 - t_0$$

and the time taken for means-ends reasoning is

$$t_{me} = t_2 - t_1$$

Further suppose that the deliberation process is *optimal* in the sense that if it selects some intention to achieve, then the achievement of this intention at time t_0 would be the best thing for the agent. So at time t_1, the agent has selected an intention to achieve that would have been optimal *if it had been achieved at t_0*. But unless $t_{deliberate}$ is vanishingly small, then the agent runs the risk that the intention selected is no longer optimal by the time the agent has fixed upon it.

Of course, selecting an intention to achieve is only part of the overall practical reasoning problem; the agent still has to determine *how* to achieve the intention, via means-ends reasoning.

As with deliberation, assume that the means-ends reasoning process enjoys optimality in the sense that if it is given an intention to achieve and it starts executing at time t_1, then it will select the course of action to achieve this intention such that this course of action would be optimal if executed at time t_1. Again, means-ends reasoning is not instantaneous: it takes time to find the best course of action to achieve the intention. How long exactly might it take to find the best action? Suppose the agent has n possible actions available to it at any given time. Then there are $n!$ possible sequences of these actions. Since $n!$ has exponential growth, this means that the most obvious technique for finding a course of action (systematically searching through the space of possible action sequences) will be impossible in practice for all but the most trivial n. The problem is exacerbated by the fact that the plan is developed on the basis of an observation made of the environment at time t_0. The environment may be very different by time t_2.

Assuming we have an agent with optimal deliberation and means-ends reasoning components, in the sense described above, it should be clear that this agent will have overall optimal behavior in the following circumstances:

1. when deliberation and means-ends reasoning take a vanishingly small amount of time; or

2. when the world is guaranteed to remain static while the agent is deliberating and performing means-ends reasoning, so that the assumptions upon which the choice of intention to achieve and plan to achieve the intention remain valid until the agent has completed deliberation and means-ends reasoning; or

3. when an intention that is optimal when achieved at time t_0 (the time at which the world is observed) is guaranteed to remain optimal until time t_2 (the

time at which the agent has found a course of action to achieve the intention).

Conditions (2) and (3) will not hold in most realistic environments. As we noted in chapter 1, the kinds of environments in which agents work will tend to be highly dynamic, and such environments will not remain static long enough for an agent to determine from first principles either an optimal intention or, given such an intention, an optimal course of action to achieve it. Similarly, most important tasks that we might assign to agents will be highly time dependent.

Let us now make the agent algorithm presented above slightly more formal. For this, we require some notation. Throughout this chapter, I make one important assumption: that the agent maintains some explicit *representation* of its beliefs, desires, and intentions. However, I will not be concerned with *how* beliefs and the like are represented. One possibility is that they are represented *symbolically*, for example as logical statements *a là* PROLOG facts [34]. Indeed, for most of this book, it is assumed that beliefs take exactly this form. However, the assumption that beliefs, desires, and intentions are symbolically represented is by no means necessary for the remainder of the book. We use B to denote a variable that holds the agent's current beliefs, and let *Bel* be the set of all such beliefs. Similarly, we use D as a variable for desires, and *Des* to denote the set of all desires. Finally, the variable I represents the agent's intentions, and *Int* is the set of all possible intentions.

Next, we need some way of representing an agent's *perception*. Consider a robotic agent, equipped with a video camera, but no other kind of sensor apparatus. Then the video feed delivered to this agent represents the information available to the agent about its environment. Any representation of its environment that the robot creates must ultimately be derived from this video feed. We refer to the video feed as the robot's *perceptual input*. In implemented agent systems, perceptual input is usually packaged into discrete bundles, which are referred to as *percepts*. We use $\rho, \rho', \rho_1, \ldots$ to represent percepts that the agent receives. Let *Per* be the set of all such percepts.

Finally, we need to say something about *plans*. Plans and intentions are closely related. We frequently use the two terms interchangeably in everyday speech, saying "I plan to..." for "I intend to..."; as Bratman puts it: "Plans are intentions writ large" [20, p.29]. In this book, when we refer to plans, we are referring to plans as *recipes* for achieving intentions. For example, one plan/recipe for achieving my intention of being at the airport might involve catching a taxi; another might involve catching a bus; and so on. Plans and planning are a major research topic in their own right — see [2] for a detailed survey. For our purposes, a simple model of plans will suffice. A plan is viewed as a tuple consisting of:

• a *pre-condition*, which defines the circumstances under which a plan is applicable — for example, one of the pre-conditions of the plan to catch a taxi to the airport is that I have sufficient funds to pay for it;

• a *post-condition*, which defines what states of affairs the plan achieves — for example, post-conditions of my plan to catch a taxi to the airport include me having less money, and me now being located at the airport;

• a *body*, which is the actual "recipe" part of the plan — for our purposes, the body is simply a sequence of actions.

We will use π (with decorations: π', π_1, ...) to denote plans, and let *Plan* be the set of all plans (over some set of actions *Ac*). We will make use of a number of auxiliary definitions for manipulating plans (some of these will not actually be required until later in this chapter):

• if π is a plan, then we write $pre(\pi)$ to denote the pre-condition of π, $post(\pi)$ to denote the post-condition of π, and $body(\pi)$ to denote the body of π;

• if π is plan, then we write $empty(\pi)$ to mean that plan π is the empty sequence (thus $empty(...)$ is a boolean-valued function);

• $execute(...)$ is a procedure that takes as input a single plan and executes it without stopping — executing a plan simply means executing each action in the plan body in turn;

• if π is a plan then by $hd(\pi)$ we mean the plan made up of the first action in the plan body of π; for example, if the body of π is $\alpha_1, ..., \alpha_n$, then the body of $hd(\pi)$ contains only the action α_1;

• if π is a plan then by $tail(\pi)$ we mean the plan made up of all but the first action in the plan body of π; for example, if the body of π is $\alpha_1, \alpha_2, ..., \alpha_n$, then the body of $tail(\pi)$ contains actions $\alpha_2, ..., \alpha_n$;

• if π is a plan, $I \subseteq Int$ is a set of intentions, and $B \subseteq Bel$ is a set of beliefs, then we write $sound(\pi, I, B)$ to mean that π is a sound plan for achieving I given beliefs B. (We will not discuss or attempt to define what makes a plan sound here — the classic paper on the subject is Lifschitz [136].)

We can now define the components of an agent's control loop. An agent's belief update process is formally modeled as a *belief revision function*. Such a belief revision function has the following signature.

$$brf : \wp(Bel) \times Per \rightarrow \wp(Bel)$$

In other words, on the basis of the current beliefs and current percept, the belief revision function determines a new set of beliefs. (As noted above, in this book we are *not* concerned with how belief revision might work; see [71].)

The agent's deliberation process is given by a function

$$deliberate : \wp(Bel) \rightarrow \wp(Int)$$

which takes a set of beliefs and returns a set of intentions — those selected by the agent to achieve, on the basis of its beliefs.

An agent's means-ends reasoning is represented by a function

$$plan : \wp(Bel) \times \wp(Int) \rightarrow Plan$$

which on the basis of an agent's current beliefs and current intentions, determines a plan to achieve the intention. Note that there is nothing in the definition of the *plan*(...) function which requires an agent to engage in *plan generation* — constructing a plan from scratch [2]. In most BDI systems, the *plan*(...) function is implemented by giving the agent a *plan library* [78]. A plan library is a pre-assembled collection of plans, which an agent designer gives to an agent. Finding a plan to achieve an intention then simply involves a single pass through the plan library to find a plan that, when executed, will have the intention as a post-condition, and will be sound given the agent's current beliefs. In implemented BDI agents, pre- and post-conditions are often represented as (lists of) atoms of first-order logic, and beliefs and intentions as ground atoms of first-order logic. Finding a plan to achieve an intention then reduces to finding a plan whose pre-condition unifies with the agent's beliefs, and whose post-condition unifies with the intention.

The agent control loop is now as shown in Figure 2.2. This algorithm highlights some limitations of this simple approach to agent control. In particular, steps (4) to (7) inclusive implicitly assume that the environment has not changed since it was observed at stage (3). Assuming that the time taken to actually execute the plan dominates the time taken to revise beliefs, deliberate, or plan, then the crucial concern is that the environment might change while the plan is being executed. The problem is that the agent remains *committed* to the intention it forms at step (5) until it has executed the plan in step (7). If the environment changes after step (3), then the assumptions upon which this plan

```
Algorithm: Agent Control Loop Version 2
1.  B := B₀;      /* B₀ are initial beliefs */
2.  while true do
3.      get next percept ρ;
4.      B := brf(B, ρ);
5.      I := deliberate(B);
6.      π := plan(B, I);
7.      execute(π)
8.  end while
```

Figure 2.2
A first refinement of the agent control loop.

depends may well be invalid by the time the plan is actually executed.

2.4   The Deliberation Process

So far, we have glossed over the problem of exactly how an agent might go about deliberating. In this section, we consider the process in more detail. It is not hard to see that in real life, deliberation typically begins by trying to understand what the *options* available to you are. Returning to the career choice example introduced above, if you gain a good first degree, then one option is that of becoming an academic; if you fail to obtain a good degree, this option is not available to you. Another option is entering industry. After deciding what the options are, you must *choose between them*, and *commit* to some. These chosen options then become intentions.

From this discussion, we can see that the *deliberate* function as discussed above can be decomposed into two distinct functional components:

- *option generation* — in which the agent generates a set of possible alternatives; and

- *filtering* — in which the agent chooses between competing alternatives, and commits to achieving them.

We represent option generation via a function, *options*, which takes the agent's current beliefs and current intentions, and from them determines a set of options that we will hereafter refer to as *desires*. The intuitive interpretation of a desire is that, in an "ideal world," an agent would like *all* its desires achieved. In any moderately realistic scenario, however, an agent will not be able to

```
Algorithm: Agent Control Loop Version 3
1.
2.   B := B₀;       /* B₀ are initial beliefs */
3.   I := I₀;       /* I₀ are initial intentions */
4.   while true do
5.        get next percept ρ;
6.        B := brf(B, ρ);
7.        D := options(B, I);
8.        I := filter(B, D, I);
9.        π := plan(B, I);
10.       execute(π)
11.  end while
```

Figure 2.3
Refining the deliberation process into option generation and filtering.

achieve all its desires. This is because desires are often mutually exclusive. For example, in the OASIS air-traffic control system, which was implemented using a BDI architecture, an agent was tasked with the problem of finding the optimal sequence in which to land aircraft at an airport [138]. The option generation process in OASIS might generate the options of landing two different aircraft on the same runway at the same time. Clearly, such options are mutually exclusive: it would be undesirable to land both aircraft simultaneously.

Formally, the signature of the option generation function *options* is as follows.

$$options : \wp(Bel) \times \wp(Int) \rightarrow \wp(Des)$$

In order to select between competing options, an agent uses a *filter* function. Intuitively, the filter function must simply select the "best" option for the agent to commit to. We represent the filter process through a function *filter*, with a signature as follows.

$$filter : \wp(Bel) \times \wp(Des) \times \wp(Int) \rightarrow \wp(Int)$$

The agent control loop incorporating explicit deliberation and means-ends reasoning is shown in Figure 2.3. Notice that desires are an *input to* the filter process, whereas intentions are an *output from* it.

2.5   Commitment Strategies

When an option successfully passes through the *filter* function and is hence chosen by the agent as an intention, we say that the agent has made a *commitment* to that option. Commitment implies *temporal persistence* — an intention, once adopted, should not immediately evaporate. A critical issue is just *how* committed an agent should be to its intentions. That is, how long should an intention persist? Under what circumstances should an intention vanish?

To motivate the discussion further, consider the following scenario:

Some time in the not-so-distant future, you are having trouble with your new household robot. You say "Willie, bring me a beer." The robot replies "OK boss." Twenty minutes later, you screech "Willie, why didn't you bring me that beer?" It answers "Well, I intended to get you the beer, but I decided to do something else." Miffed, you send the wise guy back to the manufacturer, complaining about a lack of commitment. After retrofitting, Willie is returned, marked "Model C: The Committed Assistant." Again, you ask Willie to bring you a beer. Again, it accedes, replying "Sure thing." Then you ask: "What kind of beer did you buy?" It answers: "Genessee." You say "Never mind." One minute later, Willie trundles over with a Genessee in its gripper. This time, you angrily return Willie for overcommitment. After still more tinkering, the manufacturer sends Willie back, promising no more problems with its commitments. So, being a somewhat trusting customer, you accept the rascal back into your household, but as a test, you ask it to bring you your last beer. Willie again accedes, saying "Yes, Sir." (Its attitude problem seems to have been fixed.) The robot gets the beer and starts towards you. As it approaches, it lifts its arm, wheels around, deliberately smashes the bottle, and trundles off. Back at the plant, when interrogated by customer service as to why it had abandoned its commitments, the robot replies that according to its specifications, it kept its commitments as long as required — commitments must be dropped when fulfilled or impossible to achieve. By smashing the bottle, the commitment became unachievable. [35, pp.213–214]

The mechanism an agent uses to determine when and how to drop intentions is known as a *commitment strategy*. The following three commitment strategies are commonly discussed in the literature of rational agents [187]:

- *Blind commitment*
A blindly committed agent will continue to maintain an intention until it believes the intention has actually been achieved. Blind commitment is also sometimes referred to as *fanatical* commitment.

- *Single-minded commitment*
A single-minded agent will continue to maintain an intention until it believes that either the intention has been achieved, or else that it is no longer possible

```
Algorithm: Agent Control Loop Version 4
1.
2.   B := B₀;        /* B₀ are initial beliefs */
3.   I := I₀;        /* I₀ are initial intentions */
4.   while true do
5.       get next percept ρ;
6.       B := brf(B, ρ);
7.       D := options(B, I);
8.       I := filter(B, D, I);
9.       π := plan(B, I);
10.      while not empty(π) do
11.          α := hd(π);
12.          execute(α);
13.          π := tail(π);
14.          get next percept ρ;
15.          B := brf(B, ρ);
16.          if not sound(π, I, B) then
17.              π := plan(B, I)
18.          end-if
19.      end-while
20.  end-while
```

Figure 2.4
Introducing reactivity: the agent will engage in means ends reasoning when it believes a plan has
(for whatever reason) failed.

to achieve the intention.

- *Open-minded commitment*

An open-minded agent will maintain an intention as long as it is still believed
possible.

Note that an agent has commitment both to *ends* (i.e., the state of affairs it
wishes to bring about), and *means* (i.e., the mechanism via which the agent
wishes to achieve the state of affairs). Currently, our agent control loop is overcommitted, both to means and ends. It never stops to reconsider its intentions,
and it remains committed to plans until they have been fully executed. We will
now see how this basic control loop can be refined in various ways, in order to
obtain different types of commitment.

The first modification we make allows the agent to *replan* if ever a plan
goes wrong. This reduces the commitment that an agent has towards the means
to achieve its intentions. The revised control loop is illustrated in Figure 2.4.

Using this loop, the agent will be committed to a plan to achieve its
intentions only while it believes that the plan is sound given its beliefs about

```
Algorithm: Agent Control Loop Version 5
1.
2.   B := B₀;        /* B₀ are initial beliefs */
3.   I := I₀;        /* I₀ are initial intentions */
4.   while true do
5.        get next percept ρ;
6.        B := brf(B, ρ);
7.        D := options(B, I);
8.        I := filter(B, D, I);
9.        π := plan(B, I);
10.       while not (empty(π) or succeeded(I, B) or impossible(I, B)) do
11.            α := hd(π);
12.            execute(α);
13.            π := tail(π);
14.            get next percept ρ;
15.            B := brf(B, ρ);
16.            if not sound(π, I, B) then
17.                 π := plan(B, I)
18.            end-if
19.       end-while
20. end-while
```

Figure 2.5
Dropping intentions that are either impossible or that have succeeded.

the current state of the world. If it ever determines that its plan is no longer appropriate in order to achieve the current intention, then it engages in further means-ends reasoning in order to find an alternative plan. Given that its beliefs are updated every time it executes an action, this implies at least some degree of reactivity.

This version of the control loop is clearly more attuned to the environment than previous versions, but it still remains overcommitted to intentions. This is because although the agent will replan if ever it believes the plan is no longer appropriate, it never stops to consider whether or not its intentions are appropriate. This consideration motivates the next version of the control loop, in which an agent explicitly stops to determine whether or not its intentions have succeeded or whether they are impossible. We write $succeeded(I, B)$ to mean that given beliefs B, the intentions I can be regarded as having been satisfied. Similarly, we write $impossible(I, B)$ to mean that intentions I are impossible given beliefs B. The revised control loop is then illustrated in Figure 2.5.

It is easy to see that this revised agent control loop implements single-minded commitment. The modifications required to implement open-minded commitment is straightforward, and is left to the reader. It should be stressed that, insofar as we are concerned in this book, there is no one "ideal" commitment strategy. Different circumstances call for different commitment strategies.

2.6   Intention Reconsideration

In our current algorithm, an agent will get to reconsider its intentions once every time around the outer control loop. This implies that it will reconsider its intentions when one of the following three conditions arises:

- it has completely executed a plan to achieve its current intentions; or
- it believes it has achieved its current intentions; or
- it believes its current intentions are no longer possible.

Although this ensures that the agent is neither undercommitted nor overcommitted to its intentions, it is limited in the way that it permits an agent to *reconsider* its intentions. The main problem is that it does not allow an agent to *exploit serendipity*. To see what I mean by this, consider the following scenario.

Sophie is a BDI software agent whose task is to obtain documents on behalf of a user. One day, the user instructs Sophie to obtain a soft copy of the Ph.D. thesis by A. N. Other, and Sophie creates an intention to this effect. Sophie believes that the Ph.D. is resident at A. N. Other's WWW site, and so generates an intention to download it from there. While she is planning how to achieve this intention, however, she is told that a local copy of the thesis exists. It would clearly be more efficient to obtain this version, but since there is nothing wrong with the intention of downloading the Ph.D. remotely (she believes it will succeed), she continues to do so.

In this scenario, Sophie would do better to reconsider her intentions *while she is executing the plan*. A first attempt to modify the agent control loop would involve reconsidering intentions every time the agent executed the inner loop in Figure 2.5: see Figure 2.6. Such an agent is *cautious*, in the sense that it always stops to reconsider its intentions before performing an action.

If option generation and filtering were computationally cheap processes, then this would be an acceptable strategy. Unfortunately, we know that deliberation is not cheap — it takes a considerable amount of time. While the agent is deliberating, the environment in which the agent is working is changing, possibly rendering its newly formed intentions irrelevant.

```
Algorithm: Agent Control Loop Version 6
1.
2.    B := B₀;       /* B₀ are initial beliefs */
3.    I := I₀;       /* I₀ are initial intentions */
4.    while true do
5.        get next percept ρ;
6.        B := brf(B, ρ);
7.        D := options(B, I);
8.        I := filter(B, D, I);
9.        π := plan(B, I);
10.       while not (empty(π) or succeeded(I, B) or impossible(I, B)) do
11.           α := hd(π);
12.           execute(α);
13.           π := tail(π);
14.           get next percept ρ;
15.           B := brf(B, ρ);
16.           D := options(B, I);
17.           I := filter(B, D, I);
18.           if not sound(π, I, B) then
19.               π := plan(B, I)
20.           end-if
21.       end-while
22.   end-while
```

Figure 2.6
A cautious agent, which stops to reconsider intentions before performing any action.

We are thus presented with a dilemma:

• an agent that does not stop to reconsider its intentions sufficiently often will continue attempting to achieve its intentions even after it is clear that they cannot be achieved, or that there is no longer any reason for achieving them;

• an agent that *constantly* reconsiders its attentions may spend insufficient time actually working to achieve them, and hence runs the risk of never actually achieving them.

There is clearly a trade-off to be struck between the degree of commitment and reconsideration at work here. To try to capture this trade-off, we can modify the agent to incorporate an explicit *meta-level control* component. The idea is to have a boolean-valued function, *reconsider*, such that $reconsider(I, B)$ evaluates to "true" just in case it is appropriate for the agent with beliefs B and intentions I to reconsider its intentions. The agent control loop incorporating the *reconsider*(...) function is shown in Figure 2.7.

```
Algorithm: Agent Control Loop Version 7
1.
2.    B := B₀;      /* B₀ are initial beliefs */
3.    I := I₀;      /* I₀ are initial intentions */
4.    while true do
5.        get next percept ρ;
6.        B := brf(B, ρ);
7.        D := options(B, I);
8.        I := filter(B, D, I);
9.        π := plan(B, I);
10.       while not (empty(π) or succeeded(I, B) or impossible(I, B)) do
11.           α := hd(π);
12.           execute(α);
13.           π := tail(π);
14.           get next percept ρ;
15.           B := brf(B, ρ);
16.           if reconsider(I, B) then
17.                 D := options(B, I);
18.                 I := filter(B, D, I);
19.           end-if
20.           if not sound(π, I, B) then
21.                 π := plan(B, I)
22.           end-if
23.       end-while
24.   end-while
```

Figure 2.7
An agent that attempts to strike a balance between boldness and caution: whether or not the agent chooses to reconsider intentions is determined by the boolean-valued function *reconsider*(...).

In this version of the agent control loop, the burden of deciding when to expend effort by deliberating lies with the function *reconsider*(...). It is interesting to consider the circumstances under which this function can be said to behave *optimally*. Suppose that the agent's deliberation and plan generation functions are in some sense perfect: that deliberation always chooses the "best" intentions (however that is defined for the application at hand), and planning always produces an appropriate plan. Further suppose that time expended always has a cost — the agent does not benefit by doing nothing. Then it is not difficult to see that the function *reconsider*(...) will be behaving optimally if, and only if, whenever it chooses to deliberate, the agent changes intentions [251]. For if the agent chose to deliberate but did not change intentions, then the effort expended on deliberation was wasted. Similarly, if an agent should have changed intentions, but failed to do so, then the effort expended on attempting to achieve its intentions was also wasted.

Table 2.1
Practical reasoning situations (cf. [22, p.353]).

Situation number	Chose to deliberate?	Changed intentions?	Would have changed intentions?	*reconsider*(...) optimal?
1	No	—	No	Yes
2	No	—	Yes	No
3	Yes	No	—	No
4	Yes	Yes	—	Yes

The possible interactions between meta-level control and deliberation are summarized in Table 2.1:

- In situation (1), the agent did not choose to deliberate, and as a consequence, did not choose to change intentions. Moreover, if it *had* chosen to deliberate, it would not have changed intentions. In this situation, the *reconsider*(...) function is behaving optimally.

- In situation (2), the agent did not choose to deliberate, but if it had done so, it *would* have changed intentions. In this situation, the *reconsider*(...) function is not behaving optimally.

- In situation (3), the agent chose to deliberate, but did not change intentions. In this situation, the *reconsider*(...) function is not behaving optimally.

- In situation (4), the agent chose to deliberate, and did change intentions. In this situation, the *reconsider*(...) function is behaving optimally.

Notice that there is an important assumption implicit within this discussion: that the cost of executing the *reconsider*(...) function is *much* less than the cost of the deliberation process itself. Otherwise, the *reconsider*(...) function could simply use the deliberation process as an oracle, running it as a subroutine and choosing to deliberate just in case the deliberation process changed intentions.

The nature of the trade-off was examined by David Kinny and Michael Georgeff in a number of experiments carried out using a BDI agent system [116]. The aims of Kinny and Georgeff's investigation were to:

(1) assess the feasibility of experimentally measuring agent effectiveness in a simulated environment, (2) investigate how commitment to goals contributes to effective agent behavior and (3) compare the properties of different strategies for reacting to change [116, p.82]

In Kinny and Georgeff's experiments, two different types of reconsideration strategy were used: *bold* agents, which never pause to reconsider their intentions before their current plan is fully executed, and *cautious* agents, which stop to reconsider after the execution of every action. These characteristics are defined by a *degree of boldness*, which specifies the maximum number of plan steps the agent executes before reconsidering its intentions. Dynamism in the environment is represented by the *rate of world change*, γ. Put simply, the rate of world change is the ratio of the speed of the agent's control loop to the rate of change of the world. If $\gamma = 1$, then the world will change no more than once for each time the agent can execute its control loop. If $\gamma = 2$, then the world can change twice for each pass through the agent's control loop, and so on. The performance of an agent is measured by the ratio of number of intentions that the agent managed to achieve to the number of intentions that the agent had at any time. Thus if effectiveness is 1, then the agent achieved all its intentions. If effectiveness is 0, then the agent failed to achieve any of its intentions. The main results of Kinny and Georgeff's experiments are shown in Figure 2.8.[1] This graph shows the effectiveness of an agent on the y axis against the dynamism of the world (log scale) on the x axis. The key results of Kinny and Georgeff were as follows.

• If γ is low (i.e., the environment does not change quickly), then bold agents do well compared to cautious ones. This is because cautious ones waste time reconsidering their commitments while bold agents are busy working towards — and achieving — their intentions.

• If γ is high (i.e., the environment changes frequently), then cautious agents tend to outperform bold agents. This is because they are able to recognize when intentions are doomed, and also to take advantage of serendipitous situations and new opportunities when they arise.

The bottom line is that different environment types require different intention reconsideration and commitment strategies. In static environments, agents that are strongly committed to their intentions will perform well. But in dynamic environments, the ability to react to changes by modifying intentions becomes more important, and weakly committed agents will tend to outperform bold agents.

2.7 Mental States and Computer Programs

We have been talking about programs that have a "belief-desire-intention" architecture. This is mentalistic terminology, and it is worth pausing for a

---

1 I am deeply indebted to Martijn Schut for providing this graph.

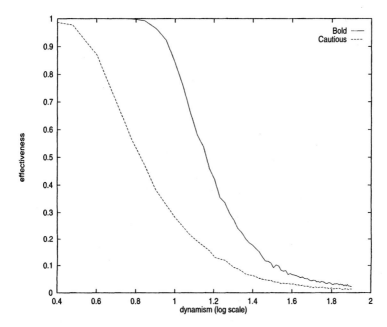

Figure 2.8
Kinny and Georgeff's intention reconsideration experiments.

moment to examine the justification for using such terms. It may seem strange
to think of computer programs in terms of mental states such as beliefs, desires,
and intentions. Is it either useful or legitimate to use mentalistic terminology to
characterize machines? As it turns out, there is an extensive literature on this
subject.

When explaining human activity, it is often useful to make statements such
as the following:

> Janine took her umbrella because she *believed* it was going to rain.
> Michael worked hard because he *wanted* to finish his book.

These statements make use of a *folk psychology*, by which human behavior is
predicted and explained through the attribution of *attitudes*, such as believing
and wanting (as in the above examples), hoping, fearing, and so on (see
e.g., [226, p.1] for a discussion of folk psychology). This folk psychology is
well established: most people reading the above statements would say they
found their meaning entirely clear, and would not give them a second glance.

The attitudes employed in such folk psychological descriptions are called the *intentional* notions.[2] The philosopher Daniel Dennett has coined the term *intentional system* to describe entities "whose behavior can be predicted by the method of attributing belief, desires and rational acumen" [43, p.49], [42]. Dennett identifies different "levels" of intentional system:

A *first-order* intentional system has beliefs and desires (etc.) but no beliefs and desires *about* beliefs and desires. [...] A *second-order* intentional system is more sophisticated; it has beliefs and desires (and no doubt other intentional states) about beliefs and desires (and other intentional states) — both those of others and its own. [43, p.243]

One can carry on this hierarchy of intentionality as far as required.

Now we have been using phrases like belief, desire, intention to talk about computer programs. An obvious question is whether it is legitimate or useful to attribute beliefs, desires, and so on to artificial agents. Isn't this just anthropomorphism? McCarthy, among others, has argued that there are occasions when the *intentional stance* is appropriate:

To ascribe *beliefs, free will, intentions, consciousness, abilities,* or *wants* to a machine is <u>legitimate</u> when such an ascription expresses the same information about the machine that it expresses about a person. It is <u>useful</u> when the ascription helps us understand the structure of the machine, its past or future behavior, or how to repair or improve it. It is perhaps never <u>logically required</u> even for humans, but expressing reasonably briefly what is actually <u>known</u> about the state of the machine in a particular situation may require mental qualities or qualities isomorphic to them. Theories of belief, knowledge and wanting can be constructed for machines in a simpler setting than for humans, and later applied to humans. Ascription of mental qualities is <u>most straightforward</u> for machines of known structure such as thermostats and computer operating systems, but is <u>most useful</u> when applied to entities whose structure is incompletely known. [148], (quoted in Shoham [205]; underlining is from [205])

What objects can be described by the intentional stance? As it turns out, almost any automaton can. For example, consider a light switch:

It is perfectly coherent to treat a light switch as a (very cooperative) agent with the capability of transmitting current at will, who invariably transmits current when it believes that we want it transmitted and not otherwise; flicking the switch is simply our way of communicating our desires. [205, p.6]

And yet most adults in the modern world would find such a description absurd — perhaps even infantile. Why is this? The answer seems to be that while the intentional stance description is perfectly consistent with the observed

---

2 Unfortunately, the word "intention" is used in several different ways in logic and the philosophy of mind. First, there is the BDI-like usage, as in "I intended to kill him." Second, an intentional notion is one of the attitudes, as above. Finally, in logic, the word intension (with an "s") means the internal content of a concept, as opposed to its extension. In what follows, the intended meaning should always be clear from context.

behavior of a light switch, and is internally consistent,

> ... it does not *buy us anything*, since we essentially understand the mechanism suffi-
> ciently to have a simpler, mechanistic description of its behavior. [205, p.6]

Put crudely, the more we know about a system, the less we need to rely
on animistic, intentional explanations of its behavior.[3] An obvious question
is then, if we have alternative, perhaps less contentious ways of explaining
systems, why should we bother with the intentional stance? Consider the
alternatives available to us. One possibility is to characterize the behavior of
a complex system by using the *physical stance* [44, p.36]. The idea of the
physical stance is to start with the original configuration of a system, and then
use the laws of physics to predict how this system will behave:

> When I predict that a stone released from my hand will fall to the ground, I am using
> the physical stance. I don't attribute beliefs and desires to the stone; I attribute mass, or
> weight, to the stone, and rely on the law of gravity to yield my prediction. [44, p.37]

Another alternative is the *design stance*. With the design stance, we use knowledge of what purpose a system is supposed to fulfill in order to predict how it
behaves. Dennett gives the example of an alarm clock [44, pp.37–39]. When
someone presents us with an alarm clock, we do not need to make use of physical laws in order to understand its behavior. We can simply make use of the
fact that all alarm clocks are designed to wake people up if we set them with
a time. No understanding of the clock's mechanism is required to justify such
an understanding — we know that *all* alarm clocks have this behavior.

However, with very complex systems, even if a complete, accurate picture of the system's architecture and working *is* available, a physical or design
stance explanation of its behavior may not be practicable. Consider a computer.
Although we might have a complete technical description of a computer available, it is hardly practicable to appeal to such a description when explaining
why a menu appears when we click a mouse on an icon. In such situations,
it may be more appropriate to adopt an intentional stance description, if that
description is consistent, and simpler than the alternatives.

---

3 Shoham observes that the move from an intentional stance to a technical description of behavior
correlates well with Piaget's model of child development, and with the scientific development
of humankind generally [205]. Children will use animistic explanations of objects — such as
light switches — until they grasp the more abstract technical concepts involved. Similarly, the
evolution of science has been marked by a gradual move from theological/animistic explanations
to mathematical ones. The author's own experiences of teaching computer programming suggest
that, when faced with completely unknown phenomena, it is not only children who adopt animistic
explanations. Indeed, it often seems easier to teach some computer concepts by using explanations
such as: "the computer doesn't know...," than to try to teach abstract principles first.

Note that the intentional stance is, in computer science terms, nothing more than an *abstraction tool*. It is a convenient shorthand for talking about complex systems, which allows us to succinctly predict and explain their behavior without having to understand how they actually work. Now, much of computer science is concerned with looking for good abstraction mechanisms, since these allow system developers to *manage complexity* with greater ease. The history of programming languages illustrates a steady move away from low-level machine-oriented views of programming towards abstractions that are closer to human experience. Procedural abstraction, abstract data types, and most recently, objects are examples of this progression. So, why not use the intentional stance as an abstraction tool in computing — to explain, understand, and, crucially, *program* complex computer systems?

There are other reasons for believing that an intentional stance will be useful for understanding and reasoning about computer programs [102]. First, and perhaps most importantly, the ability of heterogeneous, self-interested agents to communicate seems to imply the ability to talk about the beliefs, aspirations, and intentions of individual agents. For example, in order to *coordinate* their activities, agents must have information about the intentions of others [105]. This idea is closely related to Newell's *knowledge level* [166]. Later in this book, we will see how mental states such as beliefs, desires, and the like are used to give a semantics to *speech acts* [202, 35]. Second, mentalistic models are a good candidate for representing information about end users. For example, imagine a tutoring system that works with students to teach them JAVA programming. One way to build such a system is to give it a *model* of the user. Beliefs, desires, and intentions seem appropriate for the makeup of such models.

For many researchers in AI, this idea of programming computer systems in terms of "mentalistic" notions such as belief, desire, and intention is the key component of agent-based computing. The idea of programming computer systems in terms of mental states was articulated most clearly by Yoav Shoham in his *agent-oriented programming* (AOP) proposal [206]. BDI systems can be viewed as a kind of AOP.

2.8   Notes and Further Reading

Some reflections on the origins of the BDI model, and on its relationship to other models of agency, may be found in [74]. Belief-desire-intention architectures originated in the work of the Rational Agency project at Stanford Research Institute in the mid-1980s. Key figures were Michael Bratman, Phil Cohen, Michael Georgeff, David Israel, Kurt Konolige, and Martha Pollack. The origins of the model lie in the theory of human practical reasoning developed by the philosopher Michael Bratman [20], which focuses particularly on the role of intentions in practical reasoning. The conceptual framework of the BDI model is described in [22], which also describes a specific BDI agent architecture called IRMA.

The best-known implementation of the BDI model is the PRS system, developed by Georgeff and colleagues [78, 77]. The PRS has been re-implemented several times since the mid-1980s, for example in the Australian AI Institute's DMARS system [46], the University of Michigan's C++ implementation UM-PRS, and a JAVA version called JAM! [100]. JACK is a commercially available programming language, which extends the JAVA language with a number of BDI features [26].

The description of the BDI model given here draws upon [22] and [188], but is not strictly faithful to either. The most obvious difference is that I do not incorporate the notion of the "filter override" mechanism described in [22], and I also assume that plans are linear sequences of actions (which is a fairly "traditional" view of plans), rather than the hierarchically structured collections of goals used by PRS.

Plans are central to the BDI model of agency. An excellent discussion on the BDI model, focusing in particular on the role of plans in practical reasoning, is Martha Pollack's 1991 *Computers and Thought* award lecture, presented at the IJCAI-91 conference in Sydney, Australia, and published as "The Uses of Plans" [180]. Another article, which focuses on the distinction between "plans as recipes" and "plans as mental states" is [179].

It is worth emphasizing that the BDI model is only one solution to the problem of building autonomous rational agents. Many other software architectures for agent systems have been described in the literature [249, 24]. The so-called "layered" architectures are currently very popular [242]; examples include Ferguson's TOURINGMACHINES [57, 58], Müller's INTERRAP [163, 162], and the 3T architecture [17]. I mentioned in passing that belief revision is not a concern of this book: see Gärdenfors [71] for further information.

Finally, although in this book I focus on what might be called the "orthodox" BDI model, the BDI model forms a central component of many other systems, which either draw inspiration from it or implement parts of it. Examples include [61, 111, 158, 26].

3 Introduction to $\mathcal{LORA}$

In this chapter, I present an overview of the logical framework that will be used throughout the remainder of the book. This logic allows us to represent the properties of rational agents and reason about them in an unambiguous, well-defined way. The logic is called $\mathcal{LORA}$, which stands for "$\mathcal{L}$ogic $\mathcal{O}$f $\mathcal{R}$ational $\mathcal{A}$gents."

Like any logic, $\mathcal{LORA}$ has a *syntax*, a *semantics*, and a *proof theory*. The syntax of $\mathcal{LORA}$ defines a set of acceptable constructions known as *well-formed formulae* (or just *formulae*). The semantics assign a precise meaning to every formula of $\mathcal{LORA}$. Finally, the proof theory of $\mathcal{LORA}$ tells us some basic properties of the logic, and how we can establish properties of the logic.

The language of $\mathcal{LORA}$ combines four distinct components:

1. A *first-order* component, which is in essence classical first-order logic [223, 52, 73]. This component allows us to represent the properties of objects within a system under study, and how these objects stand in relation to one another.

2. A *belief-desire-intention* component, which allows us to express the beliefs, desires, and intentions of agents within a system.

3. A *temporal* component, which allows us to represent the dynamic aspects of systems — how they vary over time.

4. An *action component*, which allows us to represent the actions that agents perform, and the effects of these actions.

From a logical point of view, combining these elements into a single framework makes $\mathcal{LORA}$ rather complex. For this reason, the presentation of $\mathcal{LORA}$ is divided into two parts. The first part (this chapter), simply gives an informal introduction to the logic: the main constructs it provides, the intuitive semantics of these constructs, how these constructs can be used to express properties of agents and their environments, but most importantly, how to *read and understand* formulae of $\mathcal{LORA}$. This chapter is intended for readers whose logical background is not strong. If you are already familiar with the principles of first-order, modal, temporal, and dynamic logic, then you may wish to skim through this chapter and move quickly to the next chapter, which contains a detailed formal presentation of the language.

Table 3.1
First-order logic connectives and quantifiers.

Formula	Interpretation
$\neg\varphi$	φ is not true
$\varphi \wedge \psi$	φ is true and ψ is true
$\varphi \vee \psi$	φ is true or ψ is true
$\varphi \Rightarrow \psi$	if φ is true then ψ is true
$\varphi \Leftrightarrow \psi$	φ is true if, and only if, ψ is true
$(\tau = \tau')$	τ is the same as τ'
$\forall x \cdot \varphi(x)$	all objects x have property φ
$\exists x \cdot \varphi(x)$	there exists an object x with property φ

3.1 The First-Order Component of $\mathcal{LORA}$

The first thing to say about $\mathcal{LORA}$ is that it is an extension of classical first-order logic. Thus it contains the usual connectives of first-order logic, including "¬" (not), "∧" (and), "∨" (or), "⇒" (implies), and "⇔" (if, and only if). $\mathcal{LORA}$ also contains the first-order quantifiers "∀" (for all) and "∃" (there exists) — see Table 3.1.

To recap, let us consider some formulae of classical first-order logic, which are thus also formulae of $\mathcal{LORA}$. We may as well start with an overused example.

$$\forall x \cdot Man(x) \Rightarrow Mortal(x) \qquad (3.1)$$

This formula simply asserts that all objects x which satisfy property *Man* also satisfy the property *Mortal*. The intended interpretation of the formula is that all men are mortal.

Formally, the x in this formula is a *variable*. By default, we will use the lowercase italic roman letters x, y, and z as variables throughout the book, in order to give the reader some help in understanding formulae.

Man and *Mortal* are *predicates*. The *Man* and *Mortal* predicates each take a single *argument*, and hence they have an *arity* of one. Predicates with arity one (i.e., that take a single argument) are called *properties*, or *unary predicates*. By default, predicate symbols are written as strings of roman letters, starting with an uppercase letter. Where appropriate, predicates are *InterCapped* in the interests of readability.

The symbol "∀" is the *universal quantifier*, and is read as "for all." The symbol "⇒" is the *logical connective* for *implication*. Any formula with the shape $\varphi \Rightarrow \psi$ is read as "φ implies ψ," or "if φ then ψ." Finally, the raised dot "·" and parentheses ")" and "(" are *punctuation symbols*.

The second example illustrates the *existential quantifier*, "∃."

$$\forall x \cdot Man(x) \Rightarrow \exists y \cdot Woman(y) \wedge MotherOf(x, y) \tag{3.2}$$

This formula asserts that for every object x that satisfies the property *Man*, there exists at least one object y such that y satisfies the property of being a woman, and in addition, the *MotherOf* relationship exists between x and y. In other words, for every man x, there is a woman y such that y is the mother of x. In this example, x and y are variables, *Man* and *Woman* are predicate symbols of arity one, and *MotherOf* is a predicate of arity two. Predicates of arity two are often referred to as *two-place* predicates, or *binary* predicates.

The third example illustrates the use of *constants*.

$$\exists x \cdot Monitor(x) \wedge MonitorState(x, ready) \tag{3.3}$$

This formula asserts that there is at least one object x such that x is a *Monitor* and the state of x is *ready*. Here, *Monitor* and *MonitorState* are predicates of arity one and two respectively, x is a variable, and *ready* is a constant. A constant is just a fixed name for a particular thing. Thus formula (3.3) intuitively expresses the fact that some monitor is in a "ready" state.

$$\forall x \cdot \forall y \cdot Person(x) \wedge Person(y) \Rightarrow \neg Superior(x, y) \tag{3.4}$$

This formula asserts that for all people x and y, x is not superior to y — in other words, nobody is superior to someone else. Where we have multiple variables quantified in the same way appearing in succession, as in this example where we have the two universally quantified variables x and y, we simplify the formula as follows.

$$\forall x, y \cdot Person(x) \wedge Person(y) \Rightarrow \neg Superior(x, y) \tag{3.5}$$

We also have *equality* in our language, allowing us to *compare* terms.

$$\forall x, y \cdot USPresident(x) \wedge USPresident(y) \Rightarrow (x = y) \tag{3.6}$$

This formula asserts that if x is U.S. President and y is U.S. President, then x and y must be the same. In other words, there is only one U.S. President.

Examples (3.1)–(3.6) demonstrate some conventions that will be used throughout the remainder of the book:

• predicates will always be written as *InterCapped* strings of italic roman letters starting with an uppercase letter;

• variables will be written as the lower-case italic roman letters x, y, and z;

Table 3.2
Belief, desire, and intention modalities.

Formula	Interpretation
(Bel i φ)	agent i believes φ
(Des i φ)	agent i desires φ
(Int i φ)	agent i intends φ

- constants will be written as strings of lowercase italic roman letters; and
- parentheses (ordinary brackets, such as those surrounding this text) and other types of brackets are used where appropriate to make the intended reading of formulae clear.

Before proceeding, see if you can determine for yourself the intended interpretation of the following formulae.

- $\forall x \cdot (Vegetarian(x) \land \neg Drinks(x, beer)) \Rightarrow Skinny(x)$
- $\forall x \cdot \neg Rich(x) \Rightarrow \neg Happy(x)$
- $\forall x \cdot Pleasant(x) \Rightarrow (Illegal(x) \lor Immoral(x))$

3.2   The Belief, Desire, Intention Component of $\mathcal{LORA}$

So far, all we have is ordinary first-order logic. But $\mathcal{LORA}$ extends first-order logic in a number of important ways. First, $\mathcal{LORA}$ incorporates a whole class of extra connectives, known as *modal connectives* or *modalities*, which allow us to represent the beliefs, desires, and intentions of agents — see Table 3.2 for an overview. We will illustrate these modal connectives by way of example at first, and then discuss some technicalities associated with their use.

We will start with belief. The basic idea is to have a class of formulae with the following structure.

$$(\text{Bel } i \; \varphi) \tag{3.7}$$

Here, i is a term (i.e., a variable or a constant) that denotes an agent, and φ is any formula of $\mathcal{LORA}$. Notice that i *must* be a term standing for an agent. To give the reader some visual clues when reading formulae, I use i and j as terms denoting agents. The formula (3.7) is intended to express the fact that the agent i believes φ. To illustrate the idea, here is a simple formula about beliefs.

$$(\text{Bel } janine \; Sunny(melbourne)) \tag{3.8}$$

The intended interpretation of this formula is that the agent *janine* believes that *Sunny(melbourne)*. In other words, Janine believes it is sunny in Melbourne. Here, *janine* is a first-order logic constant, which denotes a particular agent; *Sunny(melbourne)* is simply a formula of $\mathcal{LORA}$.

$$\exists i \cdot (\text{Bel } i \text{ } Sunny(melbourne)) \tag{3.9}$$

This formula says that some agent i believes it is sunny in Melbourne — in other words, that *somebody* believes it is sunny in Melbourne. Similarly, we can say that *everyone* believes it is sunny in Melbourne.

$$\forall i \cdot (\text{Bel } i \text{ } Sunny(melbourne)) \tag{3.10}$$

We can constrain the variable i so that it only refers to English people — the intended reading of (3.11) is thus that every English person believes it is sunny in Melbourne.

$$\forall i \cdot EnglishPerson(i) \Rightarrow (\text{Bel } i \text{ } Sunny(melbourne)) \tag{3.11}$$

Note that, although Bel is written a little like an ordinary first-order logic predicate that takes two arguments, *it is actually very different*. The most obvious difference is that the arguments to an ordinary first-order predicate must all be *terms* of first-order logic: variables, constants, or functions that return some value. The first argument to the Bel modality is indeed a term, although it is a special kind of term — one that stands for an *agent*. To see why this is important, consider that although the first argument to the Bel modality in the following formula is a term, the formula does not make much sense.

$$(\text{Bel } 0.5 \text{ } Sunny(melbourne))$$

In order to prevent such nonsensical formulae, it is therefore required that the first argument to the Bel modality is a term that stands for an agent.

The second argument to the Bel modality, however, is certainly not a term. *It is actually a formula of $\mathcal{LORA}$*. To emphasize this point, consider the following formula of $\mathcal{LORA}$ — the intended interpretation is that Janine believes all Australian cities are sunny.

$$(\text{Bel } janine \text{ } \forall x \cdot AustralianCity(x) \Rightarrow Sunny(x)) \tag{3.12}$$

Just as we must be careful to ensure that the first argument to the Bel modality is a term denoting an agent, so we must be careful to ensure that the second argument is a formula. As the second argument in the following formula is a natural number, (3.13) is not a legal formula of $\mathcal{LORA}$.

(Bel *janine* 2)   (3.13)

We must therefore be careful how we construct belief, desire, and intention formulae of $\mathcal{LORA}$, to be sure that we are not breaking any logical rules. For example, although we can quantify over the first argument to the Bel predicate (the term denoting the agent), we are not allowed to quantify over the second (the formula). Thus the following is not a legal formula of $\mathcal{LORA}$.

$\exists x \cdot$ (Bel *janine x*)   (3.14)

You might absentmindedly write this formula while trying to represent the fact that there is something that Janine believes. As it turns out, statements like this cannot be represented in our language. The following misguided attempt to represent the statement "Janine believes everything Michael believes" is also illegal in $\mathcal{LORA}$.

$\forall x \cdot$ (Bel *michael x*) $\Rightarrow$ (Bel *janine x*)   (3.15)

Although some logics provide the machinery to represent such statements, they are somewhat complex, and will not be necessary for us. (A short discussion on the merits and drawbacks of such *metalogics* is provided in appendix B.)

Beliefs can be *nested*. The intended interpretation of the following formula is that Janine believes Michael believes that London is rainy.

(Bel *janine* (Bel *michael Rainy(london)*))   (3.16)

Try to understand the intended interpretation of the following formula for yourself.

(Bel *janine* $\forall i \cdot Australian(i)$ $\Rightarrow$ (Bel *i Rainy(london)*))   (3.17)

Of course, belief is just one of three modalities that we use to characterize the state of BDI agents — the other two are, not surprisingly, desires and intentions. We introduce another two modal connectives, (Des i φ) and (Int i φ), to represent desires and intentions respectively. The rules for making desire and intention formulae are the same as for making belief formulae. Thus the following formula is intended to say that Janine desires it to be sunny in Melbourne.

(Des *janine Sunny(melbourne)*)   (3.18)

Similarly, the following formula says that Michael intends to complete his lecture slides.

$$(\text{Int } michael\ Complete(slides)) \tag{3.19}$$

As with beliefs, desires and intentions can be nested. Perhaps more interesting, however, is the fact that we can nest belief, desire, and intention modalities with one another. For example, consider the following formula, which is intended to express the fact that Michael intends that Janine believes it is sunny in Melbourne.

$$(\text{Int } michael\ (\text{Bel } janine\ Sunny(melbourne))) \tag{3.20}$$

The following formula says that Michael desires that everyone will intend to own a book by Michael.

$$(\text{Des } michael\ \forall i \cdot (\text{Int } i\ OwnBookBy(michael)))) \tag{3.21}$$

The possible *relationships* between an agent's beliefs, desires, and intentions, and in particular, the relationships that a *rational* agent should enjoy, will be the focus of much of the remainder of this book.

Before proceeding, see if you can determine for yourself the intended interpretation of the following formulae:

- $\forall i,j \cdot MotherOf(i,j) \Rightarrow (\text{Bel } j\ Wonderful(i))$
- $(\text{Des } janine\ \forall i \cdot (\text{Bel } i\ Dangerous(ozoneHole)))$
- $\exists i \cdot (\text{Bel } i\ \forall j \cdot (\text{Bel } j\ Fool(i)))$
- $\exists i \cdot (\text{Int } i\ \forall j \cdot (\text{Bel } j\ (\text{Int } i\ \neg PrimeMinister(i))))$

Before presenting the temporal component, we will deal with some slightly more advanced issues connected with modalities and quantification. If you found the material presented so far hard going, you may wish to skip this section on a first reading.

Substituting Terms in Modal Contexts*

One of the most difficult issues surrounding the combination of modal operators and first-order logic is connected with the problem of *substituting terms* in the context of modal connectives. Essentially, *the standard substitution rules of first-order logic do not apply in the context of modal operators*. To understand this problem, consider the following example.[1]

Janine believes Keanu Reeves (an actor) is cute. In addition to being an actor, Keanu Reeves is also bass-player for the grunge metal band "Dogstar." Although Janine has heard of Dogstar, and knows they have a bass player, she has no idea that this bass player is Keanu Reeves. Does Janine believe the bass-player of Dogstar is cute?

We can summarize this state of affairs in the following formula of $\mathcal{LORA}$.

$$(\text{Bel } janine \ Cute(keanu)) \wedge (dogstarBassPlayer = keanu) \qquad (3.22)$$

The question is thus: Should it be possible to derive (3.23) from (3.22)?

$$(\text{Bel } janine \ Cute(dogstarBassPlayer)) \qquad (3.23)$$

Intuition suggests such a derivation is unacceptable — belief simply does not work that way. We can ask Janine whether the bass-player of Dogstar is cute, and she will happily tell us that she has no opinion either way. In ordinary first-order logic, however, the fact that we have $dogstarBassPlayer = keanu$ would allow us to substitute $dogstarBassPlayer$ for $keanu$ in a formula without affecting the truth value of the formula. We would not get far manipulating ordinary algebraic equations if we were not able to substitute equal terms! However, with belief statements — and also with other modal operators such as Des and Int — we are not allowed to do this.

To remind ourselves that Bel is not a predicate, but a modal connective, we use the LISP-like notation (Bel . . .) rather than the predicate-like Bel(. . .), and in addition we write modal operator names in an upright sans-serif font rather than the *italic roman* font used for predicates.

Quantifying in to Modal Contexts*

Combining quantification with modal operators can lead to some interesting (if somewhat arcane) situations. Consider the following formula, which its author intended to express the fact that Janine believes somewhere is sunny.

$$(\text{Bel } janine \ \exists x \cdot Sunny(x)) \qquad (3.24)$$

Now contrast (3.24) with the following formula.

$$\exists x \cdot (\text{Bel } janine \ Sunny(x)) \qquad (3.25)$$

---

1 This is a version of the well-known "morning star" puzzle [54, p.84].

Are these two formulae expressing the same or different properties? In our framework, they are different. Formula (3.24) expresses a *weaker* property than (3.25). Specifically, it is expressing the fact that Janine believes somewhere is sunny, but that she does not necessarily know where — she is not necessarily aware of the identity of the sunny place. In contrast, (3.25) expresses a stronger property. It says that there is a place x such that Janine believes of x that it is sunny. Implicitly, (3.25) says that Janine is aware of the *identity* of the sunny place. The terminology is that in (3.25), the variable x is quantified *de re*, whereas in (3.24), it is quantified *de dicto*. The practical upshot of this is that we need to be quite careful when *quantifying in* to the scope of a modal connective, to be sure that we get the interpretation we intend.

Quantifying in to modal contexts has long been recognized as one of the trickier topics in modal logic; see [101, pp.170–210] and [54, pp.83–86] for discussions.

3.3   The Temporal Component of $\mathcal{LORA}$

First-order formulae and the modal connectives introduced above allow us to express the properties of instantaneous states of affairs. For example, when we write

(Bel *janine Sunny*(*melbourne*))

it is implicitly assumed that this formula is expressing a property of some particular time. At some *later* time, it may well be that Janine no longer believes it is sunny in Melbourne. I now introduce a number of connectives that allow us to express the *dynamics* of agents and their environments — how they change over time. In order to do this, I need to say a little about the *temporal model* that underpins $\mathcal{LORA}$. We start from the assumption that the environment may be in any of a set of possible states. One of these states represents "now." The *past*, as viewed from "now" is a *linear, discrete sequence of states*. In other words, *there is only one past*. The course of future events, however, is yet to be determined. From any given time point, there will be a number of possible sequences of time points that represent *possible futures*. In other words, time *branches* into the future.

Branching time may initially seem at odds with our intuitions about the nature of the world — common sense suggests that there is really only *one* history in the real world. The branching structure is quite natural when we

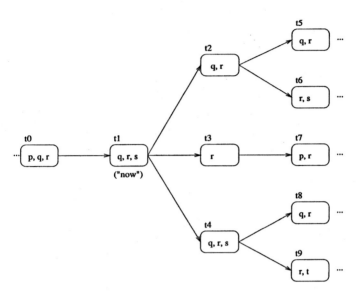

Figure 3.1
An example of a branching temporal structure.

think of representing the *choices* available to agents with respect to the actions they perform. Depending on which choices these agents make, the future may unfold in different ways. But also, we assume there is inherently some *non-determinism* in the environment. That is, the *result* of an action performed by an agent is not pre-determined — there will be a *number* of possible outcomes.

To summarize, while the past is seen as linear, the future is seen as branching. Moreover, we assume that there is no "end of time." In our model, time branches infinitely into the future. All this may sound rather abstract unless you are familiar with *temporal logics*, that is, logics for reasoning about dynamic environments. To make it more concrete, a simple temporal model is presented in Figure 3.1 (more accurately, Figure 3.1 shows *part* of a temporal model).

In this model, there are ten time points, labeled t_0 to t_9 respectively. Each time point is shown as an oval. The arrows between ovals show the progression of time, and so ovals to the right are "later" than those to the left. We take "now" — our *index* into this model — to be t_1. Thus the flow of time to the left of t_1 (the past) is linear, and to the right of t_1 (the future) is branching.

Time points are labeled with the statements that are true in them. Thus in t_1, the statements q, r, and s are all true, and all other predicates are false.

Table 3.3
Path connectives.

Formula	Interpretation
$\bigcirc \varphi$	φ is true next
$\Diamond \varphi$	φ is eventually true
$\Box \varphi$	φ is always true
$\varphi \, \mathcal{U} \, \psi$	φ is true until ψ is true
$\varphi \, \mathcal{W} \, \psi$	φ is true unless ψ is true

(Assume p is shorthand for *Sunny(melbourne)*, and so on.)

From any time point in Figure 3.1, a number of futures are possible. From t_1, for example, the following are all possible futures:

$$(t_1, t_2, t_5, \ldots)$$
$$(t_1, t_2, t_6, \ldots)$$
$$(t_1, t_3, t_7, \ldots)$$
$$(t_1, t_4, t_8, \ldots)$$
$$(t_1, t_4, t_9, \ldots)$$

We refer to these futures as *paths*. The first part of the temporal fragment of $\mathcal{LORA}$ consists of a number of modal connectives that allow us to express the properties of these paths — see Table 3.3. These path connectives have the following interpretation:

• "$\bigcirc$" means "next" — thus $\bigcirc \varphi$ is satisfied now if φ is satisfied at the next moment;

• "$\Diamond$" means "sometime" — thus $\Diamond \varphi$ is satisfied now if φ is satisfied either now or at some future moment;

• "$\Box$" means "always" — thus $\Box \varphi$ is satisfied now if φ is satisfied now and at all future moments;

• "$\mathcal{U}$" means "until" — thus $\varphi \, \mathcal{U} \, \psi$ is satisfied now if ψ is satisfied at some future moment, and φ is satisfied until then — $\mathcal{W}$ is a binary connective similar to $\mathcal{U}$, allowing for the possibility that the second argument might never be satisfied.

With respect to the path $(t_1, t_2, t_6, \ldots)$ it is easy to see that the formula $\bigcirc (q \wedge r \wedge \neg s \wedge \neg t)$ is true, since q and r are both true in time point t_2 (i.e., the next time point along) and s and t are both false in t_2. Similarly, the formula $\Diamond \neg t$ is true on this path, since t is eventually false on this path (in fact, it is false in time points t_2 and t_6). The formula $\Box r$ is true on this path, because r is true on every time point of the path. However, the formula $\Box q$ is not true

Table 3.4
Path quantifiers.

Formula	Interpretation
Aφ	φ is true on all paths
Eφ	φ is true on some path

when evaluated on this path, since while q is true in time points t_1 and t_2, it is *not* true in time point t_6. Similarly, the formula $\Diamond t$ is not true when evaluated on this path, since t is not true at any time point on this path.

With respect to the path $(t_1, t_4, t_9, \ldots)$, the formula $\bigcirc (q \wedge r \wedge s)$ is true, since q, r, and s are all true in time point t_4. The formula $q \mathcal{U} t$ is true on this path, because q is true at all time points until the time point where t is true (time point t_9).

We are allowed to combine temporal operators, so that $\Diamond (p \mathcal{U} q)$ is an allowable formula, for example. We refer to the formulae that may be built up using these path connectives as *path formulae*.

The next connectives provided by $\mathcal{LORA}$ allow us to *quantify* over paths — see Table 3.4. The idea is as follows. Consider the five paths that originate in time point t_1. Then the formula

$$\Box r \tag{3.26}$$

is true on *all* these paths. In other words, (3.26) is *inevitable*. We have a modal connective "A" that allows us to express the fact that some path formula is inevitable:

A$\Box r$

We interpret a formula Aφ as "on all paths that emerge from now, φ is true." We call "A" the *universal path quantifier*.

You might guess that, as well as having a universal path quantifier, we have an *existential* path quantifier, and indeed we do: "E." A formula Eφ is interpreted as "on some path that emerges from now, φ is true." This formula will be true in some time point t if there is at least one path (possibly more than one) rooted at t such that the path formula φ is true on this path. Thus in time point t_1, the formula

E$(q \mathcal{U} t)$

is true, since $q \mathcal{U} t$ is true on the path $(t_1, t_4, t_9, \ldots)$, which is rooted at t_1. Formulae that have no temporal operators, or that are prefixed with "A" or "E" operators are known as *state formulae*.

Before proceeding, you might want to determine for yourself the intended meaning of the following formulae. See if they are true in the temporal structure in Figure 3.1; if not, try to create a structure in which they *are* true.

- $(A \Box p) \wedge (E \Diamond \neg p)$
- $A[(\bigcirc p) \wedge (\bigcirc \Box \neg p)]$
- $A[(\bigcirc p) \wedge (\Box \neg p)]$
- $A[(p \Rightarrow q) \vee (p \Rightarrow \Box \neg r)]$

Quantifying in to Temporal Contexts*

We saw above that quantifying in to belief, desire, and intention contexts can lead to complex situations. The temporal operators of $\mathcal{LORA}$ are also modal connectives, of a kind, and they also fall prey to these problems. To see what I mean by this, consider the following (path) formula, which is intended to be read as "Tony is and always will be Prime Minister."

$$\Box PM(tony) \hspace{4cm} (3.27)$$

Now consider the following two existentially quantified versions of this formula.

$$\Box \exists x \cdot PM(x) \hspace{4cm} (3.28)$$

$$\exists x \cdot \Box PM(x) \hspace{4cm} (3.29)$$

Formula (3.28) asserts that there is always some Prime Minister. That is, whatever time point we pick, there will be an individual that has the property of being Prime Minister.

In contrast, (3.29) asserts that there is some individual who is always Prime Minister. The distinction is that in (3.28), there could be a different Prime Minister at every time point. In contrast, in (3.29), there is just one individual who is Prime Minister in every time point. It should be clear that (3.29) implies (3.28), but the converse does not hold.

A similar situation arises when we consider the "$\Diamond$" operator. Consider the following example.

$$\Diamond \forall x \cdot Free(x) \hspace{4cm} (3.30)$$

Formula (3.30) asserts that at some point in the future, everybody will be free. In other words, there will be some particular time in the future at which everybody will *simultaneously* be free. Now consider the following variation on this theme.

$$\forall x \cdot \Diamond Free(x) \tag{3.31}$$

This example asserts that everybody will be free at some time in the future, but it does not imply that everybody will *simultaneously* be free. Thus I could be free at time t_1, you could be free at time t_2, and so on. Now (3.30) implies (3.31), but the converse does not hold.

Some Common Temporal Properties*

The temporal component of $\mathcal{LORA}$ was introduced in order to allow us to specify the *dynamics* of a system: how the state of an agent, and the environment itself, change over time. The aim in this section is to consider the *types of properties* we find ourselves specifying using this temporal component. As it turns out, the most important types of such properties are *liveness* and *safety* properties.[2]

Informally, a safety property can be interpreted as saying that "something bad won't happen." More formally, a safety property states that every finite prefix of a path satisfies some requirement. For obvious reasons, safety properties are sometimes called invariance properties. The simplest kind of safety property is *global invariance*, expressed by formulae with the following shape.

$$\Box \varphi$$

A *local invariance* states that whenever φ holds, ψ must hold also. Such invariances are specified by formulae with the following shape.

$$\Box(\varphi \Rightarrow \psi)$$

Where a system terminates, *partial correctness* may be specified in terms of a precondition φ, which must hold initially, a postcondition ψ, which must hold on termination, and a condition χ, which indicates when termination has been reached.

$$\varphi \Rightarrow \Box(\chi \Rightarrow \psi)$$

---

2 The material in this section has been adapted from [49, p.1049–1054].

A *mutual exclusion* property is a global invariance of the form:

$$\Box \left(\sum_{i=1}^{n} \varphi_i \le 1 \right).$$

This formula states that at most one of the properties $\varphi_i \in \{\varphi_1, \cdots, \varphi_n\}$ should hold at any one time. The Σ notation arises if one imagines that truth is valued at 1, falsity at 0; the above formula is read "at most one of $\varphi_i \in \{\varphi_1, \ldots, \varphi_n\}$ is true." Any formula written in Σ-notation can be expanded into an ordinary formula if required; the Σ-notation may therefore be regarded as an abbreviation.

A *liveness* property is one that states that "something good will eventually happen." The simplest liveness properties have the following shape.

$$\Diamond \varphi$$

Termination is an example of liveness. Basic termination properties are specified by formulae with the following shape.

$$\varphi \Rightarrow \Diamond \chi$$

This states that every path that initially satisfies the property φ eventually satisfies property χ. Here χ is the property that holds when a path has terminated.

Another useful liveness property is *temporal implication*.

$$\Box(\varphi \Rightarrow \Diamond \psi)$$

Such formulae intuitively state that "every φ is followed by a ψ." *Responsiveness* is a classic example of temporal implication. Suppose φ represents a "request," and ψ a "response." Then the above temporal implication would state that every request is followed by a response. Another example of temporal implication is *total correctness*, which states that a system initially satisfying property φ will eventually terminate (given by χ), and on termination will satisfy property ψ.

$$\Box(\varphi \Rightarrow \Diamond(\chi \wedge \psi))$$

3.4 The Action Component of $\mathcal{LORA}$

The last component of $\mathcal{LORA}$ is probably the hardest to understand. It is the component that allows us to represent the *actions* that agents perform, and the

Table 3.5
Operators for representing actions.

Formula	Interpretation
(Happens α)	action expression α happens next
(Achvs α φ)	action α occurs, and achieves φ
(Agts α g)	group g is required to do action α

effects of these actions. Before we do this, we need to say a little about how actions fit into our temporal model.

The basic idea is that *transitions between states* are *labeled* with actions. Intuitively, it is the performance of an action by some agent that causes the change in state. We assume that actions are *atomic*: only one action is ever performed at any given time. However, we do allow for the same action performed in the same state having *multiple* possible outcomes.

To illustrate these ideas, consider Figure 3.2, in which the branching temporal structure of Figure 3.1 has been augmented by labeling state transitions with the actions that cause them. For simplicity, we will assume in this example that there is only one agent in the environment. From state t_0, the agent performs action α_1, which transforms the environment to state t_1. When the environment is in state t_1, the agent has a choice of two actions available to it. It can either perform action α_2 or it can perform α_3. If it performs α_2, then either state t_2 or state t_3 can result. If instead it chooses to perform α_3, then the only possible outcome is state t_4. From state t_2, the agent has no choice about what action to perform — it must perform α_4, and either state t_5 or state t_6 will result. From state t_3, the agent can only perform action α_5, and only state t_7 can result. Finally, when the environment is in state t_4, the agent has a choice of performing either α_6 or α_3, with t_8 or t_9 resulting respectively.

$\mathcal{LORA}$ provides a number of connectives that allow us to express the properties of actions; these are summarized in Table 3.5. In order to express the fact that some action happens, we have a modal connective "Happens." This connective is similar to $\bigcirc$, $\Diamond$, and $\square$ in that it expresses a property of a path. This operator takes a single argument, an *action expression*, and expresses the fact that this action expression is the first thing that happens on the path. For example, the formula

(Happens α_2)

is true when evaluated on the path $(t_1, t_2, t_5, \ldots)$, for the obvious reason that α_2 is the first action that happens on this path.

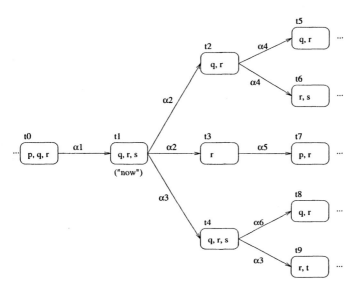

Figure 3.2
A branching temporal structure including actions that cause state transitions.

Table 3.6
Constructors for action expressions.

Expression	Interpretation
$\alpha; \alpha'$	α followed by α'
$\alpha \vert \alpha'$	either α or α'
$\alpha*$	α repeated more than once
$\varphi?$	φ is satisfied

To be precise, the symbol α_2 in the formula (Happens α_2) is actually a *term* of the language $\mathcal{LORA}$ that *stands for* the actual action α_2. $\mathcal{LORA}$ allows us to *combine* terms that stand for actions to make *action expressions* — see Table 3.6. The constructors for action expressions are very similar to the constructs that one finds in imperative programming languages such as PASCAL. Thus we can combine two action terms α and α' to make an action expression $\alpha; \alpha'$, which means α followed by α'. This *sequential composition* constructor behaves exactly like the semicolon in most imperative languages. To make this concrete, consider again the path $(t_1, t_2, t_5, \ldots)$. Then the formula

(Happens $\alpha_2; \alpha_4$)

is true on this path, since α_2 is the action that transforms t_1 to t_2, and α_4 transforms t_2 to t_5.

The *non-deterministic choice* constructor, "|," simply means that one of its arguments occurred. Thus the formula

(Happens $\alpha_2|\alpha_5$)

is true on path $(t_1, t_2, t_5, \ldots)$, since one of α_2 or α_5 occurs on the first transition. So (Happens $\alpha|\alpha'$) means that either α happens or α' happens.

The *iteration constructor*, "$*$," means that its argument occurs zero or more times in succession. With respect to Figure 3.2, consider the path $(t_1, t_2, t_5, \ldots)$. The formula

(Happens α_2*)

is trivially true on this path, since α_2 transforms t_1 to t_2. On the path $(t_1, t_4, t_9, \ldots)$, the action α_3 occurs twice in succession, and so the formula

(Happens α_3*)

is satisfied on this path.

In all programming languages, there is some notion of "test," and $\mathcal{LORA}$ also provides for this. The test constructor, "?," allows us to build action expressions that depend on the truth or falsity of formulae. To illustrate how this works, consider the following formula.

(Happens q?)   (3.32)

Formula (3.32) is true when evaluated on path $(t_1, t_2, t_5, \ldots)$, since the formula q is true on the first state of this path, t_1. However, (3.32) is false when evaluated on the path $(t_3, t_7, \ldots)$, since q is not true in t_3. It may not be obvious why we have the "test" construct. To see why, consider the following formula.

(Happens $(\varphi?; \alpha) \mid (\neg\varphi?; \alpha')$)

This formula says that either $(\varphi?; \alpha)$ will happen or $(\neg\varphi?; \alpha')$ will happen. Thus if φ is true then α will happen, else if $\neg\varphi$ is true then α' will happen. So the action expression $(\varphi?; \alpha) \mid (\neg\varphi?; \alpha')$ captures the sense of a statement

if φ then α else α'.

Similarly, consider the programming language statement

while φ do α

We can capture the sense of this in the following action expression.

$[(\varphi?; \alpha) \mid (\neg\varphi?)]*$

Similarly, the programming language statement

```
repeat α until φ
```

can be represented by the following action expression.

$\alpha; [(\neg\varphi?; \alpha) \mid \varphi?]*$

Finally, actions are usually performed by agents in order to bring about certain states of affairs. We have a modal connective

$(\text{Achvs } \alpha \ \varphi)$

which represents the fact that:

- the action expression α is *possible*, in that α occurs on some path originating from the current state;
- after α is performed, φ is guaranteed to be true.

In order to allow us to designate the agents required to perform a sequence of actions, we have an operator "Agts." This operator takes two arguments: the first is an action expression, the second is a term denoting a set of agents. Thus $(\text{Agts } \alpha \ g)$ means that the group denoted by g are precisely the agents required to perform the actions in the expression α.

Before leaving this section, it is worth commenting on the issue of *quantifying over action expressions*. There is really only one rule that needs to be remembered: We can quantify over sequences of actions, but we are not allowed to quantify over arbitrary action expressions. To see what is meant by this, consider the following formula.

$\exists \alpha \cdot (\text{Happens } \alpha)$

In this path formula, the existentially quantified variable α is a term that denotes a sequence of actions. It is *not* a term that denotes an arbitrary action expression — such terms do not exist in $\mathcal{LORA}$. This restriction has a number of implications. For example, it means that the following type of construction is not legal in $\mathcal{LORA}$.

$\exists \varphi \cdot (\text{Happens } \varphi?)$

(If we allowed this type of construction, then we would implicitly be quantifying over formulae of $\mathcal{LORA}$, which would lead to a number of serious complications.)

3.5 Groups of Agents in $\mathcal{LORA}$

$\mathcal{LORA}$ contains terms that denote *groups* of agents, and gives us a simple but powerful set-theoretic apparatus to represent the properties of such groups. The basic construct, with the obvious set-theoretic interpretation, is as follows.

$(i \in g)$

This state formula asserts that the agent denoted by i is a member of the group denoted by g. Here g is a term that stands for a (non-empty) set of agents.

As well as simply asserting that one agent is a member of a group, we have the expected set-theoretic constructions ($\subseteq$, $\subset$) for expressing subset and other relations between groups of agents.

3.6 Notes and Further Reading

$\mathcal{LORA}$ both draws upon, and extends, a number of previous formalisms. In this section, I briefly consider the relationships between the formalism presented in this chapter and other formalisms developed in the literature.

Syntactically, the logic resembles that of Cohen and Levesque [35]. Like their logic, it has modalities for representing beliefs and goals (desires), and a mechanism for describing the structure and occurrence of complex actions, with action constructors loosely based on those found in dynamic logic [93]. However, it extends their language in several respects. First, it contains terms denoting groups of agents, and provides a set-theoretic mechanism for relating agents and groups at the object-level. In addition, our language takes intentions as primitives — Cohen-Levesque argued that intentions could be reduced to beliefs and goals. A more significant difference is that the new language contains path quantifiers, for quantifying over possible future courses of events; in this respect, the language is similar to those of [185, 245, 216]. Semantically, $\mathcal{LORA}$ is very different to the logic of Cohen and Levesque. The most significant point of difference is that worlds in the Cohen and Levesque language are linear structures whereas worlds in $\mathcal{LORA}$ are themselves branching temporal structures.

A number of other logics for representing the properties of rational agents have been proposed in the literature. Among the most mature of these is the KARO framework of Meyer et al. [153, 137, 99]. KARO is perhaps best viewed as a combination of dynamic logic, doxastic (belief) logic, and a commitment logic. Meyer et al. focus in particular on the *dynamics* of mental states: how actions can change an agents beliefs, desires, and so on. $\mathcal{LORA}$ has much in common with KARO, the main difference being that $\mathcal{LORA}$ is based on temporal logic, and builds a kind of dynamic logic on top of this basic framework. In contrast, KARO builds on top of dynamic logic, and does not have explicit temporal modalities. Semantically, KARO is rather complex — even more so than $\mathcal{LORA}$. See [153, pp.32–33] for a discussion on the relationship of KARO to BDI logic.

Another well-established formal framework for reasoning about agents is that developed by Singh [216]. Singh adopts a CTL*-based branching time framework as his starting point, in which the basic structures, as in $\mathcal{LORA}$, are branching time labeled transition systems. However, Singh's formalism is unusual in that it allows for *concurrent* actions to be performed; another unusual property is that his formalism is based on *continuous* (as opposed to discrete) time. Such a temporal framework is much richer than that which underpins $\mathcal{LORA}$, although one could argue that this richness comes at the cost of complexity — the coherence constraints required to hold the technical framework together are quite elaborate [216, pp.28–37]. Using his basic model, Singh defines belief, intention, and several varieties of ability, and proves completeness for some subsets of his logic.

4 $\mathcal{LORA}$ **Defined**

It is now time to give a complete formal definition of $\mathcal{LORA}$. As I pointed out in previous chapters, $\mathcal{LORA}$ is rather baroque from a logical point of view. It extends full first-order branching time temporal logic with the addition of modalities for referring to the beliefs, desires, and intentions of agents, as well as with a dynamic logic-style apparatus for reasoning about actions.

Although the semantics of $\mathcal{LORA}$ are based upon techniques that are by now standard in the modal and temporal logic communities, the *combination* of so many logical features in the same language makes the formal definition of $\mathcal{LORA}$ somewhat complex. As a result, this chapter contains some long and involved definitions. You will not need to understand all these definitions to make sense of most of the book, but if you are interested in following the various proofs that subsequently appear, then some understanding is essential. If you *do* want to understand the technical detail, then it may be worth reading appendix B before attempting this chapter.

The logic is presented in four parts:

- In section 4.1, I formally define the syntax of the logic.

- In section 4.2, I present the semantics of the logic.

- In section 4.3 I present some *derived connectives* — widely used, useful constructs that are not primitives, but are defined in terms of primitives.

- In section 4.4, I establish some properties of the logic.

4.1 Syntax

$\mathcal{LORA}$ is a *many-sorted* logic, which permits quantification over various types of individuals: agents, (sequences of) actions, sets of agents (groups), and other individuals in the world. All of these sorts must have a corresponding set of terms (variables and individual constants) in the alphabet of the language. In addition, $\mathcal{LORA}$ contains the belief, desire, and intention modalities, the temporal connectives, the usual apparatus of first-order logic, and finally, operators for talking about membership in groups and the agents of an action. The alphabet of $\mathcal{LORA}$ thus contains the following symbols:

1. A denumerable set *Pred* of *predicate symbols*;
2. A denumerable set *Const* of *constant symbols*, the union of the following

mutually disjoint sets:

- $Const_{Ag}$ — constants that stand for agents;
- $Const_{Ac}$ — constants that stand for action sequences;
- $Const_{Gr}$ — constants that stand for sets of agents (groups); and
- $Const_U$ — constants that stand for other individuals.

3. A denumerable set *Var* of *variable symbols*, the union of the following mutually disjoint sets:

- Var_{Ag} — variables that denote agents;
- Var_{Ac} — variables that denote action sequences;
- Var_{Gr} — variables that denote sets of agents (groups); and
- Var_U — variables that denote other individuals.

4. The *modal connectives:*

- "true" — a logical constant for truth;
- "Bel" — the belief modality;
- "Des" — the desire modality;
- "Int" — the intention modality;
- "A" — the universal path quantifier;
- "$\mathcal{U}$" — the binary temporal "until" connective; and
- "$\bigcirc$" — the unary temporal "next" connective.

5. The additional operators:

- "$\in$" — group membership; and
- "Agts" — the agents of an action.

6. The *action constructors:* ";", "|", "*", and "?".

7. The *classical connectives:*

- "$\vee$" — "or" and "$\neg$" — "not".

8. The *universal quantifier:* "$\forall$".

9. The punctuation symbols ")", "(", and "·".

Associated with each predicate symbol is a natural number called its *arity*, given by the *arity* function.

arity : *Pred* → $I\!N$

Predicates of arity 0 are known as *proposition symbols*.

A *sort* is either *Ag, Ac, Gr,* or *U.* If σ is a sort, then the set *Term$_\sigma$*, of *terms of sort* σ, is defined as follows.

Term$_\sigma$ = *Var$_\sigma$* $\cup$ *Const$_\sigma$*

The set *Term*, of all terms, is defined by

Term = *Term$_{Ag}$* $\cup$ *Term$_{Ac}$* $\cup$ *Term$_{Gr}$* $\cup$ *Term$_U$*

We use τ (with decorations: $\tau', \tau_1, \ldots$) to stand for members of *Term*. To indicate that a particular term τ is of type σ, we subscript it as follows: τ_σ.

The syntax of $\mathcal{LORA}$ is then defined by the grammar in Figure 4.1 (it is assumed that predicate symbols are applied to the appropriate number of arguments).

Notice the use of parentheses in operators such as Bel, in order to make explicit the binding between a modality and its arguments. To make the intended interpretation of a formula clear, I also use parentheses and other brackets where necessary. Finally, I assume the "standard" rules of binding between logical connectives [52, pp.39–44].

4.2 Semantics

In general, syntax is easy but semantics is hard — $\mathcal{LORA}$ is no exception to this rule. The semantics of $\mathcal{LORA}$ generalize those of first-order branching time temporal logic. Although the basic underlying structures to $\mathcal{LORA}$ are essentially labeled transition systems, which have been studied in theoretical computer science for decades, the way these structures are used in $\mathcal{LORA}$ is non-standard. I will therefore spend some time introducing and motivating the use of these structures, before moving on to the formal presentation.

The Basic Components: Agents, Actions, and Time

$\mathcal{LORA}$ allows us to represent the properties of a system that may evolve in different ways, depending upon the actions performed by agents within it. We let D_{Ag} be the set of all agents, and let D_{Ac} be the set of all actions these agents may perform.

As noted in chapter 3, the model of time that underpins $\mathcal{LORA}$ is:

- discrete;
- bounded in the past (there is a "start of time");

⟨ag-term⟩	::=	any element of $Term_{Ag}$	/* agent terms */
⟨ac-term⟩	::=	any element of $Term_{Ac}$	/* action terms */
⟨gr-term⟩	::=	any element of $Term_{Gr}$	/* group terms */
⟨ac-exp⟩	::=	⟨ac-term⟩	
	|	⟨ac-exp⟩ ; ⟨ac-exp⟩	/* sequential composition */
	|	⟨ac-exp⟩ "|" ⟨ac-exp⟩	/* non-deterministic choice */
	|	⟨state-fmla⟩?	/* test actions */
	|	⟨ac-exp⟩*	/* iteration */
⟨term⟩	::=	any element of $Term$	/* arbitrary terms */
⟨pred-sym⟩	::=	any element of $Pred$	/* predicate symbols */
⟨var⟩	::=	any element of Var	/* variables */
⟨state-fmla⟩	::=	true	/* truth constant */
	|	⟨pred-sym⟩(⟨term⟩, . . . , ⟨term⟩)	/* predicates */
	|	(Bel ⟨ag-term⟩ ⟨state-fmla⟩)	/* belief formulae */
	|	(Des ⟨ag-term⟩ ⟨state-fmla⟩)	/* desire formulae */
	|	(Int ⟨ag-term⟩ ⟨state-fmla⟩)	/* intention formulae */
	|	(Agts ⟨ac-exp⟩ ⟨gr-term⟩)	/* agents of an action */
	|	(⟨term⟩ = ⟨term⟩)	/* equality */
	|	(⟨ag-term⟩ ∈ ⟨gr-term⟩)	/* group membership */
	|	A⟨path-fmla⟩	/* path quantifier */
	|	¬⟨state-fmla⟩	/* negation */
	|	⟨state-fmla⟩ ∨ ⟨state-fmla⟩	/* disjunction */
	|	∀⟨var⟩ · ⟨state-fmla⟩	/* quantification */
⟨path-fmla⟩	::=	(Happens ⟨ac-exp⟩)	/* action happens */
	|	⟨state-fmla⟩	/* state formulae */
	|	⟨path-fmla⟩ $\mathcal{U}$ ⟨path-fmla⟩	/* until */
	|	○ ⟨path-fmla⟩	/* next */
	|	¬⟨path-fmla⟩	/* negation */
	|	⟨path-fmla⟩ ∨ ⟨path-fmla⟩	/* disjunction */
	|	∀⟨var⟩ · ⟨path-fmla⟩	/* quantification */

Figure 4.1
The syntax of $\mathcal{LORA}$.

- unbounded in the future (there is no "end of time");
- linear in the past (there is only one past history); and
- branching in the future (the course of future events is yet to be determined).

In order to represent such a model, we use a *branching temporal structure*. A branching temporal structure is a *total, backwards-linear* directed graph over a set of T of *time points*. Note that a relation $\mathcal{R}$ is total if every node in $\mathcal{R}$ has at least one successor. Thus the binary relation $\mathcal{R}$ over T is total if it satisfies the following condition.

$$\forall t \cdot t \in T \Rightarrow \exists t' \cdot [t' \in T \text{ and } (t, t') \in \mathcal{R}]$$

We let $\mathcal{R} \subseteq T \times T$ be the branching temporal structure that encodes all ways in which the system can evolve. Arcs in $\mathcal{R}$ will correspond to the performance of atomic actions by agents within the system, and we therefore label these arcs with the actions that they correspond to via the function *Act*.

$$Act : \mathcal{R} \to D_{Ac}$$

Each action is associated with a single agent, given by the function *Agt*.

$$Agt : D_{Ac} \to D_{Ag}$$

Possible Worlds

The state of an agent is defined by its beliefs, desires, and intentions. The semantics of beliefs, desires, and intentions are given using possible worlds, or Kripke semantics [31]. Thus an agent's beliefs in any given situation are characterized by a set of situations — those that are consistent with the agent's beliefs. An agent is then said to believe φ if φ is true in all these possible situations. We refer to this set of "belief alternatives" as *belief-accessible situations*. Similarly, an agent's desires in any given situation are characterized as a set of situations — those that are compatible with the agent's desires. As might be expected, we refer to these as *desire-accessible situations*. Finally, an agent's intentions in a given situation are characterized by a set of *intention-accessible situations*, each of which represents a state of affairs compatible with the agent's intentions.

At this point, the semantics of our framework appear to be quite conventional. However, worlds in $\mathcal{LORA}$ are not instantaneous states but *are themselves branching time structures*. The intuition is that such structures represent an agent's uncertainty not only about how the world actually is, but also about how it will evolve.

Formally, a *world* is a pair $\langle T', \mathcal{R}' \rangle$, where $T' \subseteq T$ is a non-empty set of time points, and $\mathcal{R}' \subseteq \mathcal{R}$ is a branching time structure on T'. Let W be the set of all worlds over T. Formally, W is defined as follows.

$$W = \{\langle T', \mathcal{R}' \rangle \mid T' \subseteq T, \mathcal{R}' \subseteq \mathcal{R}, \text{ and } T' = (\text{dom } \mathcal{R}' \cup \text{ran } \mathcal{R}')\}$$

If $w \in W$ is a world, then we write T_w for the set of time points in w, and $\mathcal{R}_w$ for the branching time relation in w.

A pair $\langle w, t \rangle$, where $w \in W$ and $t \in T_w$, is known as a *situation*. If $w \in W$, then the set of all situations in w is denoted by S_w.

$$S_w = \{ \langle w, t \rangle \mid w \in W \text{ and } t \in T_w \}$$

In order to characterize the beliefs of each agent, we use a function $\mathcal{B}$, which assigns to every agent a relation over situations.

$$\mathcal{B} : D_{Ag} \to \wp(W \times T \times W).$$

I will refer to functions $\mathcal{B}$ as belief accessibility relations, even though, strictly speaking, they are functions that assign belief accessibility relations to agents. In order to simplify what follows, I write $\mathcal{B}_t^w(i)$ to denote the set of worlds accessible to agent i from situation $\langle w, t \rangle$. Formally, $\mathcal{B}_t^w(i)$ is defined as follows.

$$\mathcal{B}_t^w(i) = \{ w' \mid \langle w, t, w' \rangle \in \mathcal{B}(i) \}$$

Belief accessibility relations are required to satisfy several properties. The first is that if a world w' is accessible to an agent from situation $\langle w, t \rangle$, then t is required to be a time point in both w and w'. Formally, this requirement (which we call *world/time point compatibility*) is captured as follows.

$$\text{If } w' \in \mathcal{B}_t^w(i) \text{ then } t \in w \text{ and } t \in w'. \tag{4.1}$$

We also require that the relation that the function $\mathcal{B}$ assigns to every agent is *serial, transitive,* and *Euclidean*. $\mathcal{B}$ is said to be:

- *serial* if for all situations $\langle w, t \rangle$, there is some world w' such that $w' \in \mathcal{B}_t^w(i)$;
- *transitive* if $w' \in \mathcal{B}_t^w(i)$ and $w'' \in \mathcal{B}_t^{w'}(i)$ implies $w'' \in \mathcal{B}_t^w(i)$; and
- *Euclidean* if $w' \in \mathcal{B}_t^w(i)$ and $w'' \in \mathcal{B}_t^w(i)$ implies $w' \in \mathcal{B}_t^{w''}(i)$.

These requirements ensure that the logic of belief corresponds to the well-known modal logic system KD45 [31] — we will see a proof of this later.

To give a semantics to desires and intentions, we proceed in a similar fashion. Thus an agent's desires are given by a function $\mathcal{D}$.

$$\mathcal{D} : D_{Ag} \to \wp(W \times T \times W)$$

An agent's intentions are given by a function $\mathcal{I}$.

$$\mathcal{I} : D_{Ag} \to \wp(W \times T \times W)$$

Both $\mathcal{D}$ and $\mathcal{I}$ are assumed to assign agents serial relations. This ensures that the desire and intention modalities have a logic of KD [31]; we also require that both $\mathcal{D}$ and $\mathcal{I}$ satisfy the world/time point compatibility requirement property, analogous to (4.1) above. As with belief accessibility relations, we write $\mathcal{D}_t^w(i)$ and $\mathcal{I}_t^w(i)$ to denote the desire- and intention-accessible worlds for agent i from situation $\langle w, t \rangle$.

We now present some technical apparatus for manipulating branching time structures. Let $w \in W$ be a world. Then a *path* through w is a sequence $(t_0, t_1, \ldots)$ of time points, such that for all $u \in \mathbb{N}$, we have $(t_u, t_{u+1}) \in R_w$. Let *paths*(w) denote the set of paths through w. In the literature on branching temporal logics, paths are sometimes referred to as *fullpaths* [50]. If p is a path and $u \in \mathbb{N}$, then $p(u)$ denotes the $u + 1$'th element of p. Thus $p(0)$ is the first time point in p, $p(1)$ is the second, and so on. If p is a path and $u \in \mathbb{N}$, then the path obtained from p by removing its first u time points is denoted by $p^{(u)}$.

Domains

We now need to identify the objects that we can *refer to* using $\mathcal{LORA}$. The language will contain terms that stand for these objects, and in particular, these are the objects over which we can quantify. These objects represent the *domain* of $\mathcal{LORA}$ — the *universe of discourse*.

The domain of $\mathcal{LORA}$ contains agents, given by the set D_{Ag}, as well as actions (given by the set D_{Ac}). We will also allow quantification over *sequences of actions*, i.e., the set D_{Ac}^*, groups of agents, given by the set D_{Gr} (where $D_{Gr} \subseteq \wp(D_{Ag})$), and other objects (pints of beer, chairs, pieces of string, etc.) given by a set D_U.

Putting these components together, a *domain (of interpretation)*, D, is a structure:

$$D = \langle D_{Ag}, D_{Ac}, D_{Gr}, D_U \rangle$$

where:

- $D_{Ag} = \{1, \ldots, n\}$ is a non-empty set of agents;
- $D_{Ac} = \{\alpha, \alpha', \ldots\}$ is a non-empty set of actions;
- $D_{Gr} = \wp(D_{Ag}) \setminus \{\emptyset\}$ is a set of non-empty subsets of D_{Ag}, i.e., the set of agent groups over D_{Ag};
- D_U is a non-empty set of other individuals.

If $D = \langle D_{Ag}, D_{Ac}, D_{Gr}, D_U \rangle$ is a domain, then we denote by $\bar{D}$ the set

$$\bar{D} = D_{Ag} \cup D_{Ac}^* \cup D_{Gr} \cup D_U.$$

(Notice that $\bar{D}$ includes the set of *sequences* over D_{Ac}, rather than simply the set D_{Ac}.) If D is a domain and $u \in I\!N$, then by $\bar{D}^u$ we mean the set of u-tuples over $\bar{D}$.

$$\bar{D}^u = \underbrace{\bar{D} \times \cdots \times \bar{D}}_{u \text{ times}}$$

Denotation

In order to give a meaning to formulae of $\mathcal{LORA}$, we need various functions that associate symbols of the language with objects in the domain. The first of these is an *interpretation for predicates*. This is a function that assigns to every predicate at every situation a set of tuples that represent the extension of the predicate in that situation. Formally, an interpretation for predicates, Φ, is a function

$$\Phi : Pred \times W \times T \to \wp(\bigcup_{u \in I\!N} \bar{D}^u).$$

The function Φ is required to *preserve arity*. In other words, if the function assigns a predicate symbol P a set of u-tuples, then the arity of P should be u. Formally, this condition can be stated as follows.

If $arity(P) = u$ then $\Phi(P, w, t) \subseteq \bar{D}^u$ for all $w \in W$ and $t \in T$.

An *interpretation for constants*, C, is a function that takes a constant and a time point and returns the denotation of that constant in that time point.

$$C : Const \times T \to \bar{D}$$

This function is required to preserve sorts, in that if $a \in Const_\sigma$ and $t \in T$, then $C(a, t) \in D_\sigma$. Note that constants do not *necessarily* have a fixed interpretation: a constant a that denotes $d \in \bar{D}$ in time $t \in T$ may denote $d' \in \bar{D}$ at time $t' \in T$, where $d \neq d'$. However, in the remainder of the book, I will assume that *constants have a fixed interpretation unless otherwise stated*, as this clarifies many results.

A *variable assignment*, V, associates variables with elements of the domain.

$$V : Var \to \bar{D}$$

As with interpretations for constants, if $x \in Var_\sigma$, then $V(x) \in D_\sigma$ (i.e., variable assignments preserve sorts). In contrast to constants, the interpretation of variables is fixed across all time points.

We now introduce a derived function $[\![\ldots]\!]_{V,C}$, which gives the *denotation* of an arbitrary term. If V is a variable assignment and C is an interpretation for constants, then by $[\![\ldots]\!]_{V,C}$, we mean the function

$$[\![\ldots]\!]_{V,C} : Term \times T \to \bar{D}$$

that interprets arbitrary terms relative to V and C, as follows:

$$[\![\tau, t]\!]_{V,C} \;\hat{=}\; \begin{cases} C(\tau, t) & \text{if } \tau \in Const \\ V(\tau) & \text{otherwise.} \end{cases}$$

Since V, C, and the time point in which we are evaluating formulae will always be clear from context, reference to them will usually be suppressed: we simply write $[\![\tau]\!]$.

Models and Satisfaction Relations

A *model* for $\mathcal{LORA}$ is a structure

$$M = \langle T, \mathcal{R}, W, D, Act, Agt, \mathcal{B}, \mathcal{D}, \mathcal{I}, C, \Phi \rangle$$

where:

- T is the set of all time points;
- $\mathcal{R} \subseteq T \times T$ is a total, backwards-linear branching time relation over T;
- W is a set of worlds over T;
- $D = \langle D_{Ag}, D_{Ac}, D_{Gr}, D_U \rangle$ is a domain;
- $Act : \mathcal{R} \to D_{Ac}$ associates an action with every arc in $\mathcal{R}$;
- $Agt : D_{Ac} \to D_{Ag}$ associates an agent with every action;
- $\mathcal{B} : D_{Ag} \to \wp(W \times T \times W)$ is a *belief accessibility relation*;
- $\mathcal{D} : D_{Ag} \to \wp(W \times T \times W)$ is a *desire accessibility relation*;
- $\mathcal{I} : D_{Ag} \to \wp(W \times T \times W)$ is an *intention accessibility relation*;
- $C : Const \times T \to \bar{D}$ interprets constants; and
- $\Phi : Pred \times W \times T \to \wp(\bigcup_{u \in \mathbb{N}} \bar{D}^u)$ interprets predicates.

The semantics of the language are defined in two parts, for path formulae and state formulae respectively. The semantics of path formulae are given via the path formula satisfaction relation, "$\models_{\mathcal{P}}$", which holds between *path formulae interpretations* and path formulae. A path formula interpretation is a structure $\langle M, V, w, p \rangle$, where M is a model, V is a variable assignment, w is

$\langle M, V, w, p \rangle \models_{\mathcal{P}} \varphi$	iff $\langle M, V, w, p(0) \rangle \models_{\mathcal{S}} \varphi$ (where φ is a state formula)
$\langle M, V, w, p \rangle \models_{\mathcal{P}} \neg\varphi$	iff $\langle M, V, w, p \rangle \not\models_{\mathcal{P}} \varphi$
$\langle M, V, w, p \rangle \models_{\mathcal{P}} \varphi \vee \psi$	iff $\langle M, V, w, p \rangle \models_{\mathcal{P}} \varphi$ or $\langle M, V, w, p \rangle \models_{\mathcal{P}} \psi$
$\langle M, V, w, p \rangle \models_{\mathcal{P}} \forall x \cdot \varphi$	iff $(M, V \dagger \{x \mapsto d\}, w, p) \models_{\mathcal{P}} \varphi$ for all $d \in \bar{D}$ such that x and d are of the same sort
$\langle M, V, w, p \rangle \models_{\mathcal{P}} \varphi \mathcal{U} \psi$	iff $\exists u \in I\!N$ such that $\langle M, V, w, p^{(u)} \rangle \models_{\mathcal{P}} \psi$ and $\forall v \in I\!N$, if $(0 \leq v < u)$, then $\langle M, V, w, p^{(v)} \rangle \models_{\mathcal{P}} \varphi$
$\langle M, V, w, p \rangle \models_{\mathcal{P}} \bigcirc \varphi$	iff $\langle M, V, w, p^{(1)} \rangle \models_{\mathcal{P}} \varphi$
$\langle M, V, w, p \rangle \models_{\mathcal{P}} (\mathsf{Happens}\ \alpha)$	iff $\exists u \in I\!N$ such that $occurs(\alpha, p, 0, u)$

Figure 4.2
Rules defining the semantics of path formulae. Note that the rule for Happens makes use of the
occurs predicate, which is defined in the text.

a world in M, and p is a path through w. The rules defining the path formula
satisfaction relation are given in Figure 4.2. If $\langle M, V, w, p \rangle \models_{\mathcal{P}} \varphi$, then we say
$\langle M, V, w, p \rangle$ *satisfies* φ, or equivalently, that φ is *true* in $\langle M, V, w, p \rangle$.

The semantics of state formulae are given via the state formula satisfaction
relation, "$\models_{\mathcal{S}}$". This relation holds between state formulae interpretations
and state formulae. State formulae interpretations are structures of the form
$\langle M, V, w, t \rangle$, where M is a model, V is a variable assignment, w is a world
in M, and $t \in T_w$ is a time point in w. The rules defining this relation are
given in Figure 4.3. As with path formulae, if $\langle M, V, w, t \rangle \models_{\mathcal{S}} \varphi$, then we say
$\langle M, V, w, t \rangle$ *satisfies* φ, or φ is *true* in $\langle M, V, w, t \rangle$.

The rule for the Agts connective makes use of a function *Agts*, which
extends the *Agt* function to arbitrary action expressions.

$$Agts(\alpha, t) \hat{=} \begin{cases} \{Agt(\alpha_1), \ldots, Agt(\alpha_k)\} & \text{where } [\![\alpha, t]\!] = \alpha_1, \ldots, \alpha_k \\ Agts(\alpha_1, t) \cup Agts(\alpha_2, t) & \text{where } \alpha = \alpha_1; \alpha_2 \text{ or } \alpha = \alpha_1 \mid \alpha_2 \\ Agts(\alpha_1, t) & \text{where } \alpha = \alpha_1 * \\ \emptyset & \text{where } \alpha \text{ is of the form } \varphi? \end{cases}$$

The first case in this inductive definition deals with the sequences of actions.
The second case deals with sequential composition and non-deterministic
choice. The third case deals with iteration, and the final case with test actions.

The Semantics of Action Expressions

The semantic rules for path formulae make use of an important auxiliary
definition: *occurs*. This definition is used to define the Happens operator.
We write $occurs(\alpha, p, u, v)$ to indicate that action α occurs between "times"

$\langle M,V,w,t\rangle \models_S$ true	
$\langle M,V,w,t\rangle \models_S P(\tau_1,\ldots,\tau_n)$	iff $\langle \llbracket \tau_1 \rrbracket, \ldots, \llbracket \tau_n \rrbracket \rangle \in \Phi(P,w,t)$
$\langle M,V,w,t\rangle \models_S \neg\varphi$	iff $\langle M,V,w,t\rangle \not\models_S \varphi$
$\langle M,V,w,t\rangle \models_S \varphi \vee \psi$	iff $\langle M,V,w,t\rangle \models_S \varphi$ or $\langle M,V,w,t\rangle \models_S \psi$
$\langle M,V,w,t\rangle \models_S \forall x \cdot \varphi$	iff $\langle M,V \dagger \{x \mapsto d\},w,t\rangle \models_S \varphi$
	for all $d \in \bar{D}$ such that x and d are of the same sort
$\langle M,V,w,t\rangle \models_S (\text{Bel } i\, \varphi)$	iff $\forall w' \in W$, if $w' \in \mathcal{B}_t^w(\llbracket i \rrbracket)$, then $\langle M,V,w',t\rangle \models_S \varphi$
$\langle M,V,w,t\rangle \models_S (\text{Des } i\, \varphi)$	iff $\forall w' \in W$, if $w' \in \mathcal{D}_t^w(\llbracket i \rrbracket)$, then $\langle M,V,w',t\rangle \models_S \varphi$
$\langle M,V,w,t\rangle \models_S (\text{Int } i\, \psi)$	iff $\forall w' \in W$, if $w' \in \mathcal{I}_t^w(\llbracket i \rrbracket)$, then $\langle M,V,w',t\rangle \models_S \varphi$
$\langle M,V,w,t\rangle \models_S (\text{Agts } \alpha\, g)$	iff $Agts(\alpha,t) = \llbracket g \rrbracket$
$\langle M,V,w,t\rangle \models_S (\tau = \tau')$	iff $\llbracket \tau \rrbracket = \llbracket \tau' \rrbracket$
$\langle M,V,w,t\rangle \models_S (i \in g)$	iff $\llbracket i \rrbracket \in \llbracket g \rrbracket$
$\langle M,V,w,t\rangle \models_S \mathsf{A}\varphi$	iff $\forall p \in paths(w)$, if $p(0) = t$, then $\langle M,V,w,p\rangle \models_P \varphi$

Figure 4.3
Rules defining the semantics of state formulae.

$u,v \in I\!\!N$ on the path p. Note that *occurs* is a *meta-language* predicate. It is a predicate that we use in our presentation of $\mathcal{LORA}$, rather than a predicate that would be used in a formula of $\mathcal{LORA}$ itself.

The *occurs* predicate is best illustrated by an example. Suppose we have a path p through a world w, in which the arcs are labeled as follows.

$$p: t_0 \xrightarrow{\alpha_0} t_1 \xrightarrow{\alpha_1} t_2 \xrightarrow{\alpha_1} t_3 \xrightarrow{\alpha_1} t_4 \xrightarrow{\alpha_2} t_5 \longrightarrow \cdots$$

Then:

- *occurs*$(\alpha_0, p, 0, 1)$ holds, as the arc $(p(0), p(1))$, i.e., (t_0, t_1), is labeled with α_0;
- *occurs*$(\alpha_0; \alpha_1, p, 0, 2)$ holds, as *occurs*$(\alpha_0, p, 0, 1)$ holds (this was the first example), and *occurs*$(\alpha_1, p, 1, 2)$ holds, since the arc $(p(1), p(2))$, that is, (t_1, t_2), is labeled with the action α_1;
- *occurs*$(\alpha_0; (\alpha_1*), p, 0, 4)$ holds, as *occurs*$(\alpha_0, p, 0, 1)$ holds (this was the first example), and *occurs*$(\alpha_1*, p, 1, 4)$ holds. To see that *occurs*$(\alpha_1*, p, 1, 4)$ holds, note that *occurs*$(\alpha_1, p, 1, 2)$ holds and *occurs*$(\alpha_1*, p, 2, 4)$ holds. To see that *occurs*$(\alpha_1*, p, 2, 4)$ holds, observe that *occurs*$(\alpha_1, p, 2, 3)$ holds and *occurs*$(\alpha_1*, p, 3, 4)$ holds since *occurs*$(\alpha_1, p, 3, 4)$ holds.

I leave it to the reader to use similar reasoning to show that the following also hold.

$occurs(\alpha_1*; \alpha_2, p, 1, 5)$

$occurs(\alpha_0; (\alpha_1 \mid \alpha_2)*, p, 0, 5)$

Formally, the *occurs* predicate is defined inductively by five rules: one for each of the action expression constructors, and one for the execution of primitive actions. The first rule represents the base case, where a primitive action is executed.

$$occurs(\alpha, p, u, v) \text{ iff } v = u + k \text{ and } [\![\alpha, p(u)]\!] = \alpha_1, \ldots, \alpha_k \text{ and}$$
$$Act(p(u), p(u+1)) = \alpha_1, \ldots, Act(p(u+k-1), p(u+k)) = \alpha_k \qquad (4.2)$$
$$(\text{where } \alpha \in Term_{Ac})$$

Thus primitive action α occurs on path p between u and $u + 1$ if the arc from u to $u + 1$ is labeled with α.

The second rule captures the semantics of sequential composition. The action expression $\alpha; \alpha'$ will occur between times u and v iff there is some time point n between u and v such that α is executed between u and n, and α' is executed between n and v.

$$occurs(\alpha; \alpha', p, u, v) \text{ iff } \exists n \in \{u, \ldots, v\} \text{ such that} \qquad (4.3)$$
$$occurs(\alpha, p, u, n) \text{ and } occurs(\alpha', p, n, v)$$

The semantics of non-deterministic choice are even simpler. The action expression $\alpha \mid \alpha'$ will be executed between times u and v iff either α or α' is executed between those times.

$$occurs(\alpha \mid \alpha', p, u, v) \text{ iff } occurs(\alpha, p, u, v) \text{ or } occurs(\alpha', p, u, v) \qquad (4.4)$$

The semantics of iteration rely upon the fact that executing $\alpha*$ is the same as either: (i) doing nothing, or (ii) executing α once and then executing $\alpha*$. This leads to the following *fixed point* rule, where the right-hand side is defined in terms of the left-hand side.

$$occurs(\alpha*, p, u, v) \text{ iff } u = v \text{ or } occurs(\alpha; (\alpha*), p, u, v) \qquad (4.5)$$

Finally, we have a rule that defines the semantics of test actions. The idea is that action expression $\varphi?$ occurs between times u and v on path p if φ is satisfied on p at time u. This rule recursively makes use of the definition of whether or not a formula is satisfied; in practice, the interpretation against which the formula is being evaluated will always be clear from context.

$$occurs(\varphi?, p, u, v) \text{ iff } \langle M, V, w, p(u) \rangle \models_{\mathcal{S}} \varphi \tag{4.6}$$

4.3 Derived Connectives

In addition to the basic connectives defined above, it is useful to introduce
some *derived* constructs. These derived connectives do not add to the expressive power of the language, but are intended to make formulae more concise
and readable. We say they are "derived" because they are all defined in terms
of existing constructs of the language.

   We begin by assuming that the remaining connectives of classical logic
(i.e., "∧" — "and," "⇒" — "if... then...," and "⇔" — "if, and only if") have
been defined as normal, in terms of "¬" (not) and "∨" (or).

$$\varphi \wedge \psi \;\; \hat{=} \;\; \neg(\neg\varphi \vee \neg\psi)$$
$$\varphi \Rightarrow \psi \;\; \hat{=} \;\; (\neg\varphi \vee \psi)$$
$$\varphi \Leftrightarrow \psi \;\; \hat{=} \;\; ((\varphi \Rightarrow \psi) \wedge (\psi \Rightarrow \varphi))$$

Similarly, we assume that the existential quantifier, "∃", has been defined as
the dual of "∀".

$$\exists x \cdot \varphi \;\hat{=}\; \neg\forall x \cdot \neg\varphi$$

Derived Temporal Operators

Next, we introduce the *existential path quantifier*, "E", which is defined as the
dual of the universal path quantifier "A". Thus a formula $E\varphi$ is interpreted as
"on some path, φ," or "optionally, φ":

$$E\varphi \;\hat{=}\; \neg A\neg\varphi.$$

It is also convenient to introduce further temporal connectives. The unary connective "◊" means "sometimes." Thus the path formula $\Diamond\varphi$ will be satisfied
on some path if φ is satisfied at some point along the path. The unary "□"
connective means "now, and always." Thus $\Box\varphi$ will be satisfied on some path
if φ is satisfied at all points along the path. We also have a weak version of the
"$\mathcal{U}$" connective: $\varphi\,\mathcal{W}\,\psi$ is read "φ *unless* ψ."

$$\Diamond\varphi \;\; \hat{=} \;\; true\,\mathcal{U}\,\varphi$$
$$\Box\varphi \;\; \hat{=} \;\; \neg\Diamond\neg\varphi$$
$$\varphi\,\mathcal{W}\,\psi \;\; \hat{=} \;\; (\varphi\,\mathcal{U}\,\psi) \vee \Box\varphi.$$

Thus $\varphi \, \mathcal{W} \, \psi$ means that either: (i) φ is satisfied until ψ is satisfied; or else (ii) φ is always satisfied. It is said to be *weak* because it does not require that ψ be eventually satisfied.

Derived Operators for Reasoning about Groups

$\mathcal{LORA}$ provides us with the ability to use simple set theory to relate the properties of agents and groups of agents. The operators $\subseteq$ and $\subset$ relate groups together, and have the obvious set-theoretic interpretation; (Singleton g i) means g is a singleton group with i as the only member; (Singleton g) simply means g is a singleton.

$$(g \subseteq g') \qquad \hat{=} \quad \forall i \cdot (i \in g) \Rightarrow (i \in g')$$
$$(g \subset g') \qquad \hat{=} \quad (g \subseteq g') \wedge \neg(g = g')$$
$$(\text{Singleton } g \ i) \quad \hat{=} \quad \forall j \cdot (j \in g) \Rightarrow (j = i)$$
$$(\text{Singleton } g) \quad \hat{=} \quad \exists i \cdot (\text{Singleton } g \ i)$$

Derived Operators for Reasoning about Actions

We will abuse notation a little by writing (Agt α i) to mean that i is the only agent required to perform action α.

$$(\text{Agt } \alpha \ i) \, \hat{=} \, \forall g \cdot (\text{Agts } \alpha \ g) \Rightarrow (\text{Singleton } g \ i)$$

We will frequently need to formalize statements along the lines of "α is a good plan for φ." In order to do this, we use some definitions that closely resemble dynamic logic [93]. The first of these is the derived operator Poss. The intuition is that (Poss α φ) means that the action α occurs on *at least one* possible future, and after α is executed, φ is true.

$$(\text{Poss } \alpha \ \varphi) \, \hat{=} \, \mathsf{E}(\text{Happens } \alpha; \varphi?)$$

If you are familiar with dynamic logic, you will recognize that (Poss α φ) corresponds approximately to $\langle \alpha \rangle \varphi$. Similarly, we can capture the dynamic logic $[\alpha]\varphi$ through the Nec operator.

$$(\text{Nec } \alpha \ \varphi) \, \hat{=} \, \mathsf{A}((\text{Happens } \alpha) \Rightarrow (\text{Happens } \alpha; \varphi?))$$

Thus (Nec α φ) simply means that on all paths where α occurs, φ is true immediately after α. However, (Nec α φ) does *not* imply that α occurs on any path — it simply says that if it does, then φ follows.

The (Achvs α φ) operator is defined as a combination of Nec and Poss. (Achvs α φ) means that α does indeed happen on some path, and after α

happens, φ is guaranteed to be true.

(Achvs $\alpha\ \varphi$) $\hat{=}$ (Poss $\alpha\ \varphi$) $\wedge$ (Nec $\alpha\ \varphi$)

4.4   Some Properties of $\mathcal{LORA}$

After introducing a new logic by means of its syntax and semantics, it is usual
to illustrate the properties of the logic by means of a Hilbert-style axiom
system. However, no complete axiomatization is currently known for CTL*,
the branching temporal logic that underpins $\mathcal{LORA}$.[1] Completeness proofs for
temporal modal logics, even in the propositional case, are relatively few and far
between [54, p.307]. For these reasons, I stay primarily at the *semantic* level,
dealing with valid formulae, rather than attempt a traditional axiomatization.

We use conventional definitions of validity and satisfiability, complicated
slightly by the fact that we have essentially two languages, for path and state
formulae.

Formally, a path formula φ is said to be *satisfiable* iff for *some* $\langle M, V, w, p \rangle$,
we have $\langle M, V, w, p \rangle \models_{\mathcal{P}} \varphi$; it is said to be *valid* iff for *all* $\langle M, V, w, p \rangle$, we
have $\langle M, V, w, p \rangle \models_{\mathcal{P}} \varphi$. We indicate that φ is a valid path formula by writing

$$\models_{\mathcal{P}} \varphi$$

Similarly, the state formula φ is said to be satisfiable iff for some $\langle M, V, w, t \rangle$,
we have $\langle M, V, w, t \rangle \models_{\mathcal{S}} \varphi$; it is said to be valid iff for all $\langle M, V, w, t \rangle$, we have
$\langle M, V, w, t \rangle \models_{\mathcal{S}} \varphi$. We indicate that φ is a valid state formula by writing

$$\models_{\mathcal{S}} \varphi$$

It is easy to see that state formula validity implies path formula validity.

LEMMA 4.1:   If $\models_{\mathcal{S}} \varphi$ then $\models_{\mathcal{P}} \varphi$.

Proof State formulae are also path formulae, and the semantic rules for
evaluating them are identical.   ∎

---

1 Proving completeness for an axiomatization of CTL* has been a major open problem in temporal
logic since the logic was first formulated in the mid-1980s. Stirling reported an axiomatization
in [227], though it subsequently transpired that the completeness proof contained a bug. Mark
Reynolds from Murdoch University in Australia reported a complete axiomatization in 1998,
though at the time of writing, the work was still under review. To find out more, I urge you to
contact Mark directly.

This Lemma means that certain formulae will be valid by virtue of their shape, irrespective of whether or not they are actually path formulae or state formulae. For example, presented with a formula ψ that has the shape $\varphi \vee \neg\varphi$, we do not need to worry about whether ψ is a path formula or a state formula: whichever it is, we know it will be valid. To indicate that a formula φ is valid in this regard, we write $\models \varphi$.

We can establish a similar result with respect to satisfiability.

LEMMA 4.2:   If φ is a satisfiable state formula, then φ is a satisfiable path formula.

Since the semantics of $\mathcal{LORA}$ generalize those of classical logic, classical modes of reasoning can be used in $\mathcal{LORA}$.

THEOREM 4.1:

1. If φ is a substitution instance of a propositional logic tautology, then $\models \varphi$.
2. If $\models \varphi \Rightarrow \psi$ and $\models \varphi$, then $\models \psi$.

Proof   For (1), simply observe that the semantics of the propositional connectives "$\neg$" and "$\vee$" are identical to classical logic. Similarly, for (2) — which is simply modus ponens — the reasoning is identical to classical propositional or first-order logic.   ■

$\mathcal{LORA}$ also has the properties one would expect of a sorted first-order logic. We use the normal form $\varphi(x)$ to mean that the variable x is *free* in φ, where "free" has its standard interpretation. Additionally, $\varphi[x/y]$ is used to denote the formula obtained from φ by systematically replacing every occurrence of y in φ by x (i.e., normal first-order substitution — see, e.g., [52, pp.104–106]).

THEOREM 4.2:

1. $\models \forall x \cdot \varphi(x) \Rightarrow \varphi[\tau/x]$ (where τ is a term that does not occur free in φ, x and τ are the same sort, and φ does not contain any modal or temporal connectives).
2. $\models (\tau = \tau)$.
3. $\models (\tau = \tau') \Rightarrow (\varphi \Rightarrow \varphi[\tau'/\tau])$ (where τ' does not occur in the scope of any modal or temporal operator in φ).

Proof   (1) follows immediately from the semantics of universal quantification. (2) and (3) follow immediately from the semantics of equality. ∎

Next, we turn to the belief operator, Bel. This is essentially a normal modal necessity connective, with semantics given via a serial, Euclidean, and transitive accessibility relation [31]. Thus the logic of Bel corresponds to the well-known normal modal system "weak-S5," or KD45. Although the proofs for Theorem 4.3 are readily available in the literature, they are included here for completeness; see the further reading section for references.

THEOREM 4.3:

1. $\models_S$ (Bel i $(\varphi \Rightarrow \psi))$ $\Rightarrow$ ((Bel i φ) $\Rightarrow$ (Bel i ψ)).
2. $\models_S$ (Bel i φ) $\Rightarrow$ $\neg$(Bel i $\neg\varphi$).
3. $\models_S$ (Bel i φ) $\Rightarrow$ (Bel i (Bel i φ)).
4. $\models_S$ $\neg$(Bel i φ) $\Rightarrow$ (Bel i $\neg$(Bel i φ)).
5. If $\models_S$ φ then $\models_S$ (Bel i φ).

Proof For (1), suppose $\langle M, V, w, t \rangle \models_S$ (Bel i $(\varphi \Rightarrow \psi))$ and $\langle M, V, w, t \rangle \models_S$ (Bel i φ) for arbitrary $\langle M, V, w, t \rangle$. From the semantics of Bel, we know that $\langle M, V, w', t \rangle \models_S \varphi \Rightarrow \psi$ and $\langle M, V, w', t \rangle \models_S \varphi$ for all w' such that $w' \in \mathcal{B}_t^w([\![i]\!])$. Hence $\langle M, V, w', t \rangle \models_S \psi$, and so $\langle M, V, w, t \rangle \models_S$ (Bel i ψ). For (2), suppose not. Then for some $\langle M, V, w, t \rangle$ we have both $\langle M, V, w, t \rangle \models_S$ (Bel i φ) and $\langle M, V, w, t \rangle \models_S$ (Bel i $\neg\varphi$). Since the belief accessibility relation is serial, we know there will be at least one $w' \in \mathcal{B}_t^w([\![i]\!])$, and from the semantics of Bel, we therefore know that $\langle M, V, w', t \rangle \models_S \varphi$ and $\langle M, V, w', t \rangle \models_S \neg\varphi$, hence $\langle M, V, w', t \rangle \models_S \varphi$ and $\langle M, V, w', t \rangle \not\models_S \varphi$, which is a contradiction. For (3), assume $\langle M, V, w, t \rangle \models_S$ (Bel i φ) for arbitrary $\langle M, V, w, t \rangle$. We need to show that $\langle M, V, w, t \rangle \models_S$ (Bel i (Bel i φ)), which by the semantics of Bel amounts to showing that $\langle M, V, w', t \rangle \models_S$ (Bel i φ) for all $w' \in \mathcal{B}_t^w([\![i]\!])$, which in turn amounts to showing that $\langle M, V, w'', t \rangle \models_S$ (Bel i φ) for all $w'' \in \mathcal{B}_t^{w'}([\![i]\!])$. But since the belief accessibility relation is transitive, if $w' \in \mathcal{B}_t^w([\![i]\!])$, and $w'' \in \mathcal{B}_t^{w'}([\![i]\!])$, then $w'' \in \mathcal{B}_t^w([\![i]\!])$, and since $\langle M, V, w, t \rangle \models_S$ (Bel i φ), then by the semantics of Bel, we have $\langle M, V, w'', t \rangle \models_S$ (Bel i φ), and we are done. For (4), suppose $\langle M, V, w, t \rangle \models_S$ $\neg$(Bel i φ). Then for some $w' \in \mathcal{B}_t^w([\![i]\!])$, we have $\langle M, V, w', t \rangle \models_S \neg\varphi$. Now, consider any world $w'' \in \mathcal{B}_t^w([\![i]\!])$. The belief accessibility relation is Euclidean, and so since $w' \in \mathcal{B}_t^w([\![i]\!])$ and $w'' \in \mathcal{B}_t^w([\![i]\!])$ we have $w' \in \mathcal{B}_t^{w''}([\![i]\!])$. Hence $\langle M, V, w'', t \rangle \models_S \neg\varphi$, and since w'' was arbitrary, we therefore have $\langle M, V, w, t \rangle \models_S$ (Bel $i \neg$(Bel $i \varphi$)). For (5), assume that $\models_S \varphi$. We need to show that $\langle M, V, w, t \rangle \models_S$ (Bel $i \varphi$) for all $\langle M, V, w, t \rangle$. But since $\models_S \varphi$, then by definition φ is satisfied by all interpretation structures, and in particular, $\langle M, V, w', t \rangle \models_S \varphi$ for all $w' \in B_t^w(\llbracket i \rrbracket)$. Hence $\langle M, V, w, t \rangle \models_S$ (Bel $i \varphi$). ∎

Note that (1) in Theorem 4.3 is usually known as the "K" axiom; (2) is known as the "D" axiom; (3) as the "4" axiom, and (4) as the "5" axiom. Property (5) is known as *belief necessitation*.

    The Des and Int connectives have a logic that corresponds to the normal modal system KD. (The proofs are identical to those of Theorem 4.3, and are therefore omitted.)

THEOREM 4.4:

1. $\models_S$ (Des i ($\varphi \Rightarrow \psi$)) $\Rightarrow$ ((Des $i\,\varphi$) $\Rightarrow$ (Des $i\,\psi$)).
2. $\models_S$ (Des $i\,\varphi$) $\Rightarrow \neg$(Des $i \neg\varphi$).
3. If $\models_S \varphi$ then $\models_S$ (Des $i\,\varphi$).

THEOREM 4.5:

1. $\models_S$ (Int i ($\varphi \Rightarrow \psi$)) $\Rightarrow$ ((Int $i\,\varphi$) $\Rightarrow$ (Int $i\,\psi$)).
2. $\models_S$ (Int $i\,\varphi$) $\Rightarrow \neg$(Int $i \neg\varphi$).
3. If $\models_S \varphi$ then $\models_S$ (Int $i\,\varphi$).

Turning to the temporal connectives in $\mathcal{LORA}$, state formulae have a number of properties with respect to path quantifiers.

THEOREM 4.6:   If φ is a state formula, then: $\models_S \varphi \Leftrightarrow E\varphi \Leftrightarrow A\varphi$.

Proof Assume φ is a state formula. Then we need to prove three cases.

• $\varphi \Rightarrow E\varphi$
Assume $\langle M, V, w, t \rangle \models_S \varphi$ for arbitrary $\langle M, V, w, t \rangle$. Then for any path $p \in paths(w)$ such that $p(0) = t$, we know that $\langle M, V, w, p \rangle \models_P \varphi$, so $\langle M, V, w, t \rangle \models_S E\varphi$.

• $E\varphi \Rightarrow A\varphi$
Assume $\langle M, V, w, t \rangle \models_S E\varphi$ for arbitrary $\langle M, V, w, t \rangle$. Then by the semantics of E, we know that $\langle M, V, w, p \rangle \models_P \varphi$ for some $p \in paths(w)$ such that

$p(0) = t$. From the semantics of state formulae interpreted on paths, we thus have $\langle M, V, w, t \rangle \models_S \varphi$, and so for *any* path $p' \in paths(w)$ such that $p(0) = t$, we have $\langle M, V, w, p' \rangle \models_P \varphi$ and so from the semantics of A, we know $\langle M, V, w, t \rangle \models_S A\varphi$.

- $A\varphi \Rightarrow \varphi$

Assume $\langle M, V, w, t \rangle \models_S A\varphi$ for arbitrary $\langle M, V, w, t \rangle$. Then by the semantics of A, we know that $\langle M, V, w, p \rangle \models_P \varphi$ for all $p \in paths(w)$ such that $p(0) = t$. Since the branching time relation is total, we know there is at least one such path, and so we have $\langle M, V, w, t \rangle \models_S \varphi$.

This completes the proof. ∎

The universal path quantifier A also behaves rather like a normal modal necessity connective with logic S5.

THEOREM 4.7:

1. $\models_S A(\varphi \Rightarrow \psi) \Rightarrow ((A\varphi) \Rightarrow (A\psi))$.
2. $\models_S A\varphi \Rightarrow \neg(A\neg\varphi)$.
3. $\models_S A\varphi \Rightarrow \varphi$ (for state formulae φ).
4. $\models_S A\varphi \Rightarrow AA\varphi$.
5. $\models_S \neg A\varphi \Rightarrow A\neg A\varphi$.
6. If $\models_P \varphi$ then $\models_S A\varphi$.

Proof For (1), assume $\langle M, V, w, t \rangle \models_S A(\varphi \Rightarrow \psi)$ and $\langle M, V, w, t \rangle \models_S A\varphi$ for arbitrary $\langle M, V, w, t \rangle$. Then $\langle M, V, w, p \rangle \models_P \varphi \Rightarrow \psi$ and $\langle M, V, w, p \rangle \models_P \varphi$ for all $p \in paths(w)$ such that $p(0) = t$. Hence $\langle M, V, w, p \rangle \models_P \psi$ for all $p \in paths(w)$ such that $p(0) = t$, and so $\langle M, V, w, t \rangle \models_S A(\psi)$ and we are done. For (2), assume $\langle M, V, w, t \rangle \models_S A\varphi$ and $\langle M, V, w, t \rangle \models_S A\neg\varphi$ for arbitrary $\langle M, V, w, t \rangle$. Then from the semantics of A, we have $\langle M, V, w, p \rangle \models_P \varphi$ and $\langle M, V, w, p \rangle \models_P \neg\varphi$ for all $p \in paths(w)$ such that $p(0) = t$. (Since the branching time relation is total, we know there will be at least one such path.) Hence both $\langle M, V, w, p \rangle \models_P \varphi$ and $\langle M, V, w, p \rangle \not\models_P \neg\varphi$, which is a contradiction. For (3), simply observe that this is one implication of Theorem 4.6 (see above). For (4), assume $\langle M, V, w, t \rangle \models_S A\varphi$ for arbitrary $\langle M, V, w, t \rangle$. We need to show that $\langle M, V, w, t \rangle \models_S AA\varphi$. Since $A\varphi$ is a state formula, we know from Theorem 4.6 that $\models_S A\varphi \Leftrightarrow AA\varphi$, and so we have $\langle M, V, w, t \rangle \models_S AA\varphi$ and we are done. For (5), assume $\langle M, V, w, t \rangle \models_S \neg A\varphi$.

Then by definition, $\langle M, V, w, t \rangle \models_S$ E¬φ. Hence from Theorem 4.6, we have $\langle M, V, w, t \rangle \models_S$ AE¬φ, and so $\langle M, V, w, t \rangle \models_S$ A¬Aφ. Finally, (6) is just a version of necessitation, for which we have already seen proofs. ∎

The temporal logic component of $\mathcal{LORA}$ has been examined extensively in the literature, and we will not discuss it further here — see [143, pp.228–234] and [49, pp.1003–1005].

The following theorem captures some properties of action expressions and the Happens operator.

THEOREM 4.8:

1. $\models_\mathcal{P}$ A(Happens $\alpha; \alpha'$) ⟺ A(Happens $\alpha;$ A(Happens α')?).

2. $\models_\mathcal{P}$ (Happens $\alpha \mid \alpha'$) ⟺ (Happens α) ∨ (Happens α').

3. $\models_\mathcal{P}$ (Happens φ?) ⟺ φ.

4. $\models_\mathcal{P}$ (Happens $\alpha*$).

5. $\models_\mathcal{P}$ ∃$\alpha \cdot$ (Happens α).

Proof For (1), assume $\langle M, V, w, p \rangle \models_\mathcal{P}$ A(Happens $\alpha; \alpha'$) for arbitrary $\langle M, V, w, p \rangle$. Then by the semantics of Happens, we have some $u, v \in \mathbb{N}$ such that $occurs(\alpha, p, 0, v)$ and $occurs(\alpha', p, u, v)$. Hence $\langle M, V, w, p \rangle \models_\mathcal{P}$ A(Happens $\alpha;$ A(Happens α')?), and we are done. For (2), start by assuming $\langle M, V, w, p \rangle \models_\mathcal{P}$ (Happens $\alpha \mid \alpha'$). Then by the semantics of Happens, we must have either $occurs(\alpha, p, 0, u)$ for some $u \in \mathbb{N}$ or else $occurs(\alpha', p, 0, u)$ for some $u \in \mathbb{N}$. Hence by the semantics of ∨ and Happens, we have $\langle M, V, w, p \rangle \models_\mathcal{P}$ (Happens α)∨(Happens α'). For (3), assume $\langle M, V, w, p \rangle \models_\mathcal{P}$ (Happens φ?). Hence we have $\langle M, V, w, p(0) \rangle \models_\mathcal{P} \varphi$, and since φ must be a state formula, we have $\langle M, V, w, p(0) \rangle \models_S \varphi$ and so $\langle M, V, w, p \rangle \models_\mathcal{P} \varphi$. Part (4) follows trivially from the semantics of iteration: any action happens zero or more times. For (5), observe that time is a total branching time relation; hence there must be a path emerging from any situation, and the arcs that make up this path will be labeled with actions. (Part (5) can also be seen to be implied by (4).) ∎

The fourth part of this Theorem may seem slightly strange; it makes sense when one reads it as "every action occurs zero or more times."

4.5   Notes and Further Reading

The semantics of the first-order logic component of $\mathcal{LORA}$ are relatively standard; see Enderton's classic [52] or Genesereth and Nilsson's somewhat more accessible [73] for similar presentations.

The BDI component of $\mathcal{LORA}$ draws upon a long tradition of using modal logics to represent mental states. Jaakko Hintikka is usually credited with starting this work with the publication of his book *Knowledge and Belief* [96], building on the work of Hendrik von Wright and others. Hintikka's legacy is most clearly evident through the vast literature on epistemic logic [54, 152]. Robert Moore (building on the work of McCarthy and Hayes [151]) is often credited with bringing the tools of modal logic to bear on reasoning about agents in artificial intelligence [156, 157]. Since Moore's pioneering work, the literature on the topic has grown enormously — see [249] for a survey.

The treatment of mental states in $\mathcal{LORA}$ owes a significant debt to the intention logic developed by Phil Cohen and Hector Levesque [35]; this logic has been widely used in the agents community for formalizing everything from speech acts [36, 68] to social structure and dependence [27]. However, $\mathcal{LORA}$'s greatest debt is obviously to Anand Rao and Michael Georgeff's family of BDI logics, developed in a sequence of papers in the first half of the 1990s [186, 190, 187, 188, 189, 184, 79, 185]. In particular, $\mathcal{LORA}$ adopts their semantics for beliefs, desires, and intentions, whereby worlds in the possible worlds semantics are assumed to be themselves branching time structures. A number of BDI logics that include some apparatus for reasoning about plans have appeared in the literature, including [190, 118, 87].

The temporal fragment of $\mathcal{LORA}$ is based on CTL*, the "full" branching time temporal logic developed by Emerson and Halpern [50]; see appendix B for notes on the origins of CTL*.

The action component of the logic is loosely based on dynamic logic [93, 122]. The actual treatment of action is based on that developed by Cohen and Levesque [35].

The technical treatment of $\mathcal{LORA}$ is based on the logics in [245, 247, 248, 239]. Many of the ideas relating to use of groups directly as terms in the language are developed in these papers.

Although there are many completeness results and proof methods for modal logics with a single modality [66, 72, 30, 90] as well as temporal logics [235, 82, 62, 135], there are comparatively few completeness results or proof methods for logics that *combine* modal and temporal fragments.

Preliminary proof methods for temporal logics of knowledge and belief are described in [246, 47, 244]. With respect to BDI logics, Rao reported proof methods for linear-time BDI logics in [184] and Rao and Georgeff reported proof methods for branching time BDI logic (where the branching temporal component was restricted to CTL logic, rather than CTL*) in [185]. Klaus Schild demonstrated that BDI logic could be encoded in the μ-calculus, and established an exponential time upper bound on the satisfiability problem for (CTL-based) propositional BDI logic [200].

5 Properties of Rational Agents

In this chapter, we will see how $\mathcal{LORA}$ can be used to capture various desirable (and undesirable) properties of rational agents. The chapter focuses in particular on the possible interrelationships among the mental states of beliefs, desires, and intentions. This study has two aspects:

- A *philosophical* aspect, whereby we attempt to characterize the properties of various types of rational agents in terms of formulae of $\mathcal{LORA}$, and discuss the extent to which these formulae adequately capture our intuitive understanding of the concepts in question. For example, we might ask whether the formula schema (Int $i\,\varphi$) $\Rightarrow$ (Bel i E$\Diamond\varphi$) (if i intends φ, then i believes φ is possible) is an appropriate characterization of the relationship between intentions and beliefs.

- A *purely logical* aspect, whereby we investigate the possible interrelationships among beliefs, desires, and intentions from an abstract mathematical perspective. With such a perspective, we simply view $\mathcal{LORA}$ as a formal system that has certain properties. We pay little or no attention to the question of what these properties might *mean*. A classic question to ask in such a logical study would be "what formula characterizes this interrelationship between these accessibility relations."

It goes without saying that $\mathcal{LORA}$ will not be able to capture every nuance of the mental states under discussion. Belief, desire, and intention are in reality far too subtle, intricate, and fuzzy to be completely captured in a logic like $\mathcal{LORA}$. If such a theory was our goal, then the formalism would fail to satisfy it. However, the logic is emphatically *not* intended to serve as such a theory. Indeed, it seems certain that any formal theory which *did* fully capture all nuances of belief, desire, and intention in humans would be of curiosity value only: it would in all likelihood be too complex and involved to be of much use for anything, let alone for actually building artificial agents. Instead of serving as a "complete" theory of rational agency, therefore, the analysis in this chapter is intended to investigate the properties that an *idealized* rational agent might exhibit.

It is also worth noting that we are unable to answer many important questions that deserve to be answered about the abstract properties of our logic. In particular, complete axiomatizations — a rite of passage for any logic — are not considered. The state of the art in multimodal logics is not sufficiently advanced that we can give a complete axiomatization of $\mathcal{LORA}$. As pointed out in the introduction to this book, this is not our goal. The intention instead is to show how $\mathcal{LORA}$ can be *applied* to the problem of reasoning about rational agents.

The chapter is structured as follows. The following section establishes a number of BDI *correspondence results*. These results give us a model-theoretic characterization of various general interaction schemas. Using these results, I go on to show how we can characterize possible *pairwise interactions* between the components of an agent's mental states.

Throughout this chapter, I use the term "A-formula" to refer to formulae of $\mathcal{LORA}$ that contain no positive occurrences of the "E" path quantifier outside the scope of a belief, desire, or intention modality. Clearly, A-formulae are those that express *inevitabilities*. Without loss of generality, I assume that all A-formulae are written in the standard form $A(\varphi)$. Similarly, I use the term "E-formula" to refer to formulae that contain no positive occurrences of the "A" path quantifier outside the scope of a belief, desire, or intention modality. It should be obvious that E-formulae express *optional* properties — properties that are true in some (but not necessarily all) futures. As with A-formulae, I assume that all E-formulae are written in the standard form $E(\varphi)$. Note that Rao and Georgeff use "I-formula" and "O-formula" (for "*i*nevitable" and "*o*ptional") in the same way that I use "A-formula" and "E-formula" [185].

5.1   BDI Correspondence Theory*

Correspondence theory is perhaps the main reason for the success of Kripke-style possible worlds semantics for modal logic [31]. Correspondence theory investigates the relationships between properties of the accessibility relations in Kripke models for modal logic, and axioms of the corresponding logic. Most results take the form "formula schema φ is valid in a model M iff the accessibility relation R in M has property P." For example, in normal modal logic, it is well-known that the formula schema

$$\Box\varphi \Rightarrow \varphi$$

is valid in a model iff the accessibility relation R that is used to give a semantics to the "$\Box$" connective is reflexive (see, e.g., [31, p.80]). We can draw upon this work to establish some basic properties of $\mathcal{LORA}$ — indeed, we already did so, in the preceding chapter, to establish properties of the belief, desire, and intention modalities.

For $\mathcal{LORA}$, however, we can extend the usual correspondence results in several ways. Most obviously, we have available to us not just one, but three modalities — Bel, Des, and Int. Multimodal logics were not widely studied in classical correspondence theory, although given their importance in contemporary computer science, they are studied increasingly often [29, 139].

Also, classical correspondence results assume that the worlds over which accessibility relations operate have no internal structure. For $\mathcal{LORA}$, however, this is not the case: worlds are themselves branching time structures. Because of this, we can investigate *structural* correspondence results, which in addition to incorporating interrelationships between the accessibility relations that characterize the modal connectives, also incorporate structural properties of worlds.

Subworlds

The most obvious structural relationship that can exist between two worlds — and the most important for our purposes — is that of one world being a *subworld* of another. Intuitively, a world w is said to be a subworld of world w' if w has the same structure as w' but has fewer paths *and is otherwise identical* — see Figure 5.1. Formally, if w, w' are worlds, then w is a subworld of w' (written $w \sqsubseteq w'$) iff $paths(w) \subseteq paths(w')$ but w, w' agree on the interpretation of predicates and constants in common time points.

It is not hard to see that if $w \sqsubseteq w'$, then any A-formula that is true in w' will also be true in w. Similarly, any E-formula that is true in w must also be true in w'. These two facts turn out to be very useful in the analysis that follows, and so we prove them in the following lemmas.

LEMMA 5.1: Suppose $\langle M, V, w, t \rangle$ is an interpretation, $\mathsf{E}(\varphi)$ is an E-formula, and w, w' are two worlds in M such that $t \in T_w$ and $t \in T_{w'}$. Then if $\langle M, V, w, t \rangle \models_{\mathcal{S}} \mathsf{E}(\varphi)$ and $w \sqsubseteq w'$ then $\langle M, V, w', t \rangle \models_{\mathcal{S}} \mathsf{E}(\varphi)$.

Proof Assume $\langle M, V, w, t \rangle \models_{\mathcal{S}} \mathsf{E}(\varphi)$. We need to show that if $w \sqsubseteq w', t \in T_w$ and $t \in T_{w'}$ then $\langle M, V, w', t \rangle \models_{\mathcal{S}} \mathsf{E}(\varphi)$. From the semantics of E, we know that $\langle M, V, w, p \rangle \models_{\mathcal{P}} \varphi$ for some path $p \in paths(w)$ such that $p(0) = t$. But if $w \sqsubseteq w'$ then $p \in paths(w')$. Hence $\langle M, V, w', p \rangle \models_{\mathcal{P}} \varphi$, and since $p(0) = t$, by the semantics of E we have $\langle M, V, w', t \rangle \models_{\mathcal{S}} \mathsf{E}(\varphi)$ and we are done. ■

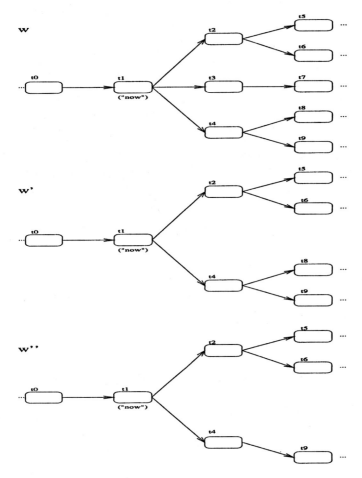

Figure 5.1
The subworld relationship: w' is a subworld of world w, that is, $w' \sqsubseteq w$; similarly, $w'' \sqsubseteq w'$.

LEMMA 5.2:   Suppose $\langle M, V, w, t \rangle$ is an interpretation, $\mathsf{A}(\varphi)$ is an A-formula, and w, w' are two worlds in M such that $t \in T_w$ and $t \in T_{w'}$. Then if $\langle M, V, w, t \rangle \models_S \mathsf{A}(\varphi)$ and $w' \sqsubseteq w$ then $\langle M, V, w', t \rangle \models_S \mathsf{A}(\varphi)$.

Proof   Assume $\langle M, V, w, t \rangle \models_S \mathsf{A}(\varphi)$ and that $t \in T_w$ and $t \in T_{w'}$. We need to show that if $w' \sqsubseteq w$ then $\langle M, V, w', t \rangle \models_S \mathsf{A}(\varphi)$. From the semantics of A, we know that $\langle M, V, w, p \rangle \models_P \varphi$ for all paths $p \in paths(w)$ such that $p(0) = t$. But if $w' \sqsubseteq w$ then if $p \in paths(w)$ then $p \in paths(w')$. Hence

$\langle M, V, w', p \rangle \models_{\mathcal{P}} \varphi$, for all $p \in paths(w')$ such that $p(0) = t$, and so from the semantics of A, we have $\langle M, V, w', t \rangle \models_{\mathcal{S}} A(\varphi)$ and we are done. ∎

Subset Correspondence Results

Given two accessibility relations R and $\bar{R}$, the most obvious relationships that could exist between them are *subset relationships*. There are three main possibilities.

$$R(\llbracket i \rrbracket) \subseteq \bar{R}(\llbracket i \rrbracket) \tag{5.1}$$
$$\bar{R}(\llbracket i \rrbracket) \subseteq R(\llbracket i \rrbracket) \tag{5.2}$$
$$R(\llbracket i \rrbracket) = \bar{R}(\llbracket i \rrbracket) \tag{5.3}$$

We can easily obtain a characterization of these relations in terms of the $\mathcal{LORA}$ formulae that they correspond to.

THEOREM 5.1:   Suppose M and M̄ are two of the modal connectives Bel, Des, and Int such that M $\neq$ M̄, defined by accessibility relations R and $\bar{R}$ respectively. Then if we have some model in which $\bar{R}(\llbracket i \rrbracket) \subseteq R(\llbracket i \rrbracket)$, then $(M\ i\ \varphi) \Rightarrow (\bar{M}\ i\ \varphi)$ is valid in that model.

Proof Assume $\bar{R}(\llbracket i \rrbracket) \subseteq R(\llbracket i \rrbracket)$, and $\langle M, V, w, t \rangle \models_{\mathcal{S}} (M\ i\ \varphi)$ for arbitrary $\langle M, V, w, t \rangle$. We need to show that $\langle M, V, w, t \rangle \models_{\mathcal{S}} (\bar{M}\ i\ \varphi)$. From the semantics of M, we know that $\langle M, V, w', t \rangle \models_{\mathcal{S}} \varphi$ for all $w' \in R_t^w(\llbracket i \rrbracket)$. Now since $\bar{R}_t^w(\llbracket i \rrbracket) \subseteq R_t^w(\llbracket i \rrbracket)$, then $\langle M, V, w'', t \rangle \models_{\mathcal{S}} \varphi$ for all $w'' \in W$ such that $w'' \in \bar{R}_t^w(\llbracket i \rrbracket)$. Hence from the semantics for M̄, we have $\langle M, V, w, t \rangle \models_{\mathcal{S}} (\bar{M}\ i\ \varphi)$ and we are done. ∎

Given this theorem, it is simple to establish the following.

THEOREM 5.2:   Suppose M and M̄ are two of the modal connectives Bel, Des, and Int such that M $\neq$ M̄, defined by accessibility relations R and $\bar{R}$ respectively. Then if we have some model in which $\bar{R}(\llbracket i \rrbracket) = R(\llbracket i \rrbracket)$, then $(M\ i\ \varphi) \Leftrightarrow (\bar{M}\ i\ \varphi)$ is valid in that model.

Proof Observe that $R(\llbracket i \rrbracket) = \bar{R}(\llbracket i \rrbracket)$ iff both $R(\llbracket i \rrbracket) \subseteq \bar{R}(\llbracket i \rrbracket)$ and $\bar{R}(\llbracket i \rrbracket) \subseteq R(\llbracket i \rrbracket)$. The result follows immediately from Theorem 5.1. ∎

The next properties we investigate are obtained by combining the subset relationships (5.1)–(5.3) with the subworld relationship that was introduced above.

The first property we consider is the *structural subset* relationship between accessibility relations. We say that accessibility relation R is a structural subset of accessibility relation $\bar{R}$ if for every R-accessible world w, there is an $\bar{R}$-accessible world w' such that w is a subworld of w'. Formally, if R and $\bar{R}$ are two accessibility relations then we write $R \subseteq_{sub} \bar{R}$ to indicate that if $w' \in R_t^w(\llbracket i \rrbracket)$, then there exists some $w'' \in \bar{R}_t^w(\llbracket i \rrbracket)$ such that $w' \sqsubseteq w''$. If $R \subseteq_{sub} \bar{R}$, then we say R is a *structural subset* of $\bar{R}$. The structural subset relationship is illustrated in Figure 5.2. In this case, we have three worlds, w, w', and w'', such that $w'' \sqsubseteq w' \sqsubseteq w$. Moreover, we have $w' \in \mathcal{B}_{t_1}^w(\llbracket i \rrbracket)$ and $w'' \in \mathcal{D}_{t_1}^w(\llbracket i \rrbracket)$. In this case, since for every desire-accessible world w' there is a belief-accessible world w'' such that $w' \sqsubseteq w''$, the desire accessibility relation $\mathcal{D}$ is a structural subset of the belief accessibility relation $\mathcal{B}$.

The following theorem characterizes the properties of structural subsets.

THEOREM 5.3:   Suppose M and $\bar{\text{M}}$ are two of the modal connectives Bel, Des, and Int such that M $\neq$ $\bar{\text{M}}$, defined by accessibility relations R and $\bar{R}$ respectively, such that $R_t^w(\llbracket i \rrbracket) \subseteq_{sub} \bar{R}_t^w(\llbracket i \rrbracket)$. Then for any A-formula $A(\varphi)$, we have $(\bar{\text{M}} \ i \ A(\varphi)) \Rightarrow (\text{M} \ i \ A(\varphi))$ is valid in that model.

Proof If $R_t^w(\llbracket i \rrbracket) \subseteq_{sub} \bar{R}_t^w(\llbracket i \rrbracket)$, then for every $w' \in R_t^w(\llbracket i \rrbracket)$, there is some $w'' \in \bar{R}_t^w(\llbracket i \rrbracket)$ such that $w' \sqsubseteq w''$. Now assume $\langle M, V, w, t \rangle \models_\mathcal{S} (\bar{\text{M}} \ i \ A(\varphi))$ and $\langle M, V, w, t \rangle \models_\mathcal{S} \neg(\text{M} \ i \ A(\varphi))$ for some $\langle M, V, w, t \rangle$. Then there must be some $w' \in R_t^w(\llbracket i \rrbracket)$ such that $\langle M, V, w', t \rangle \models_\mathcal{S} \neg A(\varphi)$. But since $R \subseteq_{sub} \bar{R}$, then there is some $w'' \in \bar{R}_t^w(\llbracket i \rrbracket)$ such that $w' \sqsubseteq w''$. Now since $\langle M, V, w, t \rangle \models_\mathcal{S}$ $(\bar{\text{M}} \ i \ A(\varphi))$ then from the semantics of $\bar{\text{M}}$, it follows that $\langle M, V, w'', t \rangle \models_\mathcal{S}$ $A(\varphi)$ and thus by Lemma 5.2, $\langle M, V, w', t \rangle \models_\mathcal{S} A(\varphi)$. This is a contradiction, so the assumption must be false. ∎

We write $\bar{R} \subseteq_{sup} R$ to indicate that if $w' \in R_t^w(\llbracket i \rrbracket)$, then there exists some $w'' \in \bar{R}_t^w(\llbracket i \rrbracket)$ such that $w'' \sqsubseteq w'$. If $R \subseteq_{sup} \bar{R}$, then we say R is a *structural superset* of $\bar{R}$. In other words, if R is a structural superset of $\bar{R}$, then for every R-accessible world w, there is an $\bar{R}$-accessible world w' such that w' is a subworld of w. In Figure 5.2, belief is a structural superset of desire. As with Theorem 5.3, we can establish a result that characterizes the structural superset property.

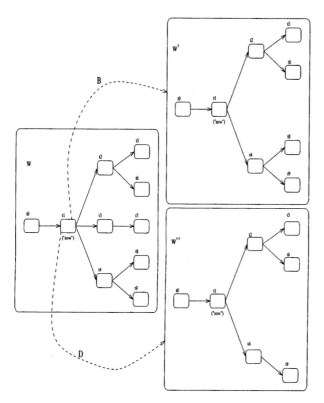

Figure 5.2
Illustrating structural subset/superset relationships: desire is a structural subset of belief
($\mathcal{D} \subseteq_{sub} \mathcal{B}$) and conversely, belief is a structural superset of desire ($\mathcal{B} \subseteq_{sup} \mathcal{D}$).

THEOREM 5.4: Suppose M and $\bar{\text{M}}$ are two of the modal connectives Bel, Des, and Int such that M $\neq$ $\bar{\text{M}}$, defined by accessibility relations R and $\bar{R}$ respectively, such that $R \subseteq_{sup} \bar{R}$. Then for any E-formula $E(\varphi)$, we have $(\bar{\text{M}} \, i \, E(\varphi)) \Rightarrow (\text{M} \, i \, E(\varphi))$ is valid in that model.

Proof Similar to Theorem 5.3. ∎

Intersection-style Correspondences

Consider the following formula schema of $\mathcal{LORA}$.

$(\text{Bel} \, i \, \varphi) \Rightarrow \neg(\text{Bel} \, i \, \neg\varphi)$

This formula schema is an instance of the "D" axiom from normal modal logic, which corresponds to the accessibility relation being serial [31, p.80]. It is usually understood as expressing the *consistency* of belief. If we turn our attention to the multimodal setting of $\mathcal{LORA}$, then we can consider related schemas, which capture consistency *between* modalities. These axiom schemas have the following general form.

$$(\mathsf{M}\ i\ \varphi) \Rightarrow \neg(\bar{\mathsf{M}}\ i\ \neg\varphi)$$

It turns out that these schemas are captured by the *intersection* of the respective accessibility relations being non-empty.

THEOREM 5.5:   Suppose M and $\bar{\mathsf{M}}$ are two of the modal connectives Bel, Des, and Int such that $\mathsf{M} \neq \bar{\mathsf{M}}$, defined by accessibility relations R and $\bar{R}$ respectively. Then if we have some model in which $\bar{R}_t^w([\![i]\!]) \cap R_t^w([\![i]\!]) \neq \emptyset$, then $(\mathsf{M}\ i\ \varphi) \Rightarrow \neg(\bar{\mathsf{M}}\ i\ \neg\varphi)$ is valid in that model, as is the contrapositive $(\bar{\mathsf{M}}\ i\ \varphi) \Rightarrow \neg(\mathsf{M}\ i\ \neg\varphi)$.

Proof I only prove that $(\mathsf{M}\ i\ \varphi) \Rightarrow \neg(\bar{\mathsf{M}}\ i\ \varphi)$ is valid; once we have this, showing that $(\bar{\mathsf{M}}\ i\ \varphi) \Rightarrow \neg(\mathsf{M}\ i\ \varphi)$ is valid is trivial (it is simply the contrapositive). Start by assuming $\bar{R}_t^w([\![i]\!]) \cap R_t^w([\![i]\!]) \neq \emptyset$, and $\langle M, V, w, t \rangle \models_S (\mathsf{M}\ i\ \varphi)$ for arbitrary $\langle M, V, w, t \rangle$. Then for all worlds $w' \in R_t^w([\![i]\!])$, we have $\langle M, V, w', t \rangle \models_S \varphi$. We need to show that $\langle M, V, w, t \rangle \models_S \neg(\bar{\mathsf{M}}\ i\ \neg\varphi)$. So assume the contrary, i.e., that $\langle M, V, w, t \rangle \models_S (\bar{\mathsf{M}}\ i\ \neg\varphi)$. Then for all worlds $w'' \in \bar{R}_t^w([\![i]\!])$, we have $\langle M, V, w'', t \rangle \models_S \neg\varphi$. But since $\bar{R}_t^w([\![i]\!]) \cap R_t^w([\![i]\!]) \neq \emptyset$, then for some $w''' \in W$, such that $w''' \in R_t^w([\![i]\!])$ and $w''' \in \bar{R}_t^w([\![i]\!])$, we must have both $\langle M, V, w''', t \rangle \models_S \varphi$ and $\langle M, V, w''', t \rangle \models_S \neg\varphi$. This is a contradiction, so the assumption must be false. ∎

Just as we were able to undertake a more fine-grained analysis of the basic interactions among beliefs, desires, and intentions by considering the structure of worlds, so we are also able to undertake a more fine-grained characterization of multimodal consistency properties by taking into account the structure of worlds.

First, we write $R_t^w([\![i]\!]) \cap_{sup} \bar{R}_t^w([\![i]\!])$ to denote the set of worlds $w' \in \bar{R}_t^w([\![i]\!])$ for which there exists some world $w'' \in R_t^w([\![i]\!])$ such that $w' \sqsubseteq w''$. Referring to Figure 5.2, we have $\mathcal{D}_{t_1}^w([\![i]\!]) \cap_{sup} \mathcal{B}_{t_1}^w([\![i]\!]) = \{w''\}$, but

$\mathcal{B}_{t_1}^w([\![i]\!]) \cap_{sup} \mathcal{D}_{t_1}^w([\![i]\!]) = \emptyset$. Formally, $R_t^w([\![i]\!]) \cap_{sup} \bar{R}_t^w([\![i]\!])$ is defined as follows.

$$R_t^w([\![i]\!]) \cap_{sup} \bar{R}_t^w([\![i]\!]) = \{w' \mid w' \in \bar{R}_t^w([\![i]\!]) \text{ and } \exists w'' \in R_t^w([\![i]\!]) \text{ s.t. } w' \sqsubseteq w''\}$$

The following theorem captures the key properties of $\cap_{sup}$.

THEOREM 5.6:   Suppose M and $\bar{\text{M}}$ are two of the modal connectives Bel, Des, and Int such that M $\neq$ $\bar{\text{M}}$, defined by accessibility relations R and $\bar{R}$ respectively. Then if we have some model in which $R_t^w([\![i]\!]) \cap_{sup} \bar{R}_t^w([\![i]\!]) \neq \emptyset$, then $(\text{M } i \text{ A}(\varphi)) \Rightarrow \neg(\bar{\text{M}} i \neg\text{A}(\varphi))$ is valid in that model.

Proof   Suppose not. Then for some $\langle M, V, w, t \rangle$ we have $R_t^w([\![i]\!]) \cap_{sup} \bar{R}_t^w([\![i]\!]) \neq \emptyset$, and $\langle M, V, w, t \rangle \models_S (\text{M } i \text{ A}(\varphi))$ and $\langle M, V, w, t \rangle \models_S (\bar{\text{M}} i \neg\text{A}(\varphi))$. Now since $R_t^w([\![i]\!]) \cap_{sup} \bar{R}_t^w([\![i]\!]) \neq \emptyset$, there exists some $w' \in \bar{R}_t^w([\![i]\!])$ such that there is some $w'' \in R_t^w([\![i]\!])$ where $w' \sqsubseteq w''$. Hence from the semantics of M, we know $\langle M, V, w'', t \rangle \models_S \text{A}(\varphi)$ and from the semantics of $\bar{\text{M}}$, we know $\langle M, V, w', t \rangle \models_S \neg\text{A}(\varphi)$. But since $w' \sqsubseteq w''$, then from Lemma 5.2 we know that $\langle M, V, w', t \rangle \models_S \text{A}(\varphi)$. This is a contradiction, so the assumption must be false. ∎

We can define $\cap_{sub}$ in the obvious way.

$$R_t^w([\![i]\!]) \cap_{sub} \bar{R}_t^w([\![i]\!]) = \{w' \mid w' \in \bar{R}_t^w([\![i]\!]) \text{ and } \exists w'' \in R_t^w([\![i]\!]) \text{ s.t. } w'' \sqsubseteq w'\}$$

The result corresponding to Theorem 5.6 is easily obtained.

THEOREM 5.7:   Suppose M and $\bar{\text{M}}$ are two of the modal connectives Bel, Des, and Int such that M $\neq$ $\bar{\text{M}}$, defined by accessibility relations R and $\bar{R}$ respectively. Then if we have some model in which $R_t^w([\![i]\!]) \cap_{sub} \bar{R}_t^w([\![i]\!]) \neq \emptyset$, then $(\text{M } i \text{ E}(\varphi)) \Rightarrow \neg(\bar{\text{M}} i \neg\text{E}(\varphi))$ is valid in that model.

Proof   Analogous to Theorem 5.6. ∎

5.2   Pairwise Interactions between Beliefs, Desires, and Intentions

Now that we have established some general correspondence results for $\mathcal{LORA}$, we can start to exploit them by considering the possible *pairwise interactions* between the modal connectives Bel, Des, and Int. Given two modal connectives M and $\bar{\text{M}}$, the most important interactions of interest between them

Table 5.1
Pairwise subset interrelationships between BDI modalities.

Relationship	Formula Schema
$\mathcal{D}_t^w(\llbracket i \rrbracket) \subseteq \mathcal{I}_t^w(\llbracket i \rrbracket)$	$(\text{Int } i \, \varphi) \Rightarrow (\text{Des } i \, \varphi)$
$\mathcal{I}_t^w(\llbracket i \rrbracket) \subseteq \mathcal{D}_t^w(\llbracket i \rrbracket)$	$(\text{Des } i \, \varphi) \Rightarrow (\text{Int } i \, \varphi)$
$\mathcal{D}_t^w(\llbracket i \rrbracket) \subseteq \mathcal{B}_t^w(\llbracket i \rrbracket)$	$(\text{Bel } i \, \varphi) \Rightarrow (\text{Des } i \, \varphi)$
$\mathcal{B}_t^w(\llbracket i \rrbracket) \subseteq \mathcal{D}_t^w(\llbracket i \rrbracket)$	$(\text{Des } i \, \varphi) \Rightarrow (\text{Bel } i \, \varphi)$
$\mathcal{B}_t^w(\llbracket i \rrbracket) \subseteq \mathcal{I}_t^w(\llbracket i \rrbracket)$	$(\text{Int } i \, \varphi) \Rightarrow (\text{Bel } i \, \varphi)$
$\mathcal{I}_t^w(\llbracket i \rrbracket) \subseteq \mathcal{B}_t^w(\llbracket i \rrbracket)$	$(\text{Bel } i \, \varphi) \Rightarrow (\text{Int } i \, \varphi)$

have the following structure.

$$(\text{M } i \, \varphi) \; \begin{array}{c} \Rightarrow \\ \Leftarrow \end{array} \; (\bar{\text{M}} \, i \, \varphi) \tag{5.4}$$

Theorem 5.1 immediately gives us a way to characterize interaction schemas of the form (5.4). Given the three modal operators Bel, Des, and Int, there are exactly six subset relationships that can exist among them, and six corresponding formula schemas. These interrelationships are summarized in Table 5.1.

Let us consider each of these formula schemas in turn.

$$(\text{Int } i \, \varphi) \Rightarrow (\text{Des } i \, \varphi) \tag{5.5}$$

Schema (5.5) says that if an agent intends something, then it desires it. Intuitively, this schema makes sense for rational agents. If we return to the view suggested in chapter 2, of desires as options, then (5.5) can be seen as a constraint on the agent's deliberation process — an agent should only commit to something as an intention if it considered it an option.

$$(\text{Des } i \, \varphi) \Rightarrow (\text{Int } i \, \varphi) \tag{5.6}$$

Schema (5.6) says that if an agent desires something, then it intends it. In other words, an agent intends all its options. If we accept (5.5) as capturing a property of rational agents, then if we also adopted (5.6), then desire and intention would be equivalent. Formula (5.6) does not therefore appear to capture any interesting properties of agents.

$$(\text{Bel } i \, \varphi) \Rightarrow (\text{Des } i \, \varphi) \tag{5.7}$$

Schema (5.7) is a well-known, if not widely-admired property of agents known as *realism*. It was introduced by Cohen and Levesque [35], where, it was argued, it captured the idea of an agent "accepting the inevitable." For example, suppose I believe that the sun will definitely rise tomorrow. Then, one could argue, it makes no sense for me to desire that the sun will not rise. For whatever I do, the sun will indeed rise tomorrow. So I may as well accept this as a desire. As a property of rational agents, realism seems too strong. Later in this chapter, we see how a finer grained analysis of the interrelationships among beliefs, desires, and intentions can lead to more reasonable types of realism.

$$(\text{Des } i \, \varphi) \Rightarrow (\text{Bel } i \, \varphi) \tag{5.8}$$

Schema (5.8) says that if an agent desires something, then it believes it. To give a concrete example, suppose I desire I am rich: should I then believe I am rich? Clearly not.

$$(\text{Int } i \, \varphi) \Rightarrow (\text{Bel } i \, \varphi) \tag{5.9}$$

Schema (5.9) says that if an agent intends something, then it believes it. Let us make this example concrete. Suppose I have an intention to write a book; does this imply I believe I *will* write it? One could argue that, in general, it is too strong a requirement for a rational agent. For example, while I can envisage many possible futures in which I proudly present my finished manuscript to a grateful and generous publisher, I can envisage equally many others in which this happy event does not take place. (The fact that you are reading this, of course, suggests that I was successful in my intention.) For example, I might win the lottery next week, in which case I would certainly reconsider my intention to write a book. Alternatively, I might be run down by a speeding bus, and so on. So while I certainly believe it is *possible* that I will succeed in my intention to write the book, I do not believe it is *inevitable* that I will do so. Bratman [20, p.31] argues that if an agent has an intention to do some action, then it is rational of the agent to believe that it will achieve it, given certain background conditions — he refers to this property as *intention-belief consistency*.

$$(\text{Bel } i \, \varphi) \Rightarrow (\text{Int } i \, \varphi) \tag{5.10}$$

Schema (5.10) says that if an agent believes something, then it intends it. Like (5.7), this is a kind of *realism* property, although it should be immediately apparent that it expresses an even stronger, and arguably less desirable property. To return to the example above, suppose that I believe that φ is true: should I then adopt φ as an intention? Clearly not. This would imply that I would choose and commit to *everything* that I believed was true. Intending some-

Table 5.2
Pairwise structural subset interrelationships.

Relationship	Formula Schema
$\mathcal{D}(\llbracket i \rrbracket) \subseteq_{sub} \mathcal{I}(\llbracket i \rrbracket)$	$(\mathsf{Int}\ i\ \mathsf{A}(\varphi)) \Rightarrow (\mathsf{Des}\ i\ \mathsf{A}(\varphi))$
$\mathcal{I}(\llbracket i \rrbracket) \subseteq_{sub} \mathcal{D}(\llbracket i \rrbracket)$	$(\mathsf{Des}\ i\ \mathsf{A}(\varphi)) \Rightarrow (\mathsf{Int}\ i\ \mathsf{A}(\varphi))$
$\mathcal{D}(\llbracket i \rrbracket) \subseteq_{sub} \mathcal{B}(\llbracket i \rrbracket)$	$(\mathsf{Bel}\ i\ \mathsf{A}(\varphi)) \Rightarrow (\mathsf{Des}\ i\ \mathsf{A}(\varphi))$
$\mathcal{B}(\llbracket i \rrbracket) \subseteq_{sub} \mathcal{D}(\llbracket i \rrbracket)$	$(\mathsf{Des}\ i\ \mathsf{A}(\varphi)) \Rightarrow (\mathsf{Bel}\ i\ \mathsf{A}(\varphi))$
$\mathcal{B}(\llbracket i \rrbracket) \subseteq_{sub} \mathcal{I}(\llbracket i \rrbracket)$	$(\mathsf{Int}\ i\ \mathsf{A}(\varphi)) \Rightarrow (\mathsf{Bel}\ i\ \mathsf{A}(\varphi))$
$\mathcal{I}(\llbracket i \rrbracket) \subseteq_{sub} \mathcal{B}(\llbracket i \rrbracket)$	$(\mathsf{Bel}\ i\ \mathsf{A}(\varphi)) \Rightarrow (\mathsf{Int}\ i\ \mathsf{A}(\varphi))$

thing implies selecting it and committing resources to achieving it. It makes no sense to suggest committing resources to achieving something that is already true.

To summarize, only formula (5.5) seems to capture a reasonable property of rational agents. While in their current form they are too strong, we can also see that weaker versions of (5.8) and (5.9) arguably also capture properties of rational agents.

Formulas (5.5)–(5.10) are a useful starting point for our analysis of the possible relationships that exist among the three components of an agent's mental state. However, it is clear that a *finer-grained* analysis of the relationships is likely to yield more intuitively reasonable results.

Attitudes to Inevitabilities

In our framework, we can also consider two important variations of (5.4). The first relates an agent's attitudes to A-formulae, i.e., formula that express *inevitable* futures.

$$(\mathsf{M}\ i\ \mathsf{A}(\varphi)) \begin{array}{c} \Rightarrow \\ \Leftarrow \end{array} (\bar{\mathsf{M}}\ i\ \mathsf{A}(\varphi)) \tag{5.11}$$

The six possible interaction schemas implied by Theorem 5.3 are summarized in Table 5.2. Consider first (5.12).

$$(\mathsf{Int}\ i\ \mathsf{A}(\varphi)) \Rightarrow (\mathsf{Des}\ i\ \mathsf{A}(\varphi)) \tag{5.12}$$

This says that if an agent intends that φ is inevitably true, then it desires that φ is inevitably true. This schema, a variant of (5.5), is obviously an appropriate property to demand of rational agents.

$$(\mathsf{Des}\ i\ \mathsf{A}(\varphi)) \Rightarrow (\mathsf{Int}\ i\ \mathsf{A}(\varphi)) \tag{5.13}$$

Schema (5.13) says that if an agent desires that φ is inevitably true, then it intends that φ is inevitably true. In other words, φ is inevitable in all the options considered by the agent. For example, suppose that in all the options that I consider, it is inevitable that I am married. Then arguably, I should adopt an intention to become inevitably married. So schema (5.13) seems to capture a reasonable property of rational agents.

$$(\text{Bel } i \, A(\varphi)) \Rightarrow (\text{Des } i \, A(\varphi)) \tag{5.14}$$

Schema (5.14) says that if an agent believes φ is inevitably true, then it desires it is inevitably true. This schema is a variant of the undesirable realism schemata, (5.7). It can be rejected as a property of rational agents for the same reason as (5.7).

$$(\text{Des } i \, A(\varphi)) \Rightarrow (\text{Bel } i \, A(\varphi)) \tag{5.15}$$

Schema (5.15) says that if an agent desires something is inevitably true, then it believes it is inevitably true. To be concrete, suppose that in all the options I consider, it is inevitable that I am married. Do I then believe I am inevitably married? No. I may well believe there is some future in which I am not married, even though in all the options I consider, it is inevitable that I am married.

$$(\text{Int } i \, A(\varphi)) \Rightarrow (\text{Bel } i \, A(\varphi)) \tag{5.16}$$

Schema (5.16) says that if an agent intends that φ is inevitably true, then it believes it is inevitably true. As we noted earlier, Bratman argues that intending φ certainly provides some support for the belief that φ [20, p.38]. Since intentions are in some sense conduct-controlling, then all other things being equal, my intention to achieve φ must make φ more likely than it would be if I did not intend φ. However, this is not to say that my intending φ is inevitable implies I believe φ is inevitable. So while (5.16) is arguably more reasonable than (5.9), it is still too strong to be a necessary property of rational agents.

$$(\text{Bel } i \, A(\varphi)) \Rightarrow (\text{Int } i \, A(\varphi)) \tag{5.17}$$

Schema (5.17) says that if an agent believes φ is inevitably true, then it intends it is inevitably true. For the same reasons as (5.10), we reject this schema as a property of rational agents.

Table 5.3
Pairwise structural superset interrelationships between modalities.

Relationship	Formula Schema
$\mathcal{D}(\llbracket i \rrbracket) \subseteq_{sup} \mathcal{I}(\llbracket i \rrbracket)$	$(\text{Int } i\, \mathsf{E}(\varphi)) \Rightarrow (\text{Des } i\, \mathsf{E}(\varphi))$
$\mathcal{I}(\llbracket i \rrbracket) \subseteq_{sup} \mathcal{D}(\llbracket i \rrbracket)$	$(\text{Des } i\, \mathsf{E}(\varphi)) \Rightarrow (\text{Int } i\, \mathsf{E}(\varphi))$
$\mathcal{D}(\llbracket i \rrbracket) \subseteq_{sup} \mathcal{B}(\llbracket i \rrbracket)$	$(\text{Bel } i\, \mathsf{E}(\varphi)) \Rightarrow (\text{Des } i\, \mathsf{E}(\varphi))$
$\mathcal{B}(\llbracket i \rrbracket) \subseteq_{sup} \mathcal{D}(\llbracket i \rrbracket)$	$(\text{Des } i\, \mathsf{E}(\varphi)) \Rightarrow (\text{Bel } i\, \mathsf{E}(\varphi))$
$\mathcal{B}(\llbracket i \rrbracket) \subseteq_{sup} \mathcal{I}(\llbracket i \rrbracket)$	$(\text{Int } i\, \mathsf{E}(\varphi)) \Rightarrow (\text{Bel } i\, \mathsf{E}(\varphi))$
$\mathcal{I}(\llbracket i \rrbracket) \subseteq_{sup} \mathcal{B}(\llbracket i \rrbracket)$	$(\text{Bel } i\, \mathsf{E}(\varphi)) \Rightarrow (\text{Int } i\, \mathsf{E}(\varphi))$

Attitudes to Options

In the preceding section, we considered the possible attitudes an agent could have to *inevitable* states of affairs. Next, we consider an agent's attitudes to *options*.

$$(\mathsf{M}\, i\, \mathsf{E}(\varphi)) \quad \overset{\Rightarrow}{\underset{\Leftarrow}{}} \quad (\bar{\mathsf{M}}\, i\, \mathsf{E}(\varphi)) \tag{5.18}$$

As with Theorem 5.1, Theorem 5.4 immediately gives us six possible interactions, summarized in Table 5.3.

Consider first (5.19).

$$(\text{Int } i\, \mathsf{E}(\varphi)) \Rightarrow (\text{Des } i\, \mathsf{E}(\varphi)) \tag{5.19}$$

In order to understand this schema, it is worth considering what it means to have an intention towards an E-formula such as $\mathsf{E}(\varphi)$. Intuitively, an agent with such an intention wants to "keep its options open." In other words, it intends to ensure that φ is always true on at least one possible future — in other words, that φ is never ruled out. There are many obvious situations where such an intention is appropriate. For example, although I have a university job, I might want to keep the option open of going into industry and taking a proper job, while not having the intention to make a job in industry *inevitable*. Intentions towards E-formulae capture exactly such commitments.

Returning to (5.19), this schema says that if an agent intends that φ is optionally true, then it desires that φ is optionally true. Clearly such an schema makes sense for rational agents.

$$(\text{Des } i\, \mathsf{E}(\varphi)) \Rightarrow (\text{Int } i\, \mathsf{E}(\varphi)) \tag{5.20}$$

Schema (5.20) says that if an agent desires that φ is true on at least one future, then it intends that φ is true on at least one future. This formula can be understood as characterizing an agent who wants to commit to all options; in other words, an agent who will never rule out options. Such a property might make sense in some situations. For example, suppose I have decided what my options are, but have insufficient information to make an informed choice among my options.

$$(\text{Bel } i \text{ E}(\varphi)) \Rightarrow (\text{Des } i \text{ E}(\varphi)) \tag{5.21}$$

Schema (5.21) says that if an agent believes φ is true on at least one future, then it desires it is true on at least one future. This schema can be seen as characterizing a weaker variant of the realism property (5.7) from the preceding section. However, it still seems in some sense too strong. For example, suppose I believe there is some future in which there will be a nuclear war. Do I also desire that there is some future in which there is a nuclear war? Clearly not. So, like the realism schemas (5.7) and (5.10), we reject (5.21) as a desirable property of rational agents.

$$(\text{Des } i \text{ E}(\varphi)) \Rightarrow (\text{Bel } i \text{ E}(\varphi)) \tag{5.22}$$

Schema (5.22) says that if an agent desires something is optionally true, then it believes it is optionally true. This formula is a variant of (5.8). However, unlike (5.8), schema (5.22) seems an entirely reasonable property for rational agents. For if I desired that I was rich in some future, while not believing that there was any possible future in which I was rich, then I would clearly be irrational.

$$(\text{Int } i \text{ E}(\varphi)) \Rightarrow (\text{Bel } i \text{ E}(\varphi)) \tag{5.23}$$

Schema (5.23) says that if an agent intends that φ is optionally true, then it believes it is optionally true. For similar reasons to (5.22), this schema is a reasonable property of rational agents.

$$(\text{Bel } i \text{ E}(\varphi)) \Rightarrow (\text{Int } i \text{ E}(\varphi)) \tag{5.24}$$

Schema (5.24) says that if an agent believes φ is optionally true, then it intends it is optionally true. As with (5.21), this is not a property we would demand of rational agents.

Table 5.4
Weak realism interactions.

Relationship	Formula Schemas
$\mathcal{D}_I^w([\![i]\!]) \cap \mathcal{I}_r^w([\![i]\!]) \neq \emptyset$	$(\text{Int } i\,\varphi) \Rightarrow \neg(\text{Des } i\,\neg\varphi)$
$\mathcal{I}_r^w([\![i]\!]) \cap \mathcal{D}_r^w([\![i]\!]) \neq \emptyset$	$(\text{Des } i\,\varphi) \Rightarrow \neg(\text{Int } i\,\neg\varphi)$
$\mathcal{B}_I^w([\![i]\!]) \cap \mathcal{D}_r^w([\![i]\!]) \neq \emptyset$	$(\text{Bel } i\,\varphi) \Rightarrow \neg(\text{Des } i\,\neg\varphi)$
$\mathcal{D}_I^w([\![i]\!]) \cap \mathcal{B}_r^w([\![i]\!]) \neq \emptyset$	$(\text{Des } i\,\varphi) \Rightarrow \neg(\text{Bel } i\,\neg\varphi)$
$\mathcal{I}_r^w([\![i]\!]) \cap \mathcal{B}_r^w([\![i]\!]) \neq \emptyset$	$(\text{Int } i\,\varphi) \Rightarrow \neg(\text{Bel } i\,\neg\varphi)$
$\mathcal{B}_I^w([\![i]\!]) \cap \mathcal{I}_r^w([\![i]\!]) \neq \emptyset$	$(\text{Bel } i\,\varphi) \Rightarrow \neg(\text{Int } i\,\neg\varphi)$

5.3   Varieties of Realism

We saw above that *realism* properties such as $(\text{Bel } i\,\varphi) \Rightarrow (\text{Des } i\,\varphi)$ are in general too strong to be regarded as reasonable properties of rational agents. In this section we will consider some weaker realism properties.

As before, this general result enables a number of specific interaction properties to be established — see Table 5.4.

The first of these properties, represented by schemas (5.25) and (5.26), says that an agent's intentions are consistent with its desires, and conversely, its desires are consistent with its intentions.

$$(\text{Int } i\,\varphi) \Rightarrow \neg(\text{Des } i\,\neg\varphi) \tag{5.25}$$

$$(\text{Des } i\,\varphi) \Rightarrow \neg(\text{Int } i\,\neg\varphi) \tag{5.26}$$

These schemas, which capture *intention-desire consistency*, appear to be reasonable properties to demand of rational agents in some, but not all circumstances. Intention-desire consistency states that an agent only ever considers options that are consistent with its intentions. Under normal circumstances, we might consider such behavior acceptable, or even desirable. For example, if I have an intention to φ then it will not normally make sense for me to entertain options that are inconsistent with φ. However, under certain circumstances, it makes sense for an agent to *reconsider* its intentions — to deliberate over them, and possibly change focus. This implies entertaining options that are not necessarily consistent with current intentions. An agent that always respects schemas (5.25) and (5.26) will never do such reconsideration.

Schemas (5.27) and (5.28) capture *belief-desire consistency*.

$$(\text{Bel } i\,\varphi) \Rightarrow \neg(\text{Des } i\,\neg\varphi) \tag{5.27}$$

$$(\text{Des } i\,\varphi) \Rightarrow \neg(\text{Bel } i\,\neg\varphi) \tag{5.28}$$

The first of the belief-desire consistency schemas, (5.27), is also known as *belief-desire weak realism*. Recall that belief-desire realism, as represented by schema (5.7) was too strong to be an acceptable version of realism. Schema (5.27) captures a weaker notion of belief-desire realism. It simply says that if an agent believes φ is already true, then an agent should not desire that φ is not true. Thus if I believe it is raining, there is no point in desiring it is not raining, since I will not be able to change what is already the case.

The second belief-desire consistency schema, (5.28), says that if an agent desires φ, then it does not believe φ is false. On first consideration, this schema seems unreasonable. For example, I may desire to be rich while believing that I am not currently rich. But when we distinguish between *present-directed* and *future-directed* desires and beliefs, the property makes sense for rational agents. It is not rational for me to have a desire to be rich at this moment while simultaneously believing that I am not rich at this moment. However, it is entirely acceptable for me to simultaneously believe that I am not rich currently while desiring to be rich at some time in the future. The second belief-desire consistency schema, (5.28), rules out the first case, but has nothing to say about the second.

$$(\text{Int } i\ \varphi) \Rightarrow \neg(\text{Bel } i\ \neg\varphi) \tag{5.29}$$

$$(\text{Bel } i\ \varphi) \Rightarrow \neg(\text{Int } i\ \neg\varphi) \tag{5.30}$$

Similar comments apply to the intention-belief consistency schemas, (5.29) and (5.30), as to the belief-desire consistency schemas, and we will therefore not comment on them here.

Weak Realism and Inevitabilities

Strong realism, as discussed above, is the most general kind of realism that we might consider. However, for the reasons we discussed above, most strong types of realism are not acceptable properties of rational agents. In this and the subsection that follows, we will discuss realism with respect to *inevitable* and *optional* formulae.

Theorem 5.6 generates the results shown in Table 5.5.

The first of these properties, (5.31), says that if an agent intends to bring about $A(\varphi)$, then it should not desire that $\neg A(\varphi)$; schema (5.32) expresses the same property for desires and intentions.

$$(\text{Int } i\ A(\varphi)) \Rightarrow \neg(\text{Des } i\ \neg A(\varphi)) \tag{5.31}$$

Table 5.5
Inevitabilities and weak realism properties.

Relationship	Formula Schemas
$\mathcal{I}_t^w(\llbracket i \rrbracket) \cap_{sup} \mathcal{D}_t^w(\llbracket i \rrbracket) \neq \emptyset$	$(\text{Int } i\, A(\varphi)) \Rightarrow \neg(\text{Des } i \,\neg A(\varphi))$
$\mathcal{D}_t^w(\llbracket i \rrbracket) \cap_{sup} \mathcal{I}_t^w(\llbracket i \rrbracket) \neq \emptyset$	$(\text{Des } i\, A(\varphi)) \Rightarrow \neg(\text{Int } i \,\neg A(\varphi))$
$\mathcal{B}_t^w(\llbracket i \rrbracket) \cap_{sup} \mathcal{D}_t^w(\llbracket i \rrbracket) \neq \emptyset$	$(\text{Bel } i\, A(\varphi)) \Rightarrow \neg(\text{Des } i \,\neg A(\varphi))$
$\mathcal{D}_t^w(\llbracket i \rrbracket) \cap_{sup} \mathcal{B}_t^w(\llbracket i \rrbracket) \neq \emptyset$	$(\text{Des } i\, A(\varphi)) \Rightarrow \neg(\text{Bel } i \,\neg A(\varphi))$
$\mathcal{I}_t^w(\llbracket i \rrbracket) \cap_{sup} \mathcal{B}_t^w(\llbracket i \rrbracket) \neq \emptyset$	$(\text{Int } i\, A(\varphi)) \Rightarrow \neg(\text{Bel } i \,\neg A(\varphi))$
$\mathcal{B}_t^w(\llbracket i \rrbracket) \cap_{sup} \mathcal{I}_t^w(\llbracket i \rrbracket) \neq \emptyset$	$(\text{Bel } i\, A(\varphi)) \Rightarrow \neg(\text{Int } i \,\neg A(\varphi))$

$$(\text{Des } i\, A(\varphi)) \Rightarrow \neg(\text{Int } i \,\neg A(\varphi)) \tag{5.32}$$

Schema (5.33) says that if an agent believes φ is inevitable, then it should not desire it is not inevitable. This captures an acceptable realism property.

$$(\text{Bel } i\, A(\varphi)) \Rightarrow \neg(\text{Des } i \,\neg A(\varphi)) \tag{5.33}$$

Schema (5.34), states that if an agent desires something is inevitable, it should not believe it is not inevitable; this seems an acceptable, though not necessarily desirable property of rational agents.

$$(\text{Des } i\, A(\varphi)) \Rightarrow \neg(\text{Bel } i \,\neg A(\varphi)) \tag{5.34}$$

Finally, schemas (5.35) and (5.36) capture weak realism between intentions and beliefs.

$$(\text{Int } i\, A(\varphi)) \Rightarrow \neg(\text{Bel } i \,\neg A(\varphi)) \tag{5.35}$$

$$(\text{Bel } i\, A(\varphi)) \Rightarrow \neg(\text{Int } i \,\neg A(\varphi)) \tag{5.36}$$

Weak Realism and Options

Table 5.6 summarizes the formula schemas corresponding to Theorem 5.7.

The first of these properties, (5.25), says that if an agent intends that φ should be optionally true, then it should not desire that φ is not optionally true. Clearly such consistency is a desirable property of rational agents.

$$(\text{Int } i\, E(\varphi)) \Rightarrow \neg(\text{Des } i \,\neg E(\varphi)) \tag{5.37}$$

Table 5.6
Options and weak realism properties.

Relationship	Formula Schemas
$\mathcal{I}_t^w([\![i]\!]) \cap_{sub} \mathcal{D}_t^w([\![i]\!]) \neq \emptyset$	$(\text{Int } i\, E(\varphi)) \Rightarrow \neg(\text{Des } i\, \neg E(\varphi))$
$\mathcal{D}_t^w([\![i]\!]) \cap_{sub} \mathcal{I}_t^w([\![i]\!]) \neq \emptyset$	$(\text{Des } i\, E(\varphi)) \Rightarrow \neg(\text{Int } i\, \neg E(\varphi))$
$\mathcal{B}_t^w([\![i]\!]) \cap_{sub} \mathcal{D}_t^w([\![i]\!]) \neq \emptyset$	$(\text{Bel } i\, E(\varphi)) \Rightarrow \neg(\text{Des } i\, \neg E(\varphi))$
$\mathcal{D}_t^w([\![i]\!]) \cap_{sub} \mathcal{B}_t^w([\![i]\!]) \neq \emptyset$	$(\text{Des } i\, E(\varphi)) \Rightarrow \neg(\text{Bel } i\, \neg E(\varphi))$
$\mathcal{I}_t^w([\![i]\!]) \cap_{sub} \mathcal{B}_t^w([\![i]\!]) \neq \emptyset$	$(\text{Int } i\, E(\varphi)) \Rightarrow \neg(\text{Bel } i\, \neg E(\varphi))$
$\mathcal{B}_t^w([\![i]\!]) \cap_{sub} \mathcal{I}_t^w([\![i]\!]) \neq \emptyset$	$(\text{Bel } i\, E(\varphi)) \Rightarrow \neg(\text{Int } i\, \neg E(\varphi))$

Schema (5.38) says that if an agent desires that φ is optional, then it does not intend that φ is not optional.

$$(\text{Des } i\, E(\varphi)) \Rightarrow \neg(\text{Int } i\, \neg E(\varphi)) \tag{5.38}$$

Schema (5.39) says that if an agent believes φ is optional, it does not desire that φ is not optional.

$$(\text{Bel } i\, E(\varphi)) \Rightarrow \neg(\text{Des } i\, \neg E(\varphi)) \tag{5.39}$$

Earlier, we argued that schema (5.7), which said that if an agent believes something it also desires it, was unacceptably strong for most agents. The previous schema (5.39), which can be seen as a weak variant of (5.7), is clearly more acceptable, as is the following schema, (5.40).

$$(\text{Des } i\, E(\varphi)) \Rightarrow \neg(\text{Bel } i\, \neg E(\varphi)) \tag{5.40}$$

Schemas (5.41) and (5.42) say that an agent's optional intentions are consistent with its beliefs, and as with the desire case, above, these schemas are clearly more acceptable than either (5.9) or (5.10).

$$(\text{Int } i\, E(\varphi)) \Rightarrow \neg(\text{Bel } i\, \neg E(\varphi)) \tag{5.41}$$

$$(\text{Bel } i\, E(\varphi)) \Rightarrow \neg(\text{Int } i\, \neg E(\varphi)) \tag{5.42}$$

5.4   Systems of BDI Logic

So far, we have only been concerned with binary relationships between modalities. But we can also consider ternary (i.e., three-way) relationships between the modalities. Given the number of different binary relationships we have

Table 5.7
Systems of BDI logic. (Source: [185, p.321].)

Name	Semantic Condition	Corresponding Formula Schema
BDI-S1	$\mathcal{B} \subseteq_{sup} \mathcal{D} \subseteq_{sup} \mathcal{I}$	$(\text{Int } i\, E(\varphi)) \Rightarrow (\text{Des } i\, E(\varphi)) \Rightarrow (\text{Bel } i\, E(\varphi))$
BDI-S2	$\mathcal{B} \subseteq_{sub} \mathcal{D} \subseteq_{sub} \mathcal{I}$	$(\text{Int } i\, A(\varphi)) \Rightarrow (\text{Des } i\, A(\varphi)) \Rightarrow (\text{Bel } i\, A(\varphi))$
BDI-S3	$\mathcal{B} \subseteq \mathcal{D} \subseteq \mathcal{I}$	$(\text{Int } i\, \varphi) \Rightarrow (\text{Des } i\, \varphi) \Rightarrow (\text{Bel } i\, \varphi)$
BDI-R1	$\mathcal{I} \subseteq_{sup} \mathcal{D} \subseteq_{sup} \mathcal{B}$	$(\text{Bel } i\, E(\varphi)) \Rightarrow (\text{Des } i\, E(\varphi)) \Rightarrow (\text{Int } i\, E(\varphi))$
BDI-R2	$\mathcal{I} \subseteq_{sub} \mathcal{D} \subseteq_{sub} \mathcal{B}$	$(\text{Bel } i\, A(\varphi)) \Rightarrow (\text{Des } i\, A(\varphi)) \Rightarrow (\text{Int } i\, A(\varphi))$
BDI-R3	$\mathcal{I} \subseteq \mathcal{D} \subseteq \mathcal{B}$	$(\text{Bel } i\, \varphi) \Rightarrow (\text{Des } i\, \varphi) \Rightarrow (\text{Int } i\, \varphi)$
BDI-W1	$\mathcal{B} \cap_{sup} \mathcal{D} \neq \emptyset$ $\mathcal{D} \cap_{sup} \mathcal{I} \neq \emptyset$ $\mathcal{B} \cap_{sup} \mathcal{I} \neq \emptyset$	$(\text{Bel } i\, A(\varphi)) \Rightarrow \neg(\text{Des } i\, \neg A(\varphi))$ $(\text{Des } i\, A(\varphi)) \Rightarrow \neg(\text{Int } i\, \neg A(\varphi))$ $(\text{Bel } i\, A(\varphi)) \Rightarrow \neg(\text{Int } i\, \neg A(\varphi))$
BDI-W2	$\mathcal{B} \cap_{sub} \mathcal{D} \neq \emptyset$ $\mathcal{D} \cap_{sub} \mathcal{I} \neq \emptyset$ $\mathcal{B} \cap_{sub} \mathcal{I} \neq \emptyset$	$(\text{Bel } i\, E(\varphi)) \Rightarrow \neg(\text{Des } i\, \neg E(\varphi))$ $(\text{Des } i\, E(\varphi)) \Rightarrow \neg(\text{Int } i\, \neg E(\varphi))$ $(\text{Bel } i\, E(\varphi)) \Rightarrow \neg(\text{Int } i\, \neg E(\varphi))$
BDI-W3	$\mathcal{B} \cap \mathcal{D} \neq \emptyset$ $\mathcal{D} \cap \mathcal{I} \neq \emptyset$ $\mathcal{B} \cap \mathcal{I} \neq \emptyset$	$(\text{Bel } i\, \varphi) \Rightarrow \neg(\text{Des } i\, \neg\varphi)$ $(\text{Des } i\, \varphi) \Rightarrow \neg(\text{Int } i\, \neg\varphi)$ $(\text{Bel } i\, \varphi) \Rightarrow \neg(\text{Int } i\, \neg\varphi)$

looked at so far, there are clearly a great many ternary relationships that we might possibly consider. However, most of these relationships are meaningless (or at best capture obscure and frankly uninteresting situations). The most important relationships for our purposes are those summarized in Table 5.7.

5.5   The Side-Effect Problem

One of the most well-known problems in the theory of intention is that of *side effects*. The side-effect problem is illustrated by the following scenario.

Janine intends to visit the dentist in order to have a tooth pulled. She is aware that as a consequence of having a tooth pulled, she will suffer pain. Does Janine intend to suffer pain?

In this example, suffering pain is a side effect of having a tooth pulled; having a tooth pulled and suffering pain come as a "package deal." However, it is generally agreed (and in particular, Bratman convincingly argues [20, p.142]), that rational agents *do not* have to intend the consequences of their intentions. In other words, Janine can intend to have a tooth pulled, believing that this will cause pain, without intending to suffer pain.

In $\mathcal{LORA}$, the side-effect problem can be captured by simply requiring the following schema to be satisfiable.

$$(\text{Int } i\ \varphi) \wedge (\text{Bel } i\ \varphi \Rightarrow \psi) \wedge \neg(\text{Int } i\ \psi) \qquad (5.43)$$

In other words, it should be possible for an agent to intend φ, believing that it is inevitable that $\varphi \Rightarrow \psi$, without intending that ψ. The following are also examples of side-effect schemas.

$$(\text{Int } i\ \varphi) \wedge (\text{Des } i\ \varphi \Rightarrow \psi) \wedge \neg(\text{Int } i\ \psi) \qquad (5.44)$$

$$(\text{Des } i\ \varphi) \wedge (\text{Bel } i\ \varphi \Rightarrow \psi) \wedge \neg(\text{Des } i\ \psi) \qquad (5.45)$$

We can prove the following general result about such consequential closure schemas.

THEOREM 5.8: Suppose M and $\bar{\text{M}}$ are two of the modal connectives Bel, Des, and Int such that M $\neq$ $\bar{\text{M}}$, defined by accessibility relations R and $\bar{R}$ respectively. Then if we have some model in which $R(\llbracket i \rrbracket) \subseteq \bar{R}(\llbracket i \rrbracket)$, then the schema

$$(\text{M } i\ \varphi) \wedge (\bar{\text{M}} i\ \varphi \Rightarrow \psi) \wedge \neg(\text{M } i\ \psi)$$

will be unsatisfiable in this model.

Proof Assume $\langle M, V, w, t \rangle \models_S (\text{M } i\ \varphi) \wedge (\bar{\text{M}} i\ \varphi \Rightarrow \psi)$ for some arbitrary $\langle M, V, w, t \rangle$. If $R(\llbracket i \rrbracket) \subseteq \bar{R}(\llbracket i \rrbracket)$, then by Theorem 5.1, the schema $(\bar{\text{M}} i\ \chi) \Rightarrow (\text{M } i\ \chi)$ will be valid. Hence $\langle M, V, w, t \rangle \models_S (\text{M } i\ \varphi \Rightarrow \psi)$. By the K axiom for the M operator and propositional reasoning, $\langle M, V, w, t \rangle \models_S (\text{M } i\ \psi)$. This contradicts the assumption. ■

Thus the consequential closure schema (5.43) will be unsatisfiable in a model if $\mathcal{I}_t^w \subseteq B_t^w$.

5.6   Notes and Further Reading

The kind of analysis undertaken in this chapter — of understanding the relationships among semantic constraints on Kripke relations and the modal logic formulae these constraints make valid — is known as *correspondence theory*, and has a long tradition in modal logic. The basic correspondence properties were identified by Kripke himself [126], and indeed the elegance of correspondence theory accounts in a large part for the continued success of this style of semantics. Basic correspondence results are described in [101] and [31].

The study of interactions among *multimodal* logics, of the kind we undertake in this chapter, is a relatively recent development. Laurent Catach's Ph.D. work, summarized in [29], was one of the first systematic, abstract studies to receive a wide audience. Catach established a correspondence theorem analogous to the general $G^{k,l,m,n}$ correspondence result of normal modal logic [31, p.88]. More recently, multimodal logics have been found to have a wide variety of applications, and this recognition has led to a rapid increase in the number of systematic studies of multimodal systems. Logical systems with multiple modalities of the same time are discussed in [54]. Alessio Lomuscio gives a comprehensive study of interaction schemas in multimodal settings, generalizing Catach's results [139, 140].

The specific properties discussed in this chapter were originally identified in Rao and Georgeff's BDI papers. The paper that "introduced" BDI logics is [187] — it showed how BDI logic could be used to capture many of our intuitions about intentions, with particular reference to the work of Cohen and Levesque [35]. Axiomatizations of the asymmetry thesis, and a justification for the temporal branching structure of BDI logic were presented in [186]. The "definitive" paper on Rao and Georgeff's formalism is [185]. This paper comprehensively studies possible axiomatizations of BDI logic, and gives some completeness results for propositional BDI logic by means of semantic tableaux systems.

6 Collective Mental States

So far in this book, we have been considering the properties of *individual* agents. In this chapter, we change the emphasis from individual agents to *multiagent systems*. I begin by discussing how we might go about characterizing the properties of *groups* of agents. Starting with mutual belief, desire, and intention, I go on to show how *joint commitment* can be defined.

6.1 Mutual Beliefs, Desires, and Intentions

The intuition behind mutual belief is straightforward. Consider a situation where you and I are in discussion, and I say to you "The door is open." Assuming there are no abnormal circumstances (i.e., you were paying attention to what I was saying, you did not suddenly lose your hearing, and so on), then the fact that I uttered this sentence will be *mutually believed* by both of us. To better understand what is meant by this, suppose φ is the statement

"Michael uttered the sentence 'The door is open.' "

Then you will believe φ.

(Bel *you* φ)

Moreover, I will also believe φ.

(Bel *me* φ)

In addition, however, since the act of me uttering the sentence was immediately visible to both of us, and both of us were witness to the fact that both of us were witness to it, it is only rational for me to believe that you believe φ.

(Bel *me* (Bel *you* φ))

The situation is of course symmetric, so you will also believe that I believe φ.

(Bel *you* (Bel *me* φ))

It is not hard to see that, if we both assume that the other observed the event, then one must carry on this nesting of beliefs.

(Bel *me* (Bel *you* (Bel *me* φ)))
(Bel *you* (Bel *me* (Bel *you* φ)))
(Bel *me* (Bel *you* (Bel *me* (Bel *you* φ))))
(Bel *you* (Bel *me* (Bel *you* (Bel *me* φ))))
(Bel *me* (Bel *you* (Bel *me* (Bel *you* (Bel *me* φ)))))
(Bel *you* (Bel *me* (Bel *you* (Bel *me* (Bel *you* φ)))))
... and so on.

We refer to this state of affairs — where I believe, you believe, I believe that you believe, you believe that I believe, I believe that you believe that I believe, and so on — as *mutual belief*. It follows that, in principle at least, mutual belief is *infinitary* in nature. If we try to write down a formula that captures mutual belief between two or more agents, then initially at least, it appears that this formula must be infinitely long. (In fact, we will see that this is not necessarily the case, as we can characterize mutual mental states in terms of *fixed points*; nevertheless, mutual beliefs are infinitary in nature.)

It is important to distinguish mutual belief from the (much simpler) case, where we have simply I believe and you believe:

(Bel *me* φ) $\wedge$ (Bel *you* φ)

Mutual belief expresses a much stronger property, which implies this weaker kind of collective mental state.

As the informal example given above illustrates, mutual mental states play an important role in communication. But, more than this, they turn out to be important in *coordination* problems. To illustrate what is meant by this, consider the following scenario, from [54, p.176].

Two divisions of an army, each commanded by a general, are camped on two hilltops overlooking a valley. In the valley awaits the enemy. It is clear that if both divisions attack the enemy simultaneously they will win the battle, while if only one division attacks, it will be defeated. As a result, neither general will attack unless he is absolutely sure that the other will attack with him. In particular, a general will not attack if he receives no messages. The commanding general of the first division wishes to coordinate a simultaneous attack (at some time the next day). The generals can communicate only by means of messengers. Normally, it takes a messenger one hour to get from one encampment to the other. However, it is possible that he will get lost in the dark or, worse yet, be captured by the enemy. Fortunately, on this particular night, everything goes smoothly. How long will it take them to coordinate an attack?

Suppose a messenger sent by general A reaches General B with a message saying "attack at dawn." Should General B attack? Although the message was in fact delivered, General A has no way of knowing that it was delivered. A must therefore consider it possible that B did not receive the message (in which case B would definitely not attack). Hence A will not attack given his current state of knowledge. Knowing this, and not willing to risk attacking alone, B cannot attack solely based on receiving A's message. Of course, B can try to improve matters by sending the messenger back to A with an acknowledgment. When A receives this acknowledgment, can he then attack? A here is in a similar position to the one B was in when he received the original message. This time B does not know that the acknowledgment was delivered.

Intuitively, the two generals are trying to bring about a state where it is mutually believed (or known) between them that the message to attack was delivered. Each successive round of communication, even if successful, only adds one level to the depth of nested belief. *No* amount of communication is sufficient to bring about the infinite nesting that mutual belief requires. As it turns out, if communication delivery is not guaranteed, then mutual belief can *never* arise in such a scenario. Ultimately, this is because, no matter how many messages and acknowledgments are sent, at least one of the generals will always be uncertain about whether or not the last message was received.

One might ask about whether *infinite* nesting of mutual belief is required. Could the two generals agree between themselves beforehand to attack after, say, only two acknowledgments? Assuming that they could meet beforehand to come to such an agreement, then this would be feasible. But the point is that whoever sent the last acknowledgment would be uncertain as to whether this was received, and would hence be attacking while unsure as to whether it was a coordinated attack or a doomed solo effort.

More pragmatically, of course, it should be noted that — as with all the formalizations of mental states that appear in this book — mutual belief and its kin represent *idealizations* of true states of affairs. In all but the most unusual of circumstances, humans are unlikely to make use of mental states that are nested to a depth of more than a few levels.

In order to formally define mutual belief, we will make use of some auxiliary definitions. First, we write (E-Bel g φ) to represent the fact that everyone in the group denoted by g believes φ.

$$(\text{E-Bel } g \; \varphi) \; \hat{=} \; \forall i \cdot (i \in g) \Rightarrow (\text{Bel } i \; \varphi)$$

If $k \in I\!N$ such that $k > 0$, we define $(\text{E-Bel}^k \ g \ \varphi)$ inductively, as follows.

$$(\text{E-Bel}^k \ g \ \varphi) \triangleq \begin{cases} (\text{E-Bel} \ g \ \varphi) & \text{if } k = 1 \\ (\text{E-Bel} \ g \ (\text{E-Bel}^{k-1} \ g \ \varphi)) & \text{otherwise.} \end{cases}$$

The mutual belief of φ in group g is then defined as follows.

$$(\text{M-Bel} \ g \ \varphi) \triangleq \bigwedge_{k>0} (\text{E-Bel}^k \ g \ \varphi)$$

In other words, $(\text{M-Bel} \ g \ \varphi)$ is the same as the following infinitary formula.

$\forall i \cdot (i \in g) \Rightarrow$
  $(\text{Bel} \ i \ \varphi) \wedge$
  $(\text{Bel} \ i \ (\text{E-Bel} \ g \ \varphi)) \wedge$
  $(\text{Bel} \ i \ (\text{E-Bel} \ g \ (\text{E-Bel} \ g \ \varphi))) \wedge$
  $\ldots$ and so on.

It turns out that there are several ways that we can characterize mutual belief. We can adopt a *model-theoretic* approach, and characterize mutual belief in terms of each agent's belief accessibility relation. Alternatively, we can characterize mutual belief as a *fixed point*.

The Semantics of Mutual Belief*

Mutual belief has a natural and quite intuitive semantic characterization, in terms of each agent's belief accessibility relation. In order to understand this characterization, let $g \subseteq D_{Ag}$ be some group of agents, $\langle w, t \rangle$ be a situation, and $w' \in W$ be a world. Then we say w' is $\mathcal{B}(g)$-reachable from $\langle w, t \rangle$ in k steps if we can reach world w' from $\langle w, t \rangle$ by following the arcs of the belief accessibility relations for agents in g for no more than k steps. Formally, w' is $\mathcal{B}(g)$-reachable from $\langle w, t \rangle$ in k steps iff there is some sequence $(w_1, \ldots, w_k)$ of worlds such that $w_1 = w$, $w_k = w'$, and for each (w_u, w_{u+1}) we have $w_{u+1} \in \mathcal{B}_t^{w_u}(i)$ for some agent $i \in g$.

THEOREM 6.1: $\langle M, V, w, t \rangle \models_{\mathcal{S}} (\text{E-Bel}^k \ g \ \varphi)$ iff $\langle M, V, w', t \rangle \models_{\mathcal{S}} \varphi$ for every world w' such that w' is $\mathcal{B}(g)$-reachable from w in k steps.

Proof The proof is by induction on k. The base case, where $k = 1$, requires that if $\langle M, V, w, t \rangle \models_{\mathcal{S}} (\text{E-Bel}^1 \ g \ \varphi)$ then $\langle M, V, w', t \rangle \models_{\mathcal{S}} \varphi$ for every $w' \in \mathcal{B}_t^{w'}(i)$, for every $i \in g$. The result follows easily from the definition of E-Bel^1. For the inductive assumption, suppose that $\langle M, V, w, t \rangle \models_{\mathcal{S}} (\text{E-Bel}^m \ g \ \varphi)$ iff

$\langle M, V, w', t \rangle \models_S \varphi$ for every world w' such that w' is $\mathcal{B}(g)$-reachable from w in m steps. We need to show that in this case, $\langle M, V, w, t \rangle \models_S (\text{E-Bel}^{m+1} \ g \ \varphi)$ iff $\langle M, V, w', t \rangle \models_S \varphi$ for every world w' such that w' is $\mathcal{B}(g)$-reachable from w in $m + 1$ steps. This follows trivially from the definition of E-Bel and the inductive assumption. ∎

We will also say that w' is $\mathcal{B}(g)$-reachable from $\langle w, t \rangle$ if w' is $\mathcal{B}(g)$-reachable from $\langle w, t \rangle$ in k steps, for some $k \in I\!N$ such that $k > 0$. We can then prove the following.

THEOREM 6.2: $\langle M, V, w, t \rangle \models_S (\text{M-Bel} \ g \ \varphi)$ iff $\langle M, V, w', t \rangle \models_S \varphi$ for every world w' such that w' is $\mathcal{B}(g)$-reachable from w.

Proof   Follows immediately from Theorem 6.1 and the definition of M-Bel. ∎

Theorems 6.1 and 6.2 characterize E-Bel^k and M-Bel graph theoretically, where each agent's accessibility relation is interpreted as a graph over possible worlds.

Mutual Mental States as Fixed Points*

The theory of fixed points is widely used in computer science, particularly in the semantics of programming languages. A fixed-point equation is one with the following form.

$$x = f(x)$$

Fixed-point equations like this often cause confusion, because they appear to be in some sense circular — the left-hand side appears to be defined in terms of the right. But such equations can have quite natural solutions. For example, the equation $x = x^2$ has solutions $x = 0$ and $x = 1$. The following Theorem tells us that mutual belief can be understood as a fixed point.

THEOREM 6.3: $\models_S (\text{M-Bel} \ g \ \varphi) \Leftrightarrow (\text{E-Bel} \ g \ \varphi \wedge (\text{M-Bel} \ g \ \varphi))$.

Proof   For the left to right implication, assume $\langle M, V, w, t \rangle \models_S (\text{M-Bel} \ g \ \varphi)$. We need to show that this implies $\langle M, V, w, t \rangle \models_S (\text{E-Bel} \ g \ \varphi \wedge (\text{M-Bel} \ g \ \varphi))$. From Theorem 6.2, we know that $\langle M, V, w', t \rangle \models_S \varphi$ for each w' that is $\mathcal{B}(g)$-reachable from w. Now consider an arbitrary $w'' \in \mathcal{B}^w_t(i)$ for some $i \in g$. Then w'' is $\mathcal{B}(g)$-reachable from w in one step, thus $\langle M, V, w'', t \rangle \models_S \varphi$. It follows that $\langle M, V, w, t \rangle \models_S$ (Bel $i\ \varphi$) for all $i \in g$, and so $\langle M, V, w, t \rangle \models_S$ (E-Bel $g\ \varphi$). Now, consider any $w''' \in W$ such that w''' is $\mathcal{B}(g)$ reachable from w''. It must be that w''' is also $\mathcal{B}(g)$-reachable from w. It follows that $\langle M, V, w''', t \rangle \models_S \varphi$, and so $\langle M, V, w'', t \rangle \models_S$ (M-Bel $g\ \varphi$). We conclude that $\langle M, V, w, t \rangle \models_S$ (E-Bel $g\ \varphi \wedge$ (M-Bel $g\ \varphi$)). The right to left implication follows from the inductive definition of M-Bel in terms of E-Bel. ∎

This Theorem tells us that (M-Bel $g\ \varphi$) can be understood as a fixed point of the function

$$f(x) = (\text{E-Bel } g\ \varphi \wedge x)$$

where the function f maps formulae of $\mathcal{LORA}$ to formulae of $\mathcal{LORA}$. (See, for example, [54, pp.402–411] for a detailed analysis of common knowledge defined as a fixed point.)

Properties of Mutual Belief

In addition to enjoying the properties discussed above, mutual belief also behaves like a KD4 modal operator.

THEOREM 6.4:

1. $\models_S$ (M-Bel $g\ \varphi \Rightarrow \psi$) $\Rightarrow$ ((M-Bel $g\ \varphi$) $\Rightarrow$ (M-Bel $g\ \psi$))
2. $\models_S$ (M-Bel $g\ \varphi$) $\Rightarrow \neg$(M-Bel $g\ \neg\varphi$)
3. $\models_S$ (M-Bel $g\ \varphi$) $\Rightarrow$ (M-Bel g (M-Bel $g\ \varphi$))
4. If $\models_S \varphi$ then $\models_S$ (M-Bel $g\ \varphi$)

Proof Parts (1) and (4) are trivial; for (2) and (3), notice that the $\mathcal{B}(g)$ reachability relation will be serial and transitive. (See e.g., [54, p.34].) ∎

In the remainder of the book, I will assume that M-Int (mutual intention) and M-Des (mutual desire) have been defined in an analogous way to M-Bel.

6.2 Mutual Mental States and Teamwork

Mutual beliefs, desires, or intentions characterize states that exist in certain idealized scenarios. In particular, as the informal example that opens this chapter illustrates, mutual belief appears to characterize many communication scenarios. In this section, we will consider the types of mutual mental states that characterize real-world joint working scenarios, and in particular, the type of mental states that characterize an agent engaged in *teamwork*. By teamwork, we mean scenarios such as the following, where a group of agents work together [133, 37, 250]:

- to lift a heavy object;
- to write a joint paper; or
- to drive in a convoy.

What sort of mental state characterizes such cooperative efforts? One possibility would be to argue that there was a "team state" that was not reducible to the individual beliefs, desires, and intentions of the participating agents. We could easily formalize such a concept, by introducing (yet) another primitive modal operator to represent team mental states, and then investigate its properties using the same techniques employed throughout this book. The problem is that intuition rejects such an approach. It seems almost superstitious to argue that there is something about team action that exists independently of the team members. I therefore adopt a *reductionist* approach, where teamwork is analyzed in terms of the individual mental states of team members.

As a first attempt at defining team mental states, we might imagine that it is sufficient for a team to have (say) a mutual intention (M-Int) towards some particular goal. Suppose we have two agents i and j cooperatively working to achieve some state of affairs φ. Then (M-Int $\{i,j\}$ φ) would expand to

(E-Int $\{i,j\}$ φ) $\wedge$
(E-Int $\{i,j\}$ (E-Int $\{i,j\}$ φ)) $\wedge$
(E-Int $\{i,j\}$ (E-Int $\{i,j\}$ (E-Int $\{i,j\}$ φ))) $\wedge$
. . . and so on.

Thus agent i's mental state is characterized by the following pattern of intentions.

(Int i φ) $\wedge$
(Int i (E-Int $\{i,j\}$ φ)) $\wedge$
(Int i (E-Int $\{i,j\}$ (E-Int $\{i,j\}$ φ))) $\wedge$
. . . and so on.

This pattern is symmetric, and so is shared by each participating agent. It seems reasonable to suppose that an agent engaged in team activity does indeed have such a pattern of intentions. For example, if you and I are together lifting a heavy object, it seems reasonable that I intend to lift it, and I intend that you intend to lift it, and I intend that you intend that I intend to lift it, and so on. But is there *more* to cooperative action than this? Levesque, Cohen, and Nunes argue that such models of mutual intention fail to capture some important characteristics of teamwork [133, 37]. In particular, they fail to capture the notion of *joint commitment*. To continue with the example of lifting a heavy object, suppose that while we are lifting it I come to believe that we will be unable to lift it for some reason. As we saw in chapter 5, a rational agent acting alone in such circumstances would drop the intention: it would be irrational for an agent to act towards an intention that was believed to be impossible. But in the teamwork case, should I simply drop my intention to lift the object with you, because I believe it is not achievable? You would hardly be inclined to say I was "cooperative" if I did so. What appears to be missing is that associated with team action is what Jennings calls *responsibility* toward the team [104, 105, 106]. Responsibility in the context of teamwork is comprised of two parts: a *commitment* and a *convention*.

A commitment is a pledge or promise that an agent makes to the group in which it is working. A commitment must, by definition, persist over time [35, pp.217–219].

A convention is a means of monitoring a commitment. A convention thus specifies the circumstances under which a commitment can be abandoned and how an agent should behave both locally and towards others when one of these conditions arises [105]. Thus a convention identifies the conditions under which the joint commitment can be dropped, and also describes how the agent should behave towards its fellow team members. For example, if an agent drops its joint commitment because it believes that the intention will never be attained, then it is part of the notion of "cooperativeness" that it informs fellow team members of this. Conventions thus provide a commonly understood frame of reference in which agents can work. By adopting a convention, every agent knows what is expected both of it, and of every other agent, as part of the collective working towards the intention, and knows that every other agent has a similar set of expectations. By adopting a particular convention, team behavior becomes more predictable. Predictability is one of the most important enablers of *coordinated* behavior [18].

We can formalize conventions quite simply. A convention is a set of *rules*, where each rule $r = \langle \rho, \gamma \rangle$ is a pair consisting of a re-evaluation condition ρ and an associated goal γ. A convention will be adopted by a group of agents g when working towards some goal φ. The idea is that if ever an agent $i \in g$

believes ρ to be true, then it must adopt γ as an intention, and keep this intention until the commitment becomes redundant.

Formally, a *convention*, c, is a finite indexed set of pairs:

$$c = \{\langle \rho_1, \gamma_1 \rangle, \ldots, \langle \rho_l, \gamma_l \rangle\}$$

where ρ_k is a state formula of $\mathcal{LORA}$ called the *re-evaluation condition*, and γ_k is a state formula of $\mathcal{LORA}$ called *goal*.

Team or joint commitments have a number of parameters. First, a team commitment is held by a group g of agents. Second, joint commitments are held with respect to some goal φ; this is the state of affairs that the group is committed to bringing about. They also have a *pre-condition*, which describes what must initially be true of the world in order for the commitment to be held. For example, in most types of team commitment, we do not expect participating agents to initially believe that the object of the commitment, φ, is true. Finally, team commitment is parameterized by a convention c. Team commitment is then informally defined as follows. A group g is has a team commitment to goal φ with respect to pre-condition ψ and convention c iff:

1. pre-condition ψ is initially satisfied; and

2. every agent $i \in g$ has an intention of φ until the termination condition is satisfied;

3. until the termination condition is satisfied, if any agent $i \in g$ believes that the re-evaluation condition of any rule in c is satisfied, then it adopts as an intention the goal corresponding to the re-evaluation condition, and maintains this goal until the termination condition is satisfied;

where the termination condition is that one of the goal parts of the convention rules is satisfied.

More formally, if

$$c = \{\langle \rho_1, \gamma_1 \rangle, \ldots \langle \rho_l, \gamma_l \rangle\}$$

is a convention, then we denote the team commitment of group g to goal φ with respect to convention c and pre-condition ψ by $(\text{Team}_c \, g \, \varphi \, \psi)$.

Formally, $(\text{Team}_c \, g \, \varphi \, \psi)$ is defined as follows:

$$(\text{Team}_c \, g \, \varphi \, \psi) \; \hat{=} \; \forall i \cdot (i \in g) \Rightarrow \psi \wedge A((\chi_1 \wedge \chi_2) \, \mathcal{U} \, \chi_3)$$

where

$$\chi_1 \triangleq (\text{Int } i \, \varphi)$$

and

$$\chi_2 \triangleq \bigwedge_{k=1}^{l} (\text{Bel } i \, \rho_k) \Rightarrow A[(\text{Int } i \, \gamma_k) \, \mathcal{U} \, \chi_3]$$

and

$$\chi_3 \triangleq \bigvee_{k=1}^{l} \gamma_k.$$

We saw in earlier chapters that a single agent can have various different kinds of commitment towards its goals. We will now see how social variants of these kinds of commitment can be encoded using our model of conventions and social commitments.

Blind Social Commitment

Recall from chapter 2 that an agent with a *blind* commitment towards some state of affairs φ will maintain φ as an intention until it believes this state of affairs is achieved. The social convention c_{blind} corresponding to blind commitment consists of a single rule.

$$c_{blind} \triangleq \{ \langle (\text{Bel } i \, \varphi), (\text{M-Bel } g \, \varphi) \rangle \}$$

The re-evaluation condition for this rule is thus that an agent i believes the goal of the teamwork has been achieved; if it ever comes to believe this, then it intends that the remainder of the team comes to believe this.

We define the pre-condition for blind commitment as ψ_{blind} as follows.

$$\psi_{blind} \triangleq \neg(\text{Bel } i \, \varphi)$$

In other words, team members do not initially believe that the goal is satisfied. Expanding out the definition of $(\text{Team}_{blind} \, g \, \varphi \, \psi)$ gives the following.

$$\forall i \cdot (i \in g) \Rightarrow$$
$$\quad \neg(\text{Bel } i \, \varphi) \wedge$$
$$\quad A\left((\text{Int } i \, \varphi) \wedge ((\text{Bel } i \, \varphi) \Rightarrow A((\text{Int } i \, \chi_1) \, \mathcal{U} \, \chi_1)) \, \mathcal{U} \, \chi_1\right)$$

where

$$\chi_1 \triangleq (\text{M-Bel } g \, \varphi).$$

Suppose an agent working in a team with such a commitment comes to believe that the goal φ is achieved. Then it must satisfy the following condition:

$$A((\text{Int } i \ (\text{M-Bel } g \ \varphi)) \mathcal{U} (\text{M-Bel } g \ \varphi))$$

Thus i should intend that g mutually believe φ until this state of affairs is achieved.

A Minimal Social Convention

Next, we specify a *minimal social convention* that is similar to the Levesque-Cohen model of joint persistent goals (JPGs) [133, p.98]. A collective with such a commitment will have a mental state in which:

- initially, every agent does not believe that the goal φ is satisfied, but believes φ is possible;
- every agent i then has a goal of φ until the termination condition is satisfied (see below);
- until the termination condition is satisfied, then:

    –if any agent i believes that the goal is achieved, then it will have a goal that this becomes a mutual belief, and will retain this goal until the termination condition is satisfied;

    –if any agent i believes that the goal is impossible, then it will have a goal that this becomes a mutual belief, and will retain this goal until the termination condition is satisfied;

- the termination condition is that it is mutually believed that either:

    –the goal φ is satisfied; or

    –the goal φ is impossible to achieve.

    Let

$$\psi_{soc} \ \hat{=} \ \neg(\text{Bel } i \ \varphi) \wedge (\text{Bel } i \ \text{E}\Diamond\varphi)$$

and

$$c_{soc} \ \hat{=} \ \left\{ \begin{array}{c} (\underbrace{(\text{Bel } i \ \varphi)}_{\rho_1}, \underbrace{(\text{M-Bel } g \ \varphi)}_{\gamma_1})), \\[2ex] (\underbrace{(\text{Bel } i \ \text{A} \Box \neg\varphi)}_{\rho_2}, \underbrace{(\text{M-Bel } g \ \text{A} \Box \neg\varphi)}_{\gamma_2})) \end{array} \right\} .$$

It is not difficult to see that $(\text{Team}_{soc}\ g\ \varphi\ \psi_{soc})$ expands to:

$$\forall i \cdot (i \in g) \Rightarrow$$
$$\neg(\text{Bel } i\ \varphi) \wedge (\text{Bel } i\ \text{E}\Diamond\varphi) \wedge$$

$$A\left[\left(\begin{array}{l}(\text{Int } i\ \varphi) \wedge \\ (\ ((\text{Bel } i\ \varphi) \Rightarrow A((\text{Int } i\ (\text{M-Bel } g\ \varphi))\,\mathcal{U}\,\chi_1))\wedge \\ \ \ \ ((\text{Bel } i\ A\,\square\,\neg\varphi) \Rightarrow A((\text{Int } i\ (\text{M-Bel } g\ A\,\square\,\neg\varphi))\,\mathcal{U}\,\chi_1)) \\ )\end{array}\right)\,\mathcal{U}\,\chi_1\right]$$

where

$$\chi_1 \triangleq [(\text{M-Bel } g\ \varphi) \vee (\text{M-Bel } g\ A\,\square\,\neg\varphi)].$$

6.3 Notes and Further Reading

The fact that mutual belief (or common knowledge) can never arise in a communication scenario where message delivery is not guaranteed is one of the most famous results in the modal logic of knowledge [89]. See [54, pp.175–232] for proofs of this and related results, and [54, pp.230–232] for historical notes on the result and related work.

The formal treatment of mutual beliefs, desires, and intentions presented in this chapter is closely based on the presentation of common knowledge in [54]. In particular, the semantics and fixed-point treatments of mutual mental states are very closely based on those of [54]. Chapters 6 and 11 of [54] are more or less completely devoted to common knowledge and the associated coordinated attack problem.

The distinction between mutually intending some state of affairs and the kinds of mental state involved in teamwork have been noted by many researchers. Searle, in particular, makes a distinction between a group of agents that are engaged in coordinated activity, but not teamwork (such as a group of agents driving on a highway), and agents that are actively engaged in team action (such a group of ballet dancers) [203]. Early attempts to formalize "team" mental states include [181, 230].

Following Levesque, Cohen, and Nunes' formalization of teamwork [133], many attempts to formalize joint intentions appeared in the literature [118, 190]. Jennings demonstrated that such models could be usefully applied to industrial coordination problems [104, 105, 106].

7 Communication

In this chapter, I show how $\mathcal{LORA}$ can be used to capture communication between agents. Communication has long been recognized as a topic of central importance in computer science, and many formalisms have been developed for representing the properties of communicating concurrent systems [98, 154]. Such formalisms have tended to focus on a number of key issues that arise when dealing with systems that can interact with one another.

Perhaps the characteristic problem in communicating concurrent systems research is that of *synchronizing* multiple processes, which was widely studied throughout the 1970s and 1980s [11]. Essentially, two processes (cf. agents) need to be synchronized if there is a possibility that they can interfere with one another in a destructive way. The classic example of such interference is the "lost update" scenario. In this scenario, we have two processes, p_1 and p_2, both of which have access to some shared variable v. Process p_1 begins to update the value of v, by first reading it, then modifying it (perhaps by simply incrementing the value that it obtained), and finally saving this updated value in v. But between p_1 reading and again saving the value of v, process p_2 updates v, by saving some value in it. When p_1 saves its modified value of v, the update performed by p_2 is thus lost, which is almost certainly not what was intended. The lost update problem is a very real issue in the design of programs that communicate through shared data structures.

Synchronization is, of course, still an issue when constructing multiagent systems of the kind under consideration in this book: we must ensure that agents do not interact with one another in damaging ways [194]. However, such low-level communication problems are generally regarded as solved for the purposes of multiagent systems research. We usually assume the presence of some underlying communication platform, which provides appropriate facilities for robust, synchronized communication between agents. This seems to be a reasonable assumption: after all, the JAVA programming language provides exactly such mechanisms.

So, if we do not treat communication in such a "low-level" way, then how *is* communication treated by the agent community? In order to understand the answer, it is helpful to first consider the way that communication is treated in the object-oriented programming community, that is, communication as method invocation. Suppose we have a JAVA system containing two objects, o_1 and o_2, and that o_1 has a publicly available method m_1. Object o_2 can communicate with o_1 by invoking method m_1. In JAVA, this would mean o_2 executing an instruction that looks something like o1.m1(arg), where arg is the argument that o_2 wants to communicate to o_1. But consider: Which object makes the decision about the execution of method m_1 — is it object o_1 or object o_2? In this scenario, object o_1 has *no control* over the execution of m_1: the decision about whether to execute m_1 lies entirely with o_2.

Now consider a similar scenario, but in an agent-oriented setting. We have two agents i and j, where i has the capability to perform action α, which corresponds loosely to a method. But there is no concept in the agent-oriented world of agent j "invoking a method" on i. This is because i is an *autonomous agent*: it has control over both its state and its behavior. It cannot be taken for granted that agent i will execute action α just because another agent j wants it to. Performing the action α may not be in the best interests of agent i. The locus of control with respect to the decision about whether to execute an action is thus very different in agent and object systems.

In general, agents can neither force other agents to perform some action, nor write data onto the internal state of other agents. This does not mean they cannot communicate, however. What they *can* do is perform actions — communicative actions — in an attempt to *influence* other agents appropriately. For example, suppose I say to you "It is raining in London," in a sincere way. Under normal circumstances, such a communication action is an attempt by me to modify your beliefs. Specifically, it is an attempt by me to bring about a state of affairs that we can characterize in $\mathcal{LORA}$ as follows.

(Bel *you Weather*(*london*, *raining*))

Of course, simply uttering the sentence "It is raining in London" is not usually enough to bring about this state of affairs, for all the reasons that were discussed above. You have control over your own beliefs (desires, intentions). You may believe that I am notoriously unreliable on the subject of the weather, or even that I am a pathological liar. But in performing the communication action of uttering "It is raining in London," I am attempting to change your internal state. Furthermore, since this utterance is an action that I perform, I am performing it for some purpose — presumably because I intend that you believe it is raining.

Speech act theory treats communication as action. It is predicated on the assumption that speech actions are performed by agents just like other actions, in the furtherance of their intentions. Speech act theory is thus broadly consistent with our view of agents as practical reasoning systems, deciding moment by moment which action to perform in order to best achieve their current intentions.

In this chapter, I show how we can model communication as speech acts in $\mathcal{LORA}$. In later chapters, I demonstrate how these speech acts can be used by agents in the cooperative problem-solving process and other social actions. I begin with an historical overview of speech act theory, focusing in particular on attempts to develop formal theories of speech acts, where communications are modeled as actions that alter the mental state of communication participants.

7.1 Speech Acts

The theory of speech acts is generally recognized to have begun with the work of the philosopher John Austin [6]. He noted that a certain class of natural language utterances — hereafter referred to as *speech acts* — had the characteristics of *actions*, in the sense that they change the state of the world in a way analogous to physical actions. It may seem strange to think of utterances changing the world in the way that physical actions do. If I pick up a block from a table (to use an overworked but traditional example), then the world has changed in an obvious way. But how does speech change the world? Austin gave as paradigm examples declaring war and saying "I now pronounce you man and wife." Stated in the appropriate circumstances, these utterances clearly change the state of the world in a very tangible way.[1]

Austin identified a number of *performative verbs*, which correspond to various different types of speech acts. Examples of such performative verbs are *request*, *inform*, and *promise*. In addition, Austin distinguished three different aspects of speech acts: the *locutionary act*, or act of making an utterance (e.g., saying "Please make some tea"), the *illocutionary act*, or action performed in saying something (e.g., "He requested me to make some tea"), and *perlocution*, or effect of the act (e.g., "He got me to make tea").

Austin referred to the conditions required for the successful completion of performatives as *felicity conditions*. He recognized three important felicity conditions:

1. There must be an accepted conventional procedure for the performative,

---

1 Notice that when referring to the effects of communication, I am ignoring "pathological" cases, such as shouting while on a ski run and causing an avalanche. Similarly, I will ignore "microscopic" effects (such as the minute changes in pressure or temperature in a room caused by speaking).

and the circumstances and persons must be as specified in the procedure.

2. The procedure must be executed correctly and completely.

3. The act must be sincere, and any *uptake* required must be completed, insofar as is possible.

Austin's work was extended by John Searle, in his 1969 book *Speech Acts* [202]. Searle identified several properties that must hold for a speech act performed between a hearer and a speaker to succeed. For example, consider a *request* by SPEAKER to HEARER to perform ACTION:

1. *Normal I/O conditions.* Normal I/O conditions state that HEARER is able to hear the request (thus must not be deaf, . . .), the act was performed in normal circumstances (not in a film or play, . . .), etc.

2. *Preparatory conditions.* The preparatory conditions state what must be true of the world in order that SPEAKER correctly choose the speech act. In this case, HEARER must be able to perform ACTION, and SPEAKER must believe that HEARER is able to perform ACTION. Also, it must not be obvious that HEARER will do ACTION anyway.

3. *Sincerity conditions.* These conditions distinguish sincere performances of the request; an insincere performance of the act might occur if SPEAKER did not really want ACTION to be performed.

Searle also attempted a systematic classification of possible types of speech acts, identifying the following five key classes:

1. *Representatives.* A representative act commits the speaker to the truth of an expressed proposition. The paradigm case is *informing*.

2. *Directives.* A directive is an attempt on the part of the speaker to get the hearer to do something. Paradigm case: *requesting*.

3. *Commissives.* Commit the speaker to a course of action. Paradigm case: *promising*.

4. *Expressives.* Express some psychological state (e.g., gratitude). Paradigm case: *thanking*.

5. *Declarations.* Effect some changes in an institutional state of affairs. Paradigm case: *declaring war*.

In the late 1960s and early 1970s, a number of researchers in AI began to build systems that could plan how to autonomously achieve goals [2]. Clearly, if such a system is required to interact with humans or other autonomous agents, then such plans must include *speech* actions. This introduced the question of how the properties of speech acts could be represented such that planning systems could reason about them. Cohen and Perrault [39] gave an account of the semantics of speech acts by using techniques developed in AI planning research [59]. The aim of their work was to develop a theory of speech acts

... by modeling them in a planning system as operators defined ... in terms of speakers' and hearers' beliefs and goals. Thus speech acts are treated in the same way as physical actions. [39]

The formalism chosen by Cohen and Perrault was the STRIPS notation, in which the properties of an action are characterized via pre- and post-conditions [59]. The idea is very similar to Hoare logic [97]. Cohen and Perrault demonstrated how the pre- and post-conditions of speech acts such as *request* could be represented in a multimodal logic containing operators for describing the *beliefs*, *abilities*, and *wants* of the participants in the speech act.

Consider the *Request* act. The aim of the *Request* act will be for a speaker to get a hearer to perform some action. Figure 7.1 defines the *Request* act. Two preconditions are stated: the "cando.pr" (can-do pre-conditions), and "want.pr" (want pre-conditions). The cando.pr states that for the successful completion of the *Request*, two conditions must hold. First, the speaker must believe that the hearer of the *Request* is able to perform the action. Second, the speaker must believe that the hearer also believes it has the ability to perform the action. The want.pr states that in order for the *Request* to be successful, the speaker must also believe it actually wants the *Request* to be performed. If the pre-conditions of the *Request* are fulfilled, then the *Request* will be successful: the result (defined by the "effect" part of the definition) will be that the hearer believes the speaker believes it wants some action to be performed.

While the successful completion of the *Request* ensures that the hearer is aware of the speaker's desires, it is not enough in itself to guarantee that the desired action is actually performed. This is because the definition of *Request* only models the illocutionary force of the act. It says nothing of the perlocutionary force. What is required is a *mediating act*. Figure 7.1 gives a definition of *CauseToWant*, which is an example of such an act. By this definition, an agent will come to believe it wants to do something if it believes that another agent believes it wants to do it. This definition could clearly be extended by adding more pre-conditions, perhaps to do with beliefs about social relationships, power structures, etc.

The *Inform* act is as basic as *Request*. The aim of performing an *Inform*

$Request(S, H, \alpha)$		
Preconditions	Cando.pr	$(S\ BELIEVE\ (H\ CANDO\ \alpha)) \wedge$ $(S\ BELIEVE\ (H\ BELIEVE\ (H\ CANDO\ \alpha)))$
	Want.pr	$(S\ BELIEVE\ (S\ WANT\ requestInstance))$
Effect		$(H\ BELIEVE\ (S\ BELIEVE\ (S\ WANT\ \alpha)))$

$CauseToWant(A_1, A_2, \alpha)$		
Preconditions	Cando.pr	$(A_1\ BELIEVE\ (A_2\ BELIEVE\ (A_2\ WANT\ \alpha)))$
	Want.pr	$\times$
Effect		$(A_1\ BELIEVE\ (A_1\ WANT\ \alpha))$

$Inform(S, H, \varphi)$		
Preconditions	Cando.pr	$(S\ BELIEVE\ \varphi)$
	Want.pr	$(S\ BELIEVE\ (S\ WANT\ informInstance))$
Effect		$(H\ BELIEVE\ (S\ BELIEVE\ \varphi))$

$Convince(A_1, A_2, \varphi)$		
Preconditions	Cando.pr	$(A_1\ BELIEVE\ (A_2\ BELIEVE\ \varphi))$
	Want.pr	$\times$
Effect		$(A_1\ BELIEVE\ \varphi)$

Figure 7.1
Definitions from Cohen and Perrault's plan-based theory of speech acts.

will be for a speaker to get a hearer to believe some statement. Like *Request*, the definition of *Inform* requires an associated mediating act to model the perlocutionary force of the act. The cando.pr of *Inform* states that the speaker must believe φ is true. The effect of the act will simply be to make the hearer believe that the speaker believes φ. The cando.pr of *Convince* simply states that the hearer must believe that the speaker believes φ. The effect is simply to make the hearer believe φ.

Speech Acts as Rational Action

While the plan-based theory of speech acts was a major step forward, it was recognized that a theory of speech acts should be rooted in a more general theory of rational action. This observation led Cohen and Levesque to develop a theory in which speech acts were modeled as actions performed by rational agents in the furtherance of their intentions [36]. The foundation upon which they built this model of rational action was their theory of intention, described in [35]. The formal theory is too complex to describe here, but as a flavor, here is the Cohen-Levesque definition of *requesting*, paraphrased in English:

A request is an attempt on the part of *spkr*, by doing *e*, to bring about a state where, ideally, (i) *addr* intends α, (relative to the *spkr* still having that goal, and *addr* still being helpfully inclined to *spkr*), and (ii) *addr* actually eventually does α, or at least brings about a state where *addr* believes it is mutually believed that it wants the ideal situation. [36, p.241]

I use the Cohen-Levesque model of speech acts as the basis on which to develop the $\mathcal{LORA}$ model of communication later in this chapter.

Agent Communication Languages: KQML and FIPA

Throughout the 1980s and 1990s, interest in multiagent systems developed rapidly [18]. An obvious problem in multiagent systems is how to get agents to communicate with one another. To this end, in the early 1990s, the DARPA Knowledge Sharing Effort (KSE) began to develop the Knowledge Query and Manipulation Language (KQML) and the associated Knowledge Interchange Format (KIF) as a common framework via which multiple expert systems (cf. agents) could exchange knowledge [170, 147].

KQML is essentially an "outer" language for messages: it defines a simple LISP-like format for messages, and 41 *performatives*, or message types, that define the intended meaning of a message. Example KQML performatives include `ask-if` and `tell`. The *content* of messages was not considered part of the KQML standard, but KIF was defined to express such content. KIF is essentially classical first-order predicate logic, recast in a LISP-like syntax.

To better understand the KQML language, consider the following example (from [147, p.354]):

```
(ask-one
    :content  (PRICE IBM ?price)
    :receiver stock-server
    :language LPROLOG
    :ontology NYSE-TICKS
)
```

The intuitive interpretation of this message is that the sender is asking about the price of IBM stock. The performative is `ask-one`, which an agent will use to ask a question of another agent where exactly one reply is needed. The various other components of this message represent its attributes. The most important of these is the `:content` field, which specifies the message content. In this case, the content simply asks for the price of IBM shares. The `:receiver` attribute specifies the intended recipient of the message, the `:language` attribute specifies that the language in which the content is expressed is called LPROLOG (the recipient is assumed to "understand" LPROLOG), and the final :ontology attribute defines the terminology used in the message.

Formal definitions of the syntax of KQML and KIF were developed by the KSE, but KQML lacked any formal semantics until Labrou and Finin's [127]. These semantics were presented using a pre- and post-condition notation, closely related to Cohen and Perrault's plan-based theory of speech acts [39]. These pre- and post-conditions were specified by Labrou and Finin using a logical language containing modalities for belief, knowledge, wanting, and intending.

The take-up of KQML by the multiagent systems community was significant. However, Cohen and Levesque (among others) criticized KQML on a number of grounds [38], the most important of which being that the language was missing an entire class of performatives — *commissives*, by which one agent makes a commitment to another. As Cohen and Levesque point out, it is difficult to see how many multiagent scenarios could be implemented without commissives, which appear to be important if agents are to *coordinate* their actions with one another.

In 1995, the Foundation for Intelligent Physical Agents (FIPA) began its work on developing standards for agent systems. The centerpiece of this initiative was the development of an ACL [60]. This ACL is superficially similar to KQML: it defines an "outer" language for messages, it defines 20 performatives (such as inform) for defining the intended interpretation of messages, and it does not mandate any specific language for message content. In addition, the concrete syntax for FIPA ACL messages closely resembles that of KQML. Here is an example of a FIPA ACL message (from [60, p.10]):

```
(inform
    :sender    agent1
    :receiver  agent2
    :content   (price good2 150)
    :language  sl
    :ontology  hpl-auction
)
```

The FIPA communication language is similar to KQML; the relationship is discussed in [60, pp.68–69]. The 20 performatives provided by the FIPA communication language are categorized in Table 7.1.

Table 7.1
Performatives provided by the FIPA communication language.

Performative	Passing Information	Requesting Information	Negotiation	Performing Actions	Error Handling
accept-proposal			×		
agree				×	
cancel		×		×	
cfp			×		
confirm	×				
disconfirm	×				
failure					×
inform	×				
inform-if	×				
inform-ref	×				
not-understood					×
propose			×		
query-if		×			
query-ref		×			
refuse				×	
reject-proposal			×		
request				×	
request-when				×	
request-whenever				×	
subscribe		×			

The FIPA ACL has been given a formal semantics, in terms of a Semantic Language (SL). The approach adopted for defining these semantics draws heavily on [36], but in particular on Sadek's enhancements to this work [23]. SL is a quantified multimodal logic, which contains modal operators for referring to the *beliefs*, *desires*, and *uncertain beliefs* of agents, as well as a simple dynamic logic-style apparatus for representing agent's actions. The semantics of the FIPA ACL map each ACL message to a formula of SL, which defines a constraint that the sender of the message must satisfy if it is to be considered as conforming to the FIPA ACL standard. FIPA refers to this constraint as the *feasibility* condition. The semantics also map each message to an SL-formula that defines the *rational effect* of the action — the "purpose" of the message: what an agent will be attempting to achieve in sending the message (cf. perlocutionary act). However, in a society of autonomous agents, the rational effect of a message cannot (and should not) be guaranteed. Hence conformance does not require the recipient of a message to respect the rational effect part of the ACL semantics — only the feasibility condition.

To illustrate the FIPA approach, I give an example of the semantics of the

FIPA `inform` performative [60, p.25]:

$\langle i, inform(j, \varphi) \rangle$
> feasibility pre-condition: $B_i\varphi \wedge \neg B_i(Bif_j\varphi \vee Uif_j\varphi)$ (7.1)
> rational effect: $B_j\varphi$

The B_i is a modal connective for referring to the beliefs of agents (rather like Bel in $\mathcal{LORA}$); *Bif* is a modal connective that allows us to express whether an agent has a definite opinion one way or the other about the truth or falsity of its parameter; and *Uif* is a modal connective that allows us to represent the fact that an agent is "uncertain" about its parameter. Thus an agent i sending an *inform* message with content φ to agent j will be respecting the semantics of the FIPA ACL if it believes φ, and it is not the case that it believes of j either that j believes whether φ is true or false, or that j is uncertain of the truth or falsity of φ.

In the remainder of this chapter, I use ideas from the work of Cohen and Perrault [39], Cohen and Levesque [36], Bretier and Sadek [23], and from the FIPA standard itself [60] to define the semantics of "inform" (representative) and "request" (directive) speech acts. In the style of [60], I then show how these two basic speech acts can be used to define a range of other possible speech acts. I begin by defining what it means for one agent to attempt to bring about some state of affairs.

7.2 Attempts

We will see below that when agents communicate with one another, they are in fact *attempting* to bring about some state of affairs. The notion of an attempt will thus be a central component of our formalization of communication. The model of attempts I adopt is based that proposed by Cohen and Levesque [36, p.240]. The idea is that an attempt by agent i to bring about a state φ is an action α, which is performed by i with the desire that after α is performed, φ is satisfied, but with the intention that at least ψ is satisfied. The ultimate aim of the attempt — the thing that i hopes to bring about — is represented by φ, whereas ψ represents "what it takes to make an honest effort" [36, p.240]. If i is successful, then bringing about ψ will be sufficient to cause φ. To make this concrete, consider the following scenario.

Alice, an academic, wishes to obtain tenure. Unfortunately, she is in competition for promotion with another colleague, Bob. She has no plan available to her that she believes will guarantee to bring about promotion. However, if the tenure committee could somehow be convinced that Bob had been faking research results, then this may be sufficient to scupper Bob's chances. To this end, she sends a letter to the tenure committee stating that Bob had been faking his results.

In this scenario, Alice is performing an action (sending the letter to the tenure committee) in an attempt to gain promotion. Alice intends that this action will cause the tenure committee to believe that Bob is a cheat, and she desires that this will be enough to foil Bob's chances. Whether or not it *is* enough will be outside Alice's control.

Formally, an attempt by i to achieve φ by performing α, at least achieving ψ, is written $\{\text{Attempt } i\ \alpha\ \varphi\ \psi\}$; following Cohen and Levesque, I use curly brackets here to indicate that attempts are complex actions, rather than predicates or modal operators [36, p.240].

$$\{\text{Attempt } i\ \alpha\ \varphi\ \psi\} \ \ \hat{=} \ \ \left[\begin{array}{l} (\text{Bel } i\ \neg\varphi)\ \wedge \\ (\text{Agt } \alpha\ i)\ \wedge \\ (\text{Des } i\ (\text{Achvs } \alpha\ \varphi))\ \wedge \\ (\text{Int } i\ (\text{Achvs } \alpha\ \psi)) \end{array} \right]?; \alpha$$

Returning to the scenario above, the action α is Alice sending the letter about Bob faking his research results; the state of affairs φ that Alice wants to bring about is being promoted, and ψ, what it takes to make a reasonable effort, is the tenure committee believing Bob is a cheat.

We now prove some properties of attempts. First, if an agent attempts to bring about some state of affairs φ by at least bringing about ψ, then it desires that φ is at least possible.

THEOREM 7.1: $\models_{\mathcal{P}} (\text{Happens } \{\text{Attempt } i\ \alpha\ \varphi\ \psi\}) \Rightarrow (\text{Des } i\ \mathsf{E}\Diamond\varphi)$

Proof Assume $\langle M, V, w, p\rangle \models_{\mathcal{P}} (\text{Happens } \{\text{Attempt } i\ \alpha\ \varphi\ \psi\})$ for arbitrary $\langle M, V, w, p\rangle$. Then by expanding out the definition of Attempt, we have $\langle M, V, w, p\rangle \models_{\mathcal{P}} (\text{Happens } (\text{Des } i\ (\text{Achvs } \alpha\ \varphi))?)$ and so $\langle M, V, w, p(0)\rangle \models_{\mathcal{P}} (\text{Des } i\ (\text{Achvs } \alpha\ \varphi))$. Now, since $\models_{\mathcal{S}} (\text{Achvs } \alpha\ \varphi) \Rightarrow \mathsf{E}\Diamond\varphi$, then from the K axiom for desires it is easy to obtain $\langle M, V, w, p(0)\rangle \models_{\mathcal{P}} (\text{Des } i\ \mathsf{E}\Diamond\varphi))$ and we are done. ∎

Similarly, if an agent attempts to bring about some state of affairs φ by at least bringing about ψ, then it believes that ψ is possible.

THEOREM 7.2: $\models_{\mathcal{P}}$ (Happens {Attempt $i\ \alpha\ \varphi\ \psi$}) $\Rightarrow$ (Des i E$\Diamond\psi$)

Proof   As Theorem 7.1.   ∎

7.3   Informing

Probably the simplest form of communication that can take place between two agents involves the exchange of information. Such information exchange will usually result in belief changes. Attempts to communicate information are known as *representative* speech acts [202]. The paradigm example of representative acts involves agents uttering simple declarative sentences. Examples include an agent saying "It is raining in London," or "Tony Blair is Prime Minister." I will say an agent performing a representative act is *informing* another agent about some state of affairs.

It is possible to identify the following properties of inform actions that we will capture in our model.

1. An inform speech act (and other speech acts) takes place between a "speaker" agent and one or more "hearer" agents.

Most theories of speech acts presuppose that they take place between just two agents: a "speaker" and a "hearer." The model of speech acts we will see below is more general than this — it allows for speech acts where the "hearer" is a group of agents. For example, consider somebody making a presentation to a group of people. The speaker is attempting to bring about some mutual belief in the mental state of the hearers.

2. Inform actions are actually *actions* that an agent may perform, just like any other action.

The model of speech acts I present here does not presuppose any particular "transport mechanism" for the communication. For example, it does not require a FIPA-like communication language for messages. Instead, *any* action that satisfies certain properties can be counted as an inform message. For example, uttering the sentence "The door is open," writing a note saying "The door is open," and simply nodding in the direction of the door can all be counted as attempts by an agent to inform a hearer that the door is open if the actor satisfies certain properties.

3. The purpose of an inform action is to modify the beliefs of agent(s) hearing the speech acts, and in particular, to cause them to believe some state of affairs. The state of affairs that the agent performing the speech act desires to bring

about is known as the *perlocutionary force* in speech act theory [202], or the *rational effect* of a message in FIPA [60]. The rational effect of an inform action is to cause some particular belief in the hearer.

4. Since the speaker of the inform act cannot normally bring about the ultimate intention of the speech act in the listener(s), they will attempt to bring about some "lesser" belief, such that this will be sufficient, if the listener(s) are so inclined, to cause the listener(s) to believe the ultimate belief.

There is something of a paradox here. If I am *completely* autonomous, and exercise *complete* control over my mental state, then *nothing* you say will have any effect on my mental state. But if nothing you say can change my state, then how can we communicate? The answer I adopt here is that if you are attempting to inform me of some state of affairs, then the best you can do is convince me that *you* believe this state of affairs. If I am then appropriately inclined, this will be sufficient to cause me to believe it.

5. Inform actions (and other speech acts) are *attempts* to bring about some intended state of affairs — they may *fail* to bring this state of affairs.

A model of speech acts that in some sense *required* an agent to bring about the intended change in mental state would be too strong. An agent can attempt to bring about such a mental state, but may fail for at least two reasons. First, the action itself may fail — for example, the communications medium may be faulty. Second, for the reasons discussed above, the hearer(s) of the speech act may simply choose to ignore it.

6. Inform actions (and other speech acts) cannot be performed *accidentally*.

To modify an example from [36, p.239], suppose a blindfolded person reaches into a bowl of flashcards, pulls out three cards, and knowingly turns them toward another person. The cards say "The door is open." One would not be inclined to say that an inform speech act took place.

It is normally required that inform actions be performed *sincerely*: that the speaker must believe the state of affairs referred to in the act. However, the model of inform speech acts presented here does not require that informs be sincere. I will instead focus on the (more general case) of agents that are simply attempting to bring about a belief in some conversation participant.

We can now formally define the Inform speech act. We write

{Inform i g α φ}

to indicate that α is an action performed by agent i in an attempt to inform group g of φ. Note the use of curly brackets here: Inform is neither a predicate nor a modal operator, but an *action*.

The definition of Inform directly builds on that of Attempt. We say agent *i* informs group *g* of φ through performing action α if α is an attempt to bring about the mutual belief in *g* of φ, by at least making it mutually believed in *g* that *i* intends that *g* mutually believe φ. Formally, this gives:

$$\{\text{Inform } i \ g \ \alpha \ \varphi\} \hat{=} \{\text{Attempt } i \ \alpha \ \psi \ \chi\}$$

where

$$\psi \hat{=} (\text{M-Bel } g \ \varphi)$$

and

$$\chi \hat{=} (\text{M-Bel } g \ (\text{Int } i \ (\text{M-Bel } g \ \varphi))).$$

In other words, action α counts an inform action between agents *i* (speaker) and group *g* (hearers) with respect to content φ if α is an attempt by *i* to cause the hearers to mutually believe φ, by at the very least causing *g* to mutually believe that *i* intends that *g* mutually believe φ.

We can prove some properties of Inform speech acts. First, we can prove that if one agent informs a group of φ, then the informant desires the hearers may come to mutually believe φ.

THEOREM 7.3: $\models_{\mathcal{P}} (\text{Happens } \{\text{Inform } i \ g \ \alpha \ \varphi\}) \Rightarrow (\text{Des } i \ \text{E}\Diamond(\text{M-Bel } g \ \varphi))$

Proof Assume $\langle M, V, w, p \rangle \models_{\mathcal{P}} (\text{Happens } \{\text{Inform } i \ g \ \alpha \ \varphi\})$ for arbitrary $\langle M, V, w, p \rangle$. From the definition of Inform, we have $\langle M, V, w, p \rangle \models_{\mathcal{P}}$ (Happens $\{\text{Attempt } i \ \alpha \ \psi \ \chi\}$) where

$$\psi \hat{=} (\text{M-Bel } g \ \varphi)$$

and

$$\chi \hat{=} (\text{M-Bel } g \ (\text{Int } i \ (\text{M-Bel } g \ \varphi))).$$

The desired result then follows immediately from Theorem 7.1. ∎

We can also prove that the informant does not believe the hearers already have a mutual belief of φ. Notice that an agent can be informing a group of agents of φ even though every agent in the group already individually believes φ. In informing the group of φ, the speaker is attempting to raise the status of this belief to the *mutual* belief of φ, which is not implied simply by everyone in a group believing φ.

THEOREM 7.4: $\models_{\mathcal{P}}$ (Happens {Inform i g α φ}) $\Rightarrow \neg$(Bel i (M-Bel g φ))

Proof   Immediate by expanding the definitions of Inform and Attempt.   ∎

Note that the case of "one-to-one" inform speech acts is covered by the multiagent definition given above. Where we wish to deal with an agent i informing a single agent j of φ, we will abuse notation slightly and write {Inform i j α φ} rather than the more cumbersome {Inform i $\{j\}$ α φ}.

7.4   Requesting

Inform speech acts are attempts by a speaker to get the hearer to *believe* some state of affairs. In contrast, *request* speech acts (directives) are attempts by a speaker to modify the *intentions* of the hearer. However, we can identify at least two different types of requests:

• Requests to *bring about some state of affairs.*
An example of such a request would be when one agent said "Keep the door closed." We call such requests "requests-that."

• Requests to *perform some particular action.*
An example of such a request would be when one agent said "Lock the door." We call such requests "requests-to."

Requests-that are more general than requests-to. In the former case (requests-that), the agent communicates an intended state of affairs, but does *not* communicate the means to achieve this state of affairs. Me asking you to keep the door closed does not tell you how I want you to keep the door closed — you may lock it, prop it closed with a chair, or sit against it. In the case of requesting to, however, the agent does not communicate the desired state of affairs at all. Instead, it communicates an action to be performed, and the state of affairs to be achieved lies implicit within the action that was communicated. It is useful to make a distinction between the two cases, and for this reason, I will formalize both. (As it turns out, it is straightforward to encode requests-to as a special case of requests-that.)

Just as we identified desirable properties of inform speech acts, so it is possible to identify the following properties of request actions.

1. A request speech act takes place between a "speaker" agent and one or more "hearer" agents.

2. Request actions are actually *actions* that an agent may perform, just like any other action.

3. The purpose of a request action is to modify the intentions of agent(s) hearing the speech act, and in particular, to cause them to intend some state of affairs (in the case of requesting-that), or to intend to perform some action (in the case of requesting-to).

4. Since the speaker of the request act cannot normally bring about the ultimate intention of the speech act directly in the listener(s), they will attempt to bring about a "lesser" belief, such that this will be sufficient, if the listener(s) are so inclined, to cause the listener(s) to intend the ultimate state of affairs (in the case of requesting-that), or to intend to perform the action (requesting-to).

5. Request actions are *attempts* to bring about some intended state of affairs — they may *fail* to bring this state of affairs.

6. Request actions cannot be performed accidentally.

Given this discussion, it is easy to formally define the RequestTh speech act. I write

$$\{\text{RequestTh } i \, g \, \alpha \, \varphi\}$$

to indicate that α is an action performed by agent i in an attempt to request that group g intends φ. Note again the use of curly brackets to indicate that RequestTh is neither a predicate nor a modal operator, but an action.

The definition of RequestTh is as follows.

$$\{\text{RequestTh } i \, g \, \alpha \, \varphi\} \,\hat{=}\, \{\text{Attempt } i \, \alpha \, \psi \, \chi\}$$

where

$$\psi \,\hat{=}\, (\text{M-Int } g \, \varphi)$$

and

$$\chi \,\hat{=}\, (\text{M-Bel } g \, (\text{Int } i \, (\text{M-Int } g \, \varphi))).$$

We can prove that the speaker does not believe the hearer already intends φ.

THEOREM 7.5: $\models_{\mathcal{P}} (\text{Happens } \{\text{RequestTh } i \, g \, \alpha \, \varphi\}) \Rightarrow \neg(\text{Bel } i \, (\text{M-Int } g \, \varphi))$

Proof Immediate from the definitions of RequestTh and Attempt. ∎

We can define the request-to speech act as a special case of requesting that. A request to perform α is thus simply a request that α is performed.

$$\{\mathsf{RequestTo}\ i\ g\ \alpha\ \alpha'\} \,\hat{=}\, \{\mathsf{RequestTh}\ i\ g\ \alpha\ \mathsf{A}\Diamond(\mathsf{Happens}\ \alpha')\}.$$

7.5   Composite Speech Acts

Inform and request speech acts are the basic mechanisms via which agents will communicate: they define the possible ways in which agents can attempt to modify one another's beliefs and intentions — their key mental states. In this section, we will see how a number of different speech acts can be defined in terms of inform and request acts. In particular, I will define some simple *conversation policies* that make use of these primitives:

Language inter-operability requires more than simply that the agents agree on the format and meaning of the various primitive [communication language] messages. As a practical matter, agents must also agree on the range of possible sequences and contexts of messages when they are interpreted in the context of larger [...] dialogues, or *conversations*. [83, p.1]

I make use of a simple graphical state-machine notation for specifying conversation policies. In this notation, nodes in the conversation policy graph correspond to states of the conversation, and arcs to the performance of speech acts. A node with an arrow entering it, but no predecessor node, is the start state. A node marked by a double circle border is an end state. I will start by considering question and answer conversations.

Questions and Answers

We have already seen that the Inform speech act is the basic mechanism via which agents can exchange information. But consider: Why should one agent inform another of anything? There are a number of possibilities why agent i should inform agent j of φ, for example:

1. Agent i has an intention that agent j believe φ for its own reasons. For example, returning to the Alice and Bob tenure example from earlier in this chapter, Alice may intend that the tenure committee believe that Bob faked research results because this will enable her intention of gaining tenure to be satisfied.

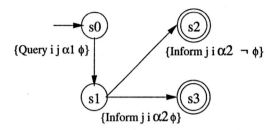

Figure 7.2
The conversation policy associated with **Query**.

2. Agent j has explicitly asked agent i the truth status of φ.

The first case is simply an instance of the more general situation, where an agent performs an action because the agent believes it is in its best interests. We will therefore focus on the second case, where one agent explicitly asks another about the truth status of some proposition.

We can easily define a Query speech act. The idea is that an agent i will perform a Query action if it has an intention of knowing the truth status of some statement φ. For example, I may want to know whether or not it is raining, and if I believe that you know whether or not it is raining, I can query you to this effect. Formally, we write $\{\text{Query } i\, j\, \varphi\}$ to denote a query action performed by a speaker i to a hearer j with the intention of discovering whether or not φ is the case. Query is defined, in the terminology of FIPA, as a *macro* action:

$$\{\text{Query } i\, j\, \alpha\, \varphi\} \, \hat{=} \, \{\text{RequestTh } i\, j\, \alpha\ (\text{Bel } i\, \varphi) \vee (\text{Bel } i\, \neg\varphi)\}$$

In other words, a Query by agent i to j with respect to statement φ is a request from i to j to bring about the belief in i that either φ is true or that φ is false.

The mechanism via which agent j can bring about such belief is the Inform speech act. This leads to the conversation policy illustrated in Figure 7.2.

Request-based Conversation Policies

When I ask you to make a cup of tea, the conversation does not usually end there. Whether or not you chose to accede to my request is up to you, but hopefully you will either confirm to me that you will carry out the request, or else explicitly tell me that you will not. To define this kind of dialogue, we will make use of two auxiliary definitions. The first, Agree, will be used to capture

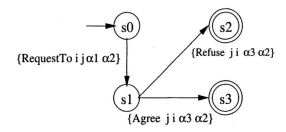

Figure 7.3
The conversation policy associated with RequestTo.

the case where you explicitly state that you intend to perform some action.

$$\{\text{Agree } i\,j\,\alpha\,\alpha'\} \;\hat{=}\; \{\text{Inform } i\,j\,\alpha\,(\text{Agt } \alpha'\ i) \wedge (\text{Int } i\ \mathsf{A}\Diamond(\text{Happens } \alpha'))\}$$

Thus agent i agreeing to perform an action α' to agent j simply means that i informs j that it is the agent of α', and that it intends that α' is performed. (Note that α is the action of informing, rather than the action being referred to in the inform.)

The Refuse speech act is used to capture the situation where i is telling j that it will not carry out an action.

$$\{\text{Refuse } i\,j\,\alpha\,\alpha'\} \;\hat{=}\; \{\text{Inform } i\,j\,\alpha\,\neg(\text{Int } i\ \mathsf{A}\Diamond(\text{Happens } \alpha'))\}$$

Using these two speech acts, we can define a conversation policy for Request speech acts. The policy is illustrated in Figure 7.3.

7.6   Notes and Further Reading

The problems associated with communicating concurrent systems have driven a significant fraction of research into theoretical computer science since the early 1980s. Two of the best-known formalisms developed in this period are Tony Hoare's Communicating Sequential Processes (CSPs) [98], and Robin Milner's Calculus of Communicating Systems (CCS) [154]. Temporal logic has also been widely used for reasoning about concurrent systems — see, for example, Pnueli [177] for an overview. A good reference, that describes the key problems in concurrent and distributed systems, is Ben-Ari [11].

Problems such as synchronization were widely studied in the early days of multiagent systems research, though they are less in the mainstream of research today. Georgeff developed formalisms for representing multiagent activities, and algorithms for synchronizing multiagent plans that drew upon synchronization techniques developed in theoretical computer science [75, 76]. Rosenschein developed similar techniques, which combined work on speech acts with CSP-like communication to synchronize multiagent plans [194]. Stuart showed how multiagent plans could be encoded as formulae of temporal logic: showing the plans were interference-free then reduced to a problem of showing that the resulting formula was satisfiable, a well-understood (if somewhat complex) logic problem [236].

The plan-based theory of speech acts developed by Cohen and Perrault made speech act theory accessible and directly usable to the artificial intelligence community [39]. In the multiagent systems community, this work is arguably the most influential single publication on the topic of speech act-like communication. Many authors have built on its basic ideas. For example, borrowing a formalism for representing the mental state of agents that was developed by Robert Moore [157], Douglas Appelt was able to implement a system that was capable of planning to perform speech acts [3, 4].

Many other approaches to speech act semantics have appeared in the literature. For example, Perrault [174] described how Reiter's default logic [193] could be used to reason about speech acts. Appelt gave a critique of Perrault's work [5, pp.167–168], and Konolige proposed a related technique using hierarchic auto-epistemic logic (HAEL) [121] for reasoning about speech acts. Galliers emphasized the links between speech acts and AMG belief revision [71]: she noted that the changes in a hearer's state caused by a speech act could be understood as analogous to an agent revising its beliefs in the presence of new information [69]. Singh developed a theory of speech acts [214, 215] using his formal framework for representing rational agents [211, 210, 212, 218, 213, 216, 217]. He introduced a predicate $comm(i,j,m)$ to represent the fact that agent i communicates message m to agent j, and then used this predicate to define the semantics of assertive, directive, commissive, and permissive speech acts.

At the time of writing (Spring 2000), there is a great deal of industrial interest in agent technology. A lot of this interest is focussed on the development of standardized agent communication languages, and in particular, on the FIPA standardization effort [67]. As noted in the text, the FIPA communication language does have a formally defined semantics, based largely on the techniques of Cohen and Levesque [36] and Sadek et al. [23]. One key issue for this work is that of *semantic conformance testing*. The conformance testing problem can be summarized as follows [241]: We are given program π_i, and an agent communication language L_C with the semantics $[\![\ldots]\!]_{L_C}$. The aim is to determine whether or not π_i respects the semantics $[\![\ldots]\!]_{L_C}$ whenever it communicates using L_C. (Syntactic conformance testing is of course trivial.)

The importance of conformance testing *has* been recognized by the ACL community [60, p.1]. However, to date, little research has been carried out either on how verifiable communication languages might be developed, or on how existing ACLs might be verified. One exception is my [241], where the issue of conformance testing is discussed from a formal point of view: I point out that ACL semantics are generally developed in such a way as to express *constraints* on the senders of messages. For example, the constraint imposed by the semantics of an "inform" message might state that the sender believes the message content. This constraint can be viewed as a *specification*. Verifying that an agent respects the semantics of the agent communication language then reduces to a conventional program verification problem: show that the agent sending the message satisfies the specification given by the communication language semantics. In [241] I pointed out that this poses the following problem for ACL conformance testing. The formalisms used to give a semantics to communication languages are typically quantified multimodal logics, similar to $\mathcal{LORA}$. However, we have no way of systematically assigning mental states to computer programs, and so we cannot verify whether or not such programs implement "mentalistic" semantics. In the $\mathcal{LORA}$ case, for example, we have no procedure that will take an arbitrary program and from that program generate a $\mathcal{LORA}$ model that represents the properties of the program. This makes it (at best) very doubtful whether one could realistically hope to do semantic conformance testing for languages with FIPA-like semantics. Recently, a number of alternative proposals have appeared for communication languages with a verifiable semantics [209, 175, 243]. See [128] for a discussion of the state of the art in agent communication languages as of early 1999.

8 Cooperation

Agents — both human and artificial — can engage in many and varied types of social interaction. Communicative acts, such as informing and requesting, are probably the simplest. In this chapter, however, we will consider *cooperative problem solving*, a much more sophisticated and structured form of social interaction. Cooperative problem solving occurs when a group of autonomous agents choose to work together to achieve a common goal. Note that we are not interested in cases where the agents working together are *not* autonomous. Client-server computing is an obvious example of non-cooperative problem solving, as are all "master-slave" systems [194].

Examples of cooperative problem solving in everyday life include a group of people working together to move a heavy object, play a symphony, build a house, or write a joint paper. In this chapter, I show how $\mathcal{LORA}$ can be used to construct a formal model of such cooperative problem solving. I begin by informally discussing what cooperative problem solving is.

8.1 What Is Cooperative Problem Solving?

Comparatively few of our intentions can be achieved without the cooperative participation of our peers. Even intentions that at first sight appear to involve just ourselves, such as traveling to an airport, require cooperation on the part of other agents on closer inspection. One of the main questions in the social sciences, and increasingly in the multiagent systems community, is how and why autonomous agents should cooperate with one another. As Castelfranchi points out, cooperation seems to be something of a paradox because it apparently involves giving up some of our autonomy [28]. In agreeing to work with you, I am effectively making my own intentions (and potentially my beliefs and desires) subservient to yours for the duration of our cooperative act. Paradox or not, cooperative action, and in particular, cooperative problem solving, does occur. In this chapter, I will present a model that attempts to account for the mental state of agents as they are engaged in the cooperative problem-solving process.

The model consists of four stages:

1. *Recognition*

The cooperative problem solving process begins when some agent recognizes the potential for cooperative action. This recognition may come about because an agent has a goal that it does not have the ability to achieve on its own, or else because the agent prefers a cooperative solution.

2. *Team formation*

During this stage, the agent that recognized the potential for cooperative action at stage (1) solicits assistance. If this stage is successful, then it will end with a group of agents having some kind of nominal commitment to collective action.

3. *Plan formation*

During this stage, the agents attempt to negotiate a joint plan that they believe will achieve the desired goal.

4. *Team action*

During this stage, the newly agreed plan of joint action is executed by the agents, which maintain a close-knit relationship throughout. This relationship is defined by a *convention*, which every agent follows.

The key theme in the model is that as cooperative problem solving progresses, the group of participating agents build up increasingly greater commitment to the process. When the process begins, there will in fact be no kind of group commitment at all — cooperation will "exist" only in the mental state of the agent that initiates the process. However, as the process proceeds, the team will build up first a commitment to the *principle* of collective action, and then to the *practice* of it.

A corollary of the fact that agents are autonomous is that cooperation may fail. If agents are not *required* to cooperate, then sometimes they will not. Even when initial cooperation is established, it can subsequently fail for many different reasons. For example, a group of agents that agree to cooperate in principle may discover that the assumptions upon which their choices were made do not in fact hold. Alternatively, events beyond the control of the team may make successful completion of their cooperation impossible. An adequate theory of cooperation must recognize that such failure is possible, identify the key points at which it may occur, and characterize the behavior of a rational agent in such circumstances.

Another aspect of the model is that it assumes communication is the main tool through which collective mental states will be assembled. Although something resembling cooperation is possible without communication [225], almost all forms of cooperative problem solving in the real world rely upon explicit, high-level communication in some form or other.

Note that in reality, the four stages are *iterative*, in that if one stage fails, the agents may return to previous stages.

8.2 Recognition

Cooperative problem solving begins when some agent in a multiagent community has a goal, and recognizes the potential for cooperative action with respect to that goal. Recognition may occur for several reasons. The paradigm case is that in which the agent is unable to achieve the goal in isolation, but believes that cooperative action can achieve it. For example, an agent may have a goal which, to achieve, requires information that is only accessible to another agent. Without the cooperation of this other agent, the goal cannot be achieved. More prosaically, an agent with a goal to move a heavy object might simply not have the strength to do this alone.

Alternatively, an agent may be able to achieve the goal on its own, but may not want to. There may be several reasons for this. First, it may believe that in working alone, it will clobber one of its other goals. For example, suppose I have a goal of lifting a heavy object. I may have the capability of lifting the object, but I might believe that in so doing, I would injure my back, thereby clobbering my goal of being healthy. In this case, a cooperative solution — involving no injury to my back — is preferable. More generally, an agent may believe that a cooperative solution will in some way be better than a solution achieved by action in isolation. For example, a solution might be obtained more quickly, or may be more accurate as a result of cooperative action.

Believing that you either cannot achieve your goal in isolation, or that (for whatever reason) you would prefer not to work alone, is part of the potential for cooperation. But it is not enough in itself to initiate the social process. For there to be potential for cooperation with respect to an agent's goal, the agent must also believe there is some group of agents that can actually achieve the goal; see Figure 8.1.

Ability

In order to precisely define the conditions that characterize the potential for cooperative action, it is necessary to introduce a number of subsidiary def-

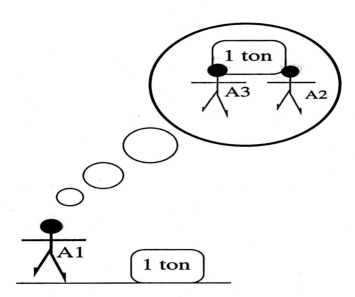

Figure 8.1
Agent A1 recognizes the potential for cooperative action.

initions. First, we require definitions of single-agent and multiagent *ability*: what it means to be *able* to bring about some state of the world. Rather than complicate $\mathcal{LORA}$ by introducing yet another primitive modality, I adapt a well-known definition of ability that was originally proposed by Moore [157].

As a first attempt to define ability, we might say an agent has the ability to achieve some state φ if it knows of an action that it can perform, which would be guaranteed to achieve the state of affairs. I will call this *first-order ability*, and define it as follows.

$$(\text{Can}^0 \, i \, \varphi) \triangleq \exists \alpha \cdot (\text{Bel} \, i \, (\text{Agt} \, \alpha \, i) \wedge (\text{Achvs} \, \alpha \, \varphi)) \wedge (\text{Agt} \, \alpha \, i) \wedge (\text{Achvs} \, \alpha \, \varphi)$$

Notice that the action α in this definition is quantified *de re* with respect to the Bel modality [101, p.183]. The significance of this is that the agent must be "aware of the identity" of the action — it must have a *rigid designator* for it. Thus it is not enough for the agent to believe that there exists *some* action that will achieve the goal. It must be aware of exactly *which* action will achieve it.

Before proceeding, we prove some results about first-order ability. First, we show that if an agent has the first-order ability to bring about some state of affairs, then that state of affairs is actually possible.

THEOREM 8.1: $\models_S (\mathsf{Can}^0 \, i \, \varphi) \Rightarrow \mathsf{E}\Diamond\varphi$

Proof Assume $\langle M, V, w, t \rangle \models_S (\mathsf{Can}^0 \, i \, \varphi)$ for arbitrary $\langle M, V, w, t \rangle$. By expanding out the definition of Can^0, we get $\langle M, V, w, t \rangle \models_S \exists\alpha \cdot (\mathsf{Achvs} \, \alpha \, \varphi)$. From this and the definition of Achvs we get $\langle M, V, w, t \rangle \models_S \mathsf{E}(\mathsf{Happens} \, \alpha) \wedge$ $\mathsf{A}(\mathsf{Happens} \, \alpha; \varphi?)$, and hence $\langle M, V, w, t \rangle \models_S \mathsf{E}\Diamond\varphi$. ■

If an agent has first-order ability to bring about a state of affairs, then it is aware of this.

THEOREM 8.2: $\models_S (\mathsf{Can}^0 \, i \, \varphi) \Rightarrow (\mathsf{Bel} \, i \, (\mathsf{Can}^0 \, i \, \varphi))$

Proof We need to show that if $\langle M, V, w, t \rangle \models_S (\mathsf{Can}^0 \, i \, \varphi)$ for arbitrary $\langle M, V, w, t \rangle$, then $\langle M, V, w', t \rangle \models_S (\mathsf{Can}^0 \, i \, \varphi)$ for all $w' \in W$ such that $w' \in \mathcal{B}_t^w(\llbracket i \rrbracket)$. Start by assuming that $\langle M, V, w, t \rangle \models_S (\mathsf{Can}^0 \, i \, \varphi)$ for arbitrary $\langle M, V, w, t \rangle$. Hence $\langle M, V, w, t \rangle \models_S \exists\alpha \cdot (\mathsf{Bel} \, i \, (\mathsf{Agt} \, \alpha \, i) \wedge (\mathsf{Achvs} \, \alpha \, \varphi))$, and so for all $w' \in W$ such that $w' \in \mathcal{B}_t^w(\llbracket i \rrbracket)$, we have $\langle M, V, w', t \rangle \models_S$ $\exists\alpha \cdot (\mathsf{Agt} \, \alpha \, i) \wedge (\mathsf{Achvs} \, \alpha \, \varphi)$. We want to show that $\langle M, V, w'', t \rangle \models_S (\mathsf{Agt} \, \alpha \, i) \wedge$ $(\mathsf{Achvs} \, \alpha \, \varphi)$ for all $w'' \in W$ such that $w'' \in \mathcal{B}_t^{w'}(\llbracket i \rrbracket)$. But since the belief accessibility relation $\mathcal{B}$ is transitive, it must be that if $w' \in \mathcal{B}_t^w(\llbracket i \rrbracket)$, and $w'' \in$ $\mathcal{B}_t^{w'}(\llbracket i \rrbracket)$, then $w'' \in \mathcal{B}_t^w(\llbracket i \rrbracket)$. Hence $\langle M, V, w'', t \rangle \models_S (\mathsf{Agt} \, \alpha \, i) \wedge (\mathsf{Achvs} \, \alpha \, \varphi)$, so $\langle M, V, w', t \rangle \models_S \exists\alpha \cdot (\mathsf{Bel} \, i \, (\mathsf{Agt} \, \alpha \, i) \wedge (\mathsf{Achvs} \, \alpha \, \varphi)) \wedge (\mathsf{Agt} \, \alpha \, i) \wedge$ $(\mathsf{Achvs} \, \alpha \, \varphi)$, and hence $\langle M, V, w', t \rangle \models_S (\mathsf{Can}^0 \, i \, \varphi)$, and we are done. ■

If an agent has the first-order ability to bring about some state of affairs, then it believes this state of affairs is possible.

THEOREM 8.3: $\models_S (\mathsf{Can}^0 \, i \, \varphi) \Rightarrow (\mathsf{Bel} \, i \, \mathsf{E}\Diamond\varphi)$

Proof Assume that $\langle M, V, w, t \rangle \models_S (\mathsf{Can}^0 \, i \, \varphi)$ for arbitrary $\langle M, V, w, t \rangle$. By Theorem 8.2, we therefore have $\langle M, V, w', t \rangle \models_S (\mathsf{Can}^0 \, i \, \varphi)$ for all $w' \in W$ such that $w' \in \mathcal{B}_t^w(\llbracket i \rrbracket)$. From Theorem 8.1, we thus have $\langle M, V, w', t \rangle \models_S$ $\mathsf{E}\Diamond\varphi$, and we are done. ■

An obvious failing of this definition when measured against our intuitions about ability is that it does not allow for an agent performing an action in order to *find out* how to bring about some state of affairs. To quote a classic example, I have the ability to telephone my friend Bill even though I do not know Bill's telephone number; I can perform an action (looking up his number in the phone book) that will furnish me with the relevant information.

This motivates a definition of *k order ability*, ($k \in I\!N, k > 0$), which allows for the possibility of an agent performing an action in order to find out how to bring about a state of affairs. The idea is that an agent will have the *k* order ability to bring about a state of affairs φ if it has the first-order ability to bring about $k - 1$ order ability to bring about φ. We formalize this as follows.

$$(\text{Can}^k \, i \, \varphi) \triangleq (\text{Can}^{k-1} \, i \, (\text{Can}^0 \, i \, \varphi)) \quad \text{for } k > 0$$

Thus

$$(\text{Can}^1 \, i \, \varphi) \triangleq (\text{Can}^0 \, i \, (\text{Can}^0 \, i \, \varphi))$$
$$(\text{Can}^2 \, i \, \varphi) \triangleq (\text{Can}^0 \, i \, (\text{Can}^0 \, i \, (\text{Can}^0 \, i \, \varphi)))$$
... and so on.

We can then define ability *simpliciter* as *k* order ability, for some $k \in I\!N$.

$$(\text{Can} \, i \, \varphi) \triangleq \bigvee_{k \geq 0} (\text{Can}^k \, i \, \varphi)$$

Notice that Can is essentially an infinitary disjunction; it has the characteristic of a least fixed point (see the discussion on fixed points in chapter 6). It is easy to see that first-order ability implies ability *simpliciter*.

THEOREM 8.4: $\models_S (\text{Can}^0 \, i \, \varphi) \Rightarrow (\text{Can} \, i \, \varphi)$

We can also prove results analogous to Theorems 8.1, 8.2, and 8.3 for Can. (Proofs for Theorems 8.5 and 8.6 are straightforward, and are therefore omitted.)

THEOREM 8.5: $\models_S (\text{Can} \, i \, \varphi) \Rightarrow E\Diamond\varphi$

THEOREM 8.6: $\models_S (\text{Can} \, i \, \varphi) \Rightarrow (\text{Bel} \, i \, E\Diamond\varphi)$

THEOREM 8.7: $\models_S (\text{Can} \, i \, \varphi) \Rightarrow (\text{Bel} \, i \, (\text{Can} \, i \, \varphi))$

Proof   The proof is by induction on the degree of ability, *k*. We show that for all $k \in I\!N$, $\models_S (\text{Can}^k \, i \, \varphi) \Rightarrow (\text{Bel} \, i \, (\text{Can}^k \, i \, \varphi))$. The inductive base ($k = 0$) is simply Theorem 8.2. The inductive assumption is that if $\langle M, V, w, t \rangle \models_S (\text{Can}^k \, i \, \varphi)$ for arbitrary $\langle M, V, w, t \rangle$, then $\langle M, V, w', t \rangle \models_S (\text{Can}^k \, i \, \varphi)$ for all $w' \in W$ such that $w' \in \mathcal{B}_t^w(\llbracket i \rrbracket)$. The inductive step is then a straightforward generalization of Theorem 8.2. ∎

To simplify future definitions, we will introduce another derived operator, Can't, which has the obvious interpretation.

$$(\text{Can't } i \; \varphi) \; \hat{=} \; \neg(\text{Can } i \; \varphi)$$

We shall assume that if an agent is unable to achieve some state of affairs, then it is aware that it is unable to achieve this.

$$\models_S (\text{Can't } i \; \varphi) \Rightarrow (\text{Bel } i \; (\text{Can't } i \; \varphi)) \tag{8.1}$$

We now need to define *multiagent ability*, which we do by simply adapting the definition of single-agent ability to the multiagent case.

$$
\begin{aligned}
(\text{J-Can}^0 \; g \; \varphi) &\;\hat{=}\; \exists \alpha \cdot (\text{M-Bel } g \; (\text{Agts } \alpha \; g) \land (\text{Achvs } \alpha \; \varphi)) \land \\
&\qquad (\text{Agts } \alpha \; g) \land (\text{Achvs } \alpha \; \varphi) \\
(\text{J-Can}^k \; g \; \varphi) &\;\hat{=}\; (\text{J-Can}^{k-1} \; g \; (\text{J-Can}^0 \; g \; \varphi)) \quad \text{for } k > 0 \\
(\text{J-Can } g \; \varphi) &\;\hat{=}\; \bigvee_{k \geq 0}(\text{J-Can}^k \; g \; \varphi)
\end{aligned}
$$

We now present some results about joint ability that are analogous to Theorems 8.1 through to 8.7. (The proofs are omitted, since these are straightforward adaptations of earlier results.)

THEOREM 8.8: $\models_S (\text{J-Can}^0 \; g \; \varphi) \Rightarrow \text{E}\Diamond\varphi$

THEOREM 8.9: $\models_S (\text{J-Can}^0 \; g \; \varphi) \Rightarrow (\text{M-Bel } g \; \text{E}\Diamond\varphi)$

THEOREM 8.10: $\models_S (\text{J-Can}^0 \; g \; \varphi) \Rightarrow (\text{M-Bel } g \; (\text{J-Can}^0 \; g \; \varphi))$

THEOREM 8.11: $\models_S (\text{J-Can}^0 \; g \; \varphi) \Rightarrow (\text{J-Can } g \; \varphi)$

THEOREM 8.12: $\models_S (\text{J-Can } g \; \varphi) \Rightarrow \text{E}\Diamond\varphi$

THEOREM 8.13: $\models_S (\text{J-Can } g \; \varphi) \Rightarrow (\text{M-Bel } g \; (\text{J-Can } g \; \varphi))$

THEOREM 8.14: $\models_S (\text{J-Can } g \; \varphi) \Rightarrow (\text{M-Bel } i \; \text{E}\Diamond\varphi)$

Potential for Cooperation Defined

We can now formally define potential for cooperation. With respect to agent i's desire φ, there is potential for cooperation iff:

1. there is some group g such that i believes that g can jointly achieve φ;

and either

2. i can't achieve φ in isolation; or

3. i believes that for every action α that it could perform that achieves φ, it has a desire of not performing α.

Note that in clause (1), an agent needs to know the identity of the group that it believes can cooperate to achieve its desire. This is perhaps an over-strong assumption. It precludes an agent attempting to find out the identity of a group that can achieve the desire, and it does not allow an agent to simply broadcast its desire in the hope of attracting help (as in the Contract Net protocol [222]). I leave such refinements to future work. Clause (2) represents the paradigm reason for an agent considering a cooperative solution: because it is unable to achieve the desire on its own. Clause (3) defines the alternative reason for an agent considering cooperation: it prefers not to perform any of the actions that might achieve the desire. (I do not consider the reasons why an agent will not want to perform a particular action — these will be domain-specific.)

To simplify the presentation that follows slightly, we will make use of an abbreviation Doesn't, to capture the sense of "something doesn't happen."

$$(\text{Doesn't } \alpha) \triangleq \text{A} \Box \neg (\text{Happens } \alpha)$$

Using the various definitions above, we can now formally state the conditions that characterize the potential for cooperation.

$$
(\text{PfC } i\, \varphi) \triangleq \begin{array}{l}
(\text{Des } i\, \varphi) \wedge \\
(\text{Bel } i\, \neg\varphi) \wedge \\
\exists g \cdot (\text{Bel } i\, (\text{J-Can } g\, \varphi)) \wedge \\
\left[\begin{array}{l}
(\text{Can't } i\, \varphi) \vee \\
(\text{Bel } i\, \forall \alpha \cdot (\text{Agt } \alpha\, i) \wedge (\text{Achvs } \alpha\, \varphi) \Rightarrow (\text{Int } i\, (\text{Doesn't } \alpha)))
\end{array} \right]
\end{array}
$$

We can prove some properties of potential for cooperation.

THEOREM 8.15: $\models_S$ (PfC $i\ \varphi$) $\Rightarrow$ (Bel i E$\Diamond\varphi$)

Proof Assume $\langle M, V, w, t \rangle \models_S$ (PfC $i\ \varphi$) for arbitrary $\langle M, V, w, t \rangle$. By expanding the definition of PfC, we get $\langle M, V, w, t \rangle \models_S \exists g \cdot$ (Bel i (J-Can $g\ \varphi$)). So for all $w' \in W$ such that $w' \in \mathcal{B}_t^w(\llbracket i \rrbracket)$, we have $\langle M, V, w', t \rangle \models_S$ (J-Can $g\ \varphi$), and so from Theorem 8.12, we have $\langle M, V, w', t \rangle \models$ E$\Diamond\varphi$. Thus $\langle M, V, w, t \rangle \models_S$ (Bel i E$\Diamond\varphi$). ∎

Assuming an agent is aware of its desires, and there is potential for cooperation with respect to one of its desires, then the agent is aware of this.

THEOREM 8.16: $\models_S$ (PfC $i\ \varphi$) $\Rightarrow$ (Bel i (PfC $i\ \varphi$)) (assuming agent i is aware of its desires).

Proof Assume $\langle M, V, w, t \rangle \models_S$ (PfC $i\ \varphi$), for arbitrary $\langle M, V, w, t \rangle$. We need to show that $\langle M, V, w, t \rangle \models_S$ (Bel $i\ \chi$), for each conjunct in the definition of potential for cooperation:

- $\langle M, V, w, t \rangle \models_S$ (Bel i (Des $i\ \varphi$))
From the fact that i is aware of its desires.

- $\langle M, V, w, t \rangle \models_S$ (Bel i (Bel $i\ \neg\varphi$))
Immediate from axiom 4 for belief modalities.

- $\langle M, V, w, t \rangle \models_S$ (Bel $i\ \exists g \cdot$ (Bel i (J-Can $g\ \varphi$)))
Immediate from axiom 4 for belief modalities.

- $\langle M, V, w, t \rangle \models_S$ (Bel i (Can't $i\ \varphi$) $\vee$ (Bel $i\ \forall\alpha \cdot$ (Agt $\alpha\ i$) $\wedge$ (Achvs $\alpha\ \varphi$) $\Rightarrow$ (Des i (Doesn't α))))
There are two cases to consider. For the first case, assume that $\langle M, V, w, t \rangle \models_S$ (Can't $i\ \varphi$). Then by the assumption that agents are aware of what they cannot achieve, $\langle M, V, w, t \rangle \models_S$ (Bel i (Can't $i\ \varphi$)).
For the second case, assume $\langle M, V, w, t \rangle \models_S$ (Bel $i\ \forall\alpha \cdot$ (Agt $\alpha\ i$) $\wedge$ (Achvs $\alpha\ \varphi$) $\Rightarrow$ (Des i (Doesn't α))). In this case, $\langle M, V, w, t \rangle \models_S$ (Bel i (Bel $i\ \forall\alpha \cdot$ (Agt $\alpha\ i$) $\wedge$ (Achvs $\alpha\ \varphi$) $\Rightarrow$ (Des i (Doesn't α)))) follows from axiom 4 for belief modalities.

This completes the proof. ∎

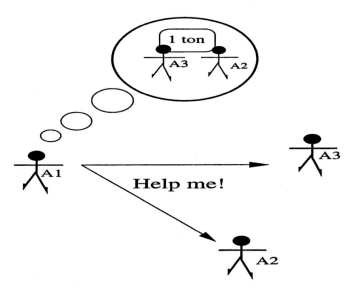

Figure 8.2
Agent A1 attempts to build a team to help with its problem.

8.3   Team Formation

Having identified the potential for cooperative action with respect to one of its
desires, what is a rational agent to do? Such an agent should attempt to *solicit*
assistance from a group of agents that it believes can achieve the desire. If the
agent is successful, then at the conclusion of this *team formation* stage, the
agent will have brought about in such a group a mental state wherein each
member of the group has a nominal commitment to collective action. The
group will not yet have fixed upon an action to perform, and in fact will not
share any kind of commitment other than to the *principle* of joint action. In
particular, there will not yet be a joint intention: this comes later.

How does an agent go about forming a team? The most important point to
note is that it cannot *guarantee* that it will be successful in forming a team: it
can only *attempt* it; see Figure 8.2.

The team formation stage can then be characterized as the following assumption about rational agents: an agent i, who believes that there is potential
for cooperative action with respect to its desire φ, will attempt to bring about
in some group g (which it believes can jointly achieve φ):

1. the mutual intention to achieve φ; and

2. the mutual belief that g can indeed achieve φ.

In other words, agent i will *request* g to carry out φ, and *inform* g that they are able to do it.

It is implicit within this assumption that agents are *veracious* with respect to their desires, i.e., that they will try to influence the group by revealing their true desire. I do not consider cases where agents are mendacious (i.e., they lie about their desires), or when agents do not reveal their desires. The interested reader is referred to [68, pp.159–165] for a discussion and formalization of such considerations.

It is useful to introduce a definition that captures the commitment that agents have to collective action if team formation is successful. We write

(PreTeam $g\ \varphi$)

to indicate that: (i) it is mutually believed in g that g can jointly achieve φ; and (ii) g mutually intend φ.

(PreTeam $g\ \varphi$) $\hat{=}$ (M-Bel g (J-Can $g\ \varphi$)) $\wedge$ (M-Int $g\ \varphi$)

The following result captures a key property of PreTeam.

THEOREM 8.17: $\models_S$ (PreTeam $g\ \varphi$) $\Rightarrow$ (M-Bel g E$\Diamond\varphi$)

Proof   Assume that $\langle M, V, w, t \rangle \models_S$ (PreTeam $g\ \varphi$) for arbitrary $\langle M, V, w, t \rangle$. The definition of PreTeam gives $\langle M, V, w, t \rangle \models_S$ (M-Bel g (J-Can $g\ \varphi$)). Theorem 8.12 tells us that $\models$ (J-Can $g\ \varphi$) $\Rightarrow$ E$\Diamond\varphi$, and from necessitation for M-Bel operators, we therefore know that $\models_S$ (M-Bel g ((J-Can $g\ \varphi$) $\Rightarrow$ E$\Diamond\varphi$)). From the K axiom for M-Bel and propositional reasoning, we can therefore conclude that $\langle M, V, w, t \rangle \models_S$ (M-Bel g E$\Diamond\varphi$).   ∎

We will define a composite speech act FormTeam, the purpose of which is to bring about a PreTeam mental state.

{FormTeam $i\ g\ \alpha\ \varphi$} $\hat{=}$ {Inform $i\ g\ \alpha$ (J-Can $g\ \varphi$)}; {Request $i\ g\ \alpha\ \varphi$}

Thus performing an action {FormTeam $i\ g\ \alpha\ \varphi$} involves first informing g that they are able to achieve φ, and then requesting g to achieve φ. (Notice that for simplicity, I assume the same action α is used for both the inform and request speech acts.)

Using this composite speech act, we can give the assumption that characterizes the behavior of an agent who recognizes the potential for cooperative
action with respect to one of its desires.

$$\models_S \forall i \cdot (\mathsf{PfC}\ i\ \varphi) \Rightarrow \mathsf{A}\exists g \cdot \exists \alpha \cdot (\mathsf{Happens}\ \{\mathsf{FormTeam}\ i\ g\ \alpha\ \varphi\}) \qquad (8.2)$$

If team formation is successful, then for the first time there will be a *social*
commitment: a commitment by a group of agents on behalf of another agent.

8.4   Plan Formation

If an agent is successful in its attempt to solicit assistance, then there will be a
group of agents with a mutual intention to cooperative action, and the mutual
belief that they can achieve the desire. But collective action cannot actually
begin until the group agrees on what they will actually do. Hence the next
stage: plan formation.

We saw above that a group will not form a collective unless they believe
they can actually achieve the desire. This, in turn, implies there is at least one
action known to the group that will take them "closer" to the goal (see the
definition of J-Can, above). However, it is possible that there are many agents
that know of actions the group can perform in order to take them closer to the
goal. Moreover, some members of the collective may have objections to one
or more of these actions. One of the desiderata for our model is that agents are
autonomous — they have control over their internal state, and will not simply
perform an action because another agent wants them to [249]. It is therefore
necessary for the collective to come to some agreement about exactly which
course of action they will follow. Such an agreement is reached via *negotiation*.

Negotiation usually involves agents making reasoned arguments for and
against courses of action; making proposals and counter proposals; suggesting
modifications or amendments to plans; and continuing in this way until all the
participants have agreed on a final result.[1] Negotiation has long been recognized as a process of some importance in multiagent systems [228, 195, 123].
Unfortunately, these analyses demonstrate that negotiation is also extremely
complex — a rigorous attempt at formalization is quite beyond the scope of
this book (see the "Notes and Further Reading" section for references). Instead, we simply offer some observations about the weakest conditions under
which negotiation can be said to have occurred.

---

1 It may also involve agents lying, though we shall not consider such cases here.

What can we say about negotiating a plan? First, we note that negotiation may *fail*: the collective may simply be unable to reach agreement, due to some irreconcilable differences.

In this case, the minimum condition required for us to be able to say that negotiation occurred at all is that *at least one* agent proposed a course of action that it believed would take the collective closer to the goal. However, negotiation may also succeed. In this case, we expect a team action stage to follow immediately — we shall say no more about team action here, as this is the subject of the next section.

We shall now make the above discussion more precise. First, we define *joint attempts*: what it means for a group of agents to collectively attempt something. As might be expected, joint attempts are a generalization of single-agent attempts. An attempt by a group of agents g to bring about a state φ is an action α, of which g are the agents, performed with the mutual desire that after α is performed, φ is satisfied, or at least ψ is satisfied (where ψ represents what it takes to make a reasonable effort).

$$\{\text{J-Attempt } g\ \alpha\ \varphi\ \psi\} \;\hat{=}\; \left[\begin{array}{l} (\text{M-Bel } g\ \neg\varphi)\ \wedge \\ (\text{Agts } \alpha\ g)\ \wedge \\ (\text{M-Des } g\ (\text{Achvs } \alpha\ \varphi))\ \wedge \\ (\text{M-Int } g\ (\text{Achvs } \alpha\ \psi)) \end{array} \right] ?;\alpha$$

We can now state the minimum conditions required for negotiation to have occurred. Intuitively, the group will try to bring about a state where they have agreed on a common plan, and intend to act on it. Failing that, they will bring about a state where at least one of them has proposed a plan that it believed would achieve the desired goal. More formally, if group g are a pre-team with respect to agent i's desire φ, then g will eventually jointly attempt to bring about a state in which g are a team with respect to i's desire φ, or, failing that, to at least bring about a state where some agent $j \in g$ has made g mutually aware of its belief that some action α can be performed by g in order to achieve φ. Formally, this assumption is as follows:

$$\models_{\mathcal{S}} (\text{PreTeam } g\ \varphi) \Rightarrow \text{A}\Diamond\exists\alpha \cdot (\text{Happens } \{\text{J-Attempt } g\ \alpha\ \psi\ \chi\}) \qquad (8.3)$$

where

$$\psi \;\hat{=}\; (\text{Team}_{soc}\ g\ \varphi\ \psi_{soc})$$

and

$$\chi \hat{=} \exists j \cdot \exists \alpha \cdot (j \in g) \wedge (\text{M-Bel } g \text{ (Bel } j \text{ (Agts } \alpha \text{ } g) \wedge (\text{Achvs } \alpha \text{ } \varphi))).$$

Recall that Team$_{soc}$ was defined in chapter 6, to capture the notion of a "team" mental state.

We can make some other assumptions about agent behavior during negotiation. Most importantly, we assume that agents will *attempt to bring about their preferences*. For example, if an agent has an objection to some plan, then it will attempt to prevent this plan being carried out. Similarly, if it has a preference for some plan, then it will attempt to bring this plan about. More precisely, if group g are a pre-team with respect to agent i's desire φ, and there is some action α such that it is mutually believed in g that α achieves φ, and that g are the agents of α, then every agent $j \in g$ that has a preference that α does/does not occur will attempt to ensure that α does/does not occur, by at least making g mutually aware of its preference for/against α. Note that we are once again assuming that agents are veracious; that they attempt to influence the team by revealing their true preferences, rather than by lying about their preferences, or not revealing their true preferences. An agent can attempt to cause a team to perform some action by simply making use of the RequestTh speech act, as defined in chapter 7.

If the plan formation phase is successful then the team will have a full joint commitment to the joint goal, and will have agreed to the means by which they will pursue their joint goal. Ideally, we would also like to specify that the group negotiate a convention for monitoring progress of the team action, but this is beyond the scope of this book.

If a collective is successful in its attempt to negotiate a plan, then we expect that collective to follow up negotiation with action. This gives us the fourth, and final stage in our model: team action. Team action will take place when the group of agents have a joint intention towards some state of affairs, have a mutually agreed action that will achieve this state of affairs, and have some convention in place to monitor the progress of the team action. We have already seen examples of this type of team action in chapter 6.

8.5   Notes and Further Reading

Many attempts to formally define ability have appeared in the literature. The earliest discussion on the subject in the artificial intelligence literature is probably that by McCarthy and Hayes, in their well-known work [151]. The best-known definition of ability, (and the one upon which the definition in this book is based) is that developed by Robert Moore [156, 157]. Other examples include the work of Brown [25], Singh's definitions of ability and cooperative ability [212, 216], and the work of Werner [234] and Morgenstern [160, 161].

The model of cooperative problem solving presented here is based on one I developed jointly with Nick Jennings [247, 248, 250]. These papers were the first to present the four-stage model of cooperative problem solving, and the first to formally define such notions as potential for cooperation. The logic used in this earlier work is an ancestor of $\mathcal{LORA}$, with the main difference being that $\mathcal{LORA}$ uses the BDI model of Rao and Georgeff; in the original formulation, the logic more closely resembled that of Cohen and Levesque [35, 36].

Afsaneh Haddadi, building on [247, 248, 250], developed a formalization of cooperation plans [86, 87]. She further developed the concept of potential for cooperation that was presented in [247, 248, 250], and discussed how cooperation plans specified in a BDI logic might be implemented in a practical BDI system.

A number of attempts have appeared in the literature to formalize multi-agent argumentation. One of the first was [124]; since then, Parsons and colleagues have presented several such models [169, 207]. Kraus et al. present a detailed logical formalization of argumentation using a BDI-like logic in [125].

The best-developed alternative to the model of cooperative action presented in this chapter is the "SharedPlans" model developed by Grosz and Kraus [84, 85]. Expressed in a rich logic that combines multimodal and first-order elements, the primary emphasis in SharedPlans is on giving an account of how the plans of individual agents can be reconciled with those of a team.

9 Logic and Agent Theory

Mathematical logic is one of the most important tools available in computer science and AI today. In this chapter, we will step back from our attempts to formalize the properties of rational agents to see what role logic can play in the *engineering* of rational agents.

Broadly speaking, logic has played a role in three aspects of software engineering:

- as a *specification language*;
- as a *programming language*; and
- as a *verification language*.

In the sections that follow, we will discuss the use of logics such as $\mathcal{LORA}$ in these three processes.

9.1 Specification

The software development process begins by establishing the client's requirements. When this process is complete, a *specification* is developed, which sets out the functionality of the new system. Temporal and dynamic logics, closely related to $\mathcal{LORA}$, have found wide applicability in the specification of systems. An obvious question is therefore whether logics such as $\mathcal{LORA}$ might be used as specification languages.

A specification expressed in $\mathcal{LORA}$ would be a formula φ. The idea is that such a specification would express the desirable behavior of a system. To see how this might work, consider the following formula of $\mathcal{LORA}$, intended to form part of a specification of a process control system.

$$(\text{Bel } i \; Open(valve32)) \Rightarrow (\text{Int } i \; (\text{Bel } j \; Open(valve32)))$$

This formula says that if i believes valve 32 is open, then i should intend that j believes valve 32 is open. A rational agent i with such an intention can select a speech act to perform in order to inform j of this state of affairs. It should be intuitively clear how a system specification might be constructed using such formulae, to define the intended behavior of a system.

One of the main desirable features of a software specification language is that it should not dictate *how* a specification should be satisfied by an implementation. It should be clear that the specification above has exactly these properties. It does not dictate how agent i should go about making j aware that valve 32 is open. We simply expect i to behave as a rational agent given such an intention.

There are a number of problems with the use of languages such as $\mathcal{LORA}$ for specification. The most worrying of these is with respect to their semantics. The semantics for the modal connectives (for beliefs, desires, and intentions) are given in the normal modal logic tradition of possible worlds [31]. So, for example, an agent's beliefs in some state are characterized by a set of different states, each of which represents one possibility for how the world could actually be, given the information available to the agent. In much the same way, an agent's desires in some state are characterized by a set of states that are consistent with the agent's desires. Intentions are represented similarly. There are several advantages to the possible worlds model: it is well studied and well understood, and the associated mathematics of correspondence theory is extremely elegant. These attractive features make possible worlds the semantics of choice for almost every researcher in formal agent theory. However, there are also a number of serious drawbacks to possible worlds semantics. First, possible worlds semantics imply that agents are logically perfect reasoners, (in that their deductive capabilities are sound and complete), and they have infinite resources available for reasoning. No real agent, artificial or otherwise, has these properties. (See appendix B for a discussion of this.)

Second, possible worlds semantics are generally *ungrounded*. That is, there is usually no precise relationship between the abstract accessibility relations that are used to characterize an agent's state, and any concrete computational model. As we shall see in later sections, this makes it difficult to go from a formal specification of a system in terms of beliefs, desires, and so on, to a concrete computational system. Similarly, given a concrete computational system, there is generally no way to determine what the beliefs, desires, and intentions of that system are. If temporal modal logics such as $\mathcal{LORA}$ are to be taken seriously as *specification* languages, then this is a significant problem.

9.2 Implementation

Specification is not (usually!) the end of the story in software development. Once given a specification, we must implement a system that is correct with respect to this specification. The next issue we consider is this move from abstract specification to concrete computational model. There are at least three possibilities for achieving this transformation:

1. manually refine the specification into an executable form via some principled but informal refinement process (as is the norm in most current software development);

2. directly execute or animate the abstract specification; or

3. translate or compile the specification into a concrete computational form using an automatic translation technique.

In the subsections that follow, we shall investigate each of these possibilities in turn.

Refinement

At the time of writing, most software developers use structured but informal techniques to transform specifications into concrete implementations. Probably the most common techniques in widespread use are based on the idea of top-down refinement. In this approach, an abstract system specification is *refined* into a number of smaller, less abstract subsystem specifications, which together satisfy the original specification. If these subsystems are still too abstract to be implemented directly, then they are also refined. The process recurses until the derived subsystems are simple enough to be directly implemented. Throughout, we are obliged to demonstrate that each step represents a true refinement of the more abstract specification that preceded it. This demonstration may take the form of a formal proof, if our specification is presented in, say, Z [224] or VDM [110]. More usually, justification is by informal argument. Object-oriented analysis and design techniques, which also tend to be structured but informal, are also increasingly playing a role in the development of systems (see, e.g., [19]).

For *functional* systems, which simply compute a function of some input and then terminate, the refinement process is well understood, and comparatively straightforward. Such systems can be specified in terms of pre- and post-conditions (e.g., using Hoare logic [97]). Refinement calculi exist, which enable the system developer to take a pre- and post-condition specification, and from it systematically derive an implementation through the use of proof rules [159]. Part of the reason for this comparative simplicity is that there is often an easily understandable relationship between the pre- and post-conditions that characterize an operation and the program structures required to implement it.

For agent systems, which fall into the category of Pnuelian reactive systems (see the discussion in chapter 1), refinement is not so straightforward. This is because such systems must be specified in terms of their *ongoing* behavior — they cannot be specified simply in terms of pre- and post-conditions. In contrast to pre- and post-condition formalisms, it is not so easy to determine what program structures are required to realize such specifications. As a consequence, researchers have only just begun to investigate refinement and design technique for agent-based systems.

Case Study: A Methodology for BDI Agents

In [117], Kinny et al. propose a four-stage design methodology for systems of BDI agents. The methodology is closely linked to a specific realization of the BDI model: the PRS architecture [78]. The methodology may be summarized as follows:

1. Identify the relevant *roles* in the application domain, and on the basis of these, develop an *agent class hierarchy*. An example role might be weather monitor, whereby agent i is required to make agent j aware of the prevailing weather conditions every hour.

2. Identify the responsibilities associated with each role, the services required by and provided by the role, and then determine the *goals* associated with each service. With respect to the above example, the goals would be to find out the current weather, and to make agent j aware of this information.

3. For each goal, determine the plans that may be used to achieve it, and the context conditions under which each plan is appropriate. With respect to the above example, a plan for the goal of making agent j aware of the weather conditions might involve sending a message to j.

4. Determine the belief structure of the system — the information requirements for each plan and goal. With respect to the above example, we might propose a unary predicate $WindSpeed(x)$ to represent the fact that the current wind speed is x. A plan to determine the current weather conditions would need to be able to represent this information.

Note that the analysis process will be iterative, as in more traditional methodologies. The outcome will be a model that closely corresponds to the PRS agent architecture. As a result, the move from end-design to implementation using PRS is relatively simple.

Directly Executing Agent Specifications

One major disadvantage with manual refinement methods is that they introduce the possibility of error. If no proofs are provided, to demonstrate that each refinement step is indeed a true refinement, then the correctness of the implementation process depends upon little more than the intuitions of the developer. This is clearly an undesirable state of affairs for applications in which correctness is a major issue. One possible way of circumventing this problem, which has been widely investigated in mainstream computer science, is to get rid of the refinement process altogether, and *directly execute* the specification.

It might seem that suggesting the direct execution of complex agent specification languages is naive — it is exactly the kind of suggestion that detractors of logic-based AI hate. One should therefore be very careful about what claims or proposals one makes. However, in certain circumstances, the direct execution of agent specification languages *is* possible.

What does it mean, to execute a formula φ of logic L? It means generating a logical model, M, for φ, such that $M \models \varphi$ [64]. If this could be done without interference from the environment — if the agent had complete control over its environment — then execution would reduce to constructive theorem-proving, where we show that φ is satisfiable by building a model for φ. In reality, of course, agents are *not* interference-free: they must iteratively construct a model in the presence of input from the environment. Execution can then be seen as a two-way iterative process:

- environment makes something true;
- agent responds by doing something, i.e., making something else true in the model;
- environment responds, making something else true;
- ...

Execution of logical languages and theorem-proving are thus closely related. This tells us that the execution of sufficiently rich (quantified) languages is not possible (since any language equal in expressive power to first-order logic is undecidable).

A useful way to think about execution is as if the agent is *playing a game* against the environment. The specification represents the goal of the game: the agent must keep the goal satisfied, while the environment tries to prevent the agent from doing so. The game is played by agent and environment taking turns to build a little more of the model. If the specification ever becomes false in the (partial) model, then the agent loses. In real reactive systems, the game is never over: the agent must continue to play forever. Of course, some specifications (logically inconsistent ones) cannot ever be satisfied. A *winning strategy* for building models from (satisfiable) agent specifications in the presence of arbitrary input from the environment is an execution algorithm for the logic.

Case Study: Concurrent METATEM

Concurrent METATEM is a programming language for multiagent systems, that is based on the idea of directly executing linear time temporal logic agent specifications [65, 63]. A Concurrent METATEM system contains a number of concurrently executing agents, each of which is programmed by giving it a temporal logic specification of the behavior it is intended the agent should exhibit. An agent specification has the form $\bigwedge_i P_i \Rightarrow F_i$, where P_i is a temporal logic formula referring only to the present or past, and F_i is a temporal logic formula referring to the present or future. The $P_i \Rightarrow F_i$ formulae are known as *rules*. The basic idea for executing such a specification may be summed up in the following slogan:

on the basis of the past *do* the future.

Thus each rule is continually matched against an internal, recorded *history*, and if a match is found, then the rule *fires*. If a rule fires, then any variables in the future time part are instantiated, and the future time part then becomes a *commitment* that the agent will subsequently attempt to satisfy. Satisfying a commitment typically means making some predicate true within the agent. Here is a simple example of a Concurrent METATEM agent definition:

⬤ $ask(x) \Rightarrow \Diamond give(x)$
$(\neg ask(x) \, \mathcal{Z} \, (give(x) \wedge \neg ask(x))) \Rightarrow \neg give(x)$
$give(x) \wedge give(y) \Rightarrow (x = y)$

The agent in this example is a controller for a resource that is infinitely renewable, but which may only be possessed by one agent at any given time. The controller must therefore enforce mutual exclusion. The predicate $ask(x)$ means that agent x has asked for the resource. The predicate $give(x)$ means that the resource controller has given the resource to agent x. The resource controller is assumed to be the only agent able to "give" the resource. However, many agents may ask for the resource simultaneously. The three rules that define this agent's behavior may be summarized as follows:

- Rule 1: if someone asks, then eventually give;
- Rule 2: don't give unless someone has asked since you last gave; and
- Rule 3: if you give to two people, then they must be the same person (i.e., don't give to more than one person at a time).

Concurrent METATEM agents can communicate by asynchronous broadcast message passing, though the details are not important here.

Compiling Agent Specifications

An alternative to direct execution is *compilation*. In this scheme, we take our abstract specification, and transform it into a concrete computational model via some automatic synthesis process. The main perceived advantages of compilation over direct execution are in run-time efficiency. Direct execution of an agent specification, as in Concurrent METATEM, above, typically involves manipulating a symbolic representation of the specification at run time. This manipulation generally corresponds to reasoning of some form, which is computationally costly (and in many cases, simply impracticable for systems that must operate in anything like real time). In contrast, compilation approaches aim to reduce abstract symbolic specifications to a much simpler computational model, which requires no symbolic representation. The "reasoning" work is thus done off-line, at compile-time; execution of the compiled system can then be done with little or no run-time symbolic reasoning. As a result, execution is much faster. The advantages of compilation over direct execution are thus those of compilation over interpretation in mainstream programming.

Compilation approaches usually depend upon the close relationship between models for temporal/modal logic (which are typically labeled graphs of some kind), and automata-like finite state machines. Crudely, the idea is to take a specification φ, and do a *constructive proof* of the implementability of φ, wherein we show that the specification is satisfiable by systematically attempting to build a model for it. If the construction process succeeds, then the specification is satisfiable, and we have a model to prove it. Otherwise, the specification is unsatisfiable. If we have a model, then we "read off" the automaton that implements φ from its corresponding model. The most common approach to constructive proof is the *semantic tableaux* method of Smullyan [223].

In mainstream computer science, the compilation approach to automatic program synthesis has been investigated by a number of researchers. Perhaps the closest to our view is the work of Pnueli and Rosner [178] on the automatic synthesis of reactive systems from branching time temporal logic specifications. The goal of their work is to generate reactive systems, which share many of the properties of our agents (the main difference being that reactive systems are not generally required to be capable of rational decision making in the way we described above). To do this, they specify a reactive system in terms of a first-order branching time temporal logic formula $\forall x \, \exists y \, A\varphi(x, y)$: the predicate φ characterizes the relationship between inputs to the system (x) and outputs (y). Inputs may be thought of as sequences of environment states, and outputs as corresponding sequences of actions. The A is the universal path quantifier. The specification is intended to express the fact that in all possible futures, the desired relationship φ holds between the inputs to the system, x, and its outputs, y. The synthesis process itself is rather complex: it involves generating a Rabin tree automaton, and then checking this automaton for emptiness. Pnueli and Rosner show that the time complexity of the synthesis process is double exponential in the size of the specification, i.e., $O(2^{2^{c.n}})$, where c is a constant and $n = |\varphi|$ is the size of the specification φ. The size of the synthesized program (the number of states it contains) is of the same complexity.

The Pnueli-Rosner technique is rather similar to (and in fact depends upon) techniques developed by Wolper, Vardi, and colleagues for synthesizing Büchi automata from linear temporal logic specifications [232]. Büchi automata are those that can recognize *ω-regular expressions*: regular expressions that may contain infinite repetition. A standard result in temporal logic theory is that a formula φ of linear time temporal logic is satisfiable if and only if there exists a Büchi automaton that accepts just the sequences that satisfy φ. Intuitively, this is because the sequences over which linear time temporal logic is interpreted can be viewed as ω-regular expressions. This result yields a decision procedure for linear time temporal logic: to determine whether a formula φ is satisfiable, construct an automaton that accepts just the (infinite) sequences that correspond to models of φ; if the set of such sequences is empty, then φ is unsatisfiable. The technique for constructing an automaton from the corresponding formula is closely based on Wolper's tableau proof method for temporal logic [236].

Similar automatic synthesis techniques have also been deployed to develop concurrent system skeletons from temporal logic specifications. Manna and Wolper present an algorithm that takes as input a linear time temporal logic specification of the *synchronization* part of a concurrent system, and generates as output a program skeleton (based upon Hoare's CSP formalism [98]) that realizes the specification [146]. The idea is that the functionality of a concurrent system can generally be divided into two parts: a functional part, which actually performs the required computation in the program, and a synchronization part, which ensures that the system components cooperate in the correct way. For example, the synchronization part will be responsible for any mutual exclusion that is required. The synthesis algorithm (like the synthesis algorithm for Büchi automata, above) is based on Wolper's tableau proof method for temporal logic [236]. Very similar work is reported by Clarke and Emerson [32]: they synthesize synchronization skeletons from branching time temporal logic (CTL) specifications.

Case Study: Situated Automata

Perhaps the best-known example of this approach to agent development is the *situated automata* paradigm of Rosenschein and Kaelbling [196, 114, 197]. In this approach, an agent has two main components:

- a *perception* part, which is responsible for observing the environment and updating the internal state of the agent; and

- an *action* part, which is responsible for deciding what action to perform, based on the internal state of the agent.

Rosenschein and Kaelbling developed two programs to support the development of the perception and action components of an agent respectively. The RULER program takes a declarative perception specification and compiles it down to a finite state machine. The specification is given in terms of a theory of knowledge. The semantics of knowledge in the declarative specification language are given in terms of possible worlds, in the way described above. Crucially, however, the possible worlds underlying this logic are given a precise computational interpretation, in terms of the states of a finite state machine. It is this precise relationship that permits the synthesis process to take place.

The action part of an agent in Rosenschein and Kaelbling's framework is specified in terms of *goal reduction rules*, which encode information about how to achieve goals. The GAPPS program takes as input a goal specification, and a set of goal reduction rules, and generates as output a set of *situation action rules*, which may be thought of as a lookup table, defining what the agent should do under various circumstances, in order to achieve the goal. The process of deciding what to do is then very simple in computational terms, involving no reasoning at all. (A similar technique, called *universal plans*, was developed by Schoppers [201].)

9.3   Verification

Once we have developed a concrete system, we need to show that this system is correct with respect to our original specification. This process is known as *verification*, and it is particularly important if we have introduced any informality into the development process. For example, any manual refinement, done without a formal proof of refinement correctness, creates the possibility of a faulty transformation from specification to implementation. Verification is the process of convincing ourselves that the transformation was sound. We can divide approaches to the verification of systems into two broad classes: (1) *axiomatic*; and (2) *semantic* (model checking). In the subsections that follow, we shall look at the way in which these two approaches have evidenced themselves in agent-based systems.

Axiomatic Approaches

Axiomatic approaches to program verification were the first to enter the mainstream of computer science, with the work of Hoare in the late 1960s [97]. Axiomatic verification requires that we can take our concrete program, and from this program systematically derive a logical theory that represents the behavior of the program. Call this the program theory. If the program theory is expressed in the same logical language as the original specification, then verification reduces to a proof problem: show that the specification is a theorem of (equivalently, is a logical consequence of) the program theory.

The development of a program theory is made feasible by *axiomatizing* the programming language in which the system is implemented. For example, Hoare logic gives us more or less an axiom for every statement type in a simple PASCAL-like language. Once given the axiomatization, the program theory can be derived from the program text in a systematic way.

Perhaps the most relevant work from mainstream computer science is the specification and verification of reactive systems using temporal logic, in the way pioneered by Pnueli, Manna, and colleagues [145]. The idea is that the computations of reactive systems are infinite sequences, which correspond to models for linear temporal logic.[1] Temporal logic can be used both to develop a system specification, and to axiomatize a programming language. This axiomatization can then be used to systematically derive the theory of a

---

1 The set of all computations of a reactive system is a tree-like structure, corresponding to a model for branching time temporal logic [50].

program from the program text. Both the specification and the program theory will then be encoded in temporal logic, and verification hence becomes a proof problem in temporal logic.

Comparatively little work has been carried out within the agent-based systems community on axiomatizing multiagent environments. I shall review just one approach.

Case Study: Axiomatizing Two Multiagent Languages

In [237], an axiomatic approach to the verification of multiagent systems was proposed. Essentially, the idea was to use a temporal belief logic to axiomatize the properties of two multiagent programming languages. Given such an axiomatization, a program theory representing the properties of the system could be systematically derived in the way indicated above.

A temporal belief logic was used for two reasons. First, a temporal component was required because, as we observed above, we need to capture the ongoing behavior of a multiagent system. A belief component was used because the agents we wish to verify are each symbolic AI systems in their own right. That is, each agent is a symbolic reasoning system, which includes a representation of its environment and desired behavior. A belief component in the logic allows us to capture the symbolic representations present within each agent.

The two multiagent programming languages that were axiomatized in the temporal belief logic were Shoham's AGENT0 [206], and Fisher's Concurrent METATEM (see above). The basic approach was as follows:

1. First, a simple abstract model was developed of symbolic AI agents. This model captures the fact that agents are symbolic reasoning systems, capable of communication. The model gives an account of how agents might change state, and what a computation of such a system might look like.

2. The histories traced out in the execution of such a system were used as the semantic basis for a temporal belief logic. This logic allows us to express properties of agents modeled at stage (1).

3. The temporal belief logic was used to axiomatize the properties of a multiagent programming language. This axiomatization was then used to develop the program theory of a multiagent system.

4. The proof theory of the temporal belief logic was used to verify properties of the system [246].

Note that this approach relies on the operation of agents being sufficiently simple that their properties can be axiomatized in the logic. It works for Shoham's AGENT0 and Fisher's Concurrent METATEM largely because these languages have a simple semantics, closely related to rule-based systems, which in turn have a simple logical semantics. For more complex agents, an axiomatization is not so straightforward. Also, capturing the semantics of concurrent execution of agents is not easy (it is, of course, an area of ongoing research in computer science generally).

Semantic Approaches: Model Checking

Ultimately, axiomatic verification reduces to a proof problem. Axiomatic approaches to verification are thus inherently limited by the difficulty of this proof problem. Proofs are hard enough, even in classical logic; the addition of temporal and modal connectives to a logic makes the problem considerably harder. For this reason, more efficient approaches to verification have been sought. One particularly successful approach is that of *model checking* [33]. As the name suggests, whereas axiomatic approaches generally rely on syntactic proof, model-checking approaches are based on the semantics of the specification language.

The model-checking problem, in abstract, is quite simple: given a formula φ of language L, and a model M for L, determine whether or not φ is valid in M, i.e., whether or not $M \models_L \varphi$. Verification by model checking has been studied in connection with temporal logic [134]. The technique once again relies upon the close relationship between models for temporal logic and finite-state machines. Suppose that φ is the specification for some system, and π is a program that claims to implement φ. Then, to determine whether or not π truly implements φ, we proceed as follows:

- take π, and from it generate a model M_π that corresponds to π, in the sense that M_π encodes all the possible computations of π;
- determine whether or not $M_\pi \models \varphi$, i.e., whether the specification formula φ is valid in M_π; the program π satisfies the specification φ just in case the answer is "yes."

The main advantage of model checking over axiomatic verification is in complexity: model checking using the branching time temporal logic CTL [32] can be done in time $O(|\varphi| \times |M|)$, where $|\varphi|$ is the size of the formula to be checked, and $|M|$ is the size of the model against which φ is to be checked — the number of states it contains.

Case Study: Model Checking BDI Systems

In [189], Rao and Georgeff present an algorithm for model checking BDI systems. More precisely, they give an algorithm for taking a logical model for their (propositional) BDI logic, and a formula of the language, and determining whether the formula is valid in the model. The technique is closely based on model-checking algorithms for normal modal logics [92]. They show that despite the inclusion of three extra modalities (for beliefs, desires, and intentions) into the CTL branching time framework, the algorithm is still quite efficient, running in polynomial time. So the second step of the two-stage model-checking process described above can still be done efficiently. Similar algorithms have been reported for BDI-like logics in [13].

The main problem with model-checking approaches for BDI is that it is not clear how the first step might be realized for BDI logics. Where does the logical model characterizing an agent actually come from? Can it be derived from an arbitrary program π, as in mainstream computer science? To do this, we would need to take a program implemented in, say, PASCAL, and from it derive the belief-, desire-, and intention-accessibility relations that are used to give a semantics to the BDI component of the logic. Because, as we noted earlier, there is no clear relationship between the BDI logic and the concrete computational models used to implement agents, it is not clear how such a model could be derived.

9.4 Notes and Further Reading

This chapter is an updated and extended version of [240], which examined the possibility of using logic to engineer agent-based systems. Since this article was published, several other authors have proposed the use of agents in software engineering (see, e.g., [107]).

Structured but informal refinement techniques are the mainstay of real-world software engineering. If agent-oriented techniques are ever to become widely used outside the academic community, then informal, structured methods for agent-based development will be essential. One possibility for such techniques, followed by Luck and d'Inverno, is to use a standard specification technique (in their case, Z), and use traditional refinement methods (in their case, object-oriented development) to transform the specification into an implementation [141]. This approach has the advantage of being familiar to a much larger user-base than entirely new techniques, but suffers from the disadvantage of presenting the user with no features that make it particularly well-suited to agent specification. It seems certain that there will be much more work on manual refinement techniques for agent-based systems in the immediate future, but exactly what form these techniques will take is not clear.

With respect to the possibility of directly executing agent specifications, a number of problems suggest themselves. The first is that of finding a concrete computational interpretation for the agent specification language in question. To see what we mean by this, consider models for the agent specification language in Concurrent METATEM. These are very simple: essentially just linear discrete sequences of states. Temporal logic is (among other things) simply a language for expressing *constraints* that must hold between successive states. Execution in Concurrent METATEM is thus a process of generating constraints as past-time antecedents are satisfied, and then trying to build a next state that satisfies these constraints. Constraints are expressed in temporal logic, which implies that they may only be in certain, regular forms. Because of this, it is possible to devise an algorithm that is guaranteed to build a next state if it is possible to do so. Such an algorithm is described in [8].

The agent specification language upon which Concurrent METATEM is based thus has a concrete computational model, and a comparatively simple execution algorithm. Contrast this state of affairs with languages like $\mathcal{LORA}$, where we have not only a temporal dimension to the logic, but also modalities for referring to beliefs, desires, and so on. In general, models for these logics have *ungrounded* semantics. That is, the semantic structures that underpin these logics (typically accessibility relations for each of the modal operators) have no concrete computational interpretation. As a result, it is not clear how such agent specification languages might be executed.

Another obvious problem is that execution techniques based on theorem-proving are inherently limited when applied to sufficiently expressive (first-order) languages, as first-order logic is undecidable. However, complexity is a problem even in the propositional case. For "vanilla" propositional logic, the decision problem for satisfiability is NP-complete [54, p.72]; for linear temporal logic, the problem is PSPACE-complete [220]; for simple modal logics of knowledge, the problem is NP-complete, and for more complex modal logics of knowledge, the problem is EXPTIME-complete [54, p.73]; for logics that *combine* temporal and (S5) modal aspects, the decision problem varies from PSPACE-complete in the simplest case to Π_1^1-complete, (and hence *undecid-*

able) in the propositional case, depending on what semantic assumptions are made [54, p.289].

Despite these problems, the undoubted attractions of direct execution have led to a number of attempts to devise executable logic-based agent languages. Rao, one of the main figures behind BDI, proposed an executable subset of BDI logic in his AGENTSPEAK(L) language [183]. Building on this work, Hindriks and colleagues developed the 3APL agent programming language [94, 95]. Lespérance, Reiter, Levesque, and colleagues developed the GOLOG language throughout the latter half of the 1990s as an executable subset of the situation calculus [130, 131]. Fagin and colleagues have proposed *knowledge-based programs* as a paradigm for executing logical formulae which contain epistemic modalities [54, 55]. Although considerable work has been carried out on the properties of knowledge-based programs, comparatively little research to date has addressed the problem of how such programs might be actually executed.

Turning to automatic synthesis, we find that the techniques described above have been developed primarily for propositional specification languages. If we attempt to extend these techniques to more expressive, first-order specification languages, then we again find ourselves coming up against the undecidability of quantified logic. Even in the propositional case, the theoretical complexity of theorem-proving for modal and temporal logics is likely to limit the effectiveness of compilation techniques: given an agent specification of size 1,000, a synthesis algorithm that runs in exponential time when used off-line is no more useful than an execution algorithm that runs in exponential time on-line.

Another problem with respect to synthesis techniques is that they typically result in finite-state, automata-like machines, which are less powerful than Turing machines. In particular, the systems generated by the processes outlined above cannot modify their behavior at run-time. In short, they cannot learn. While for many applications, this is acceptable — even desirable — for equally many others, it is not. In expert assistant agents, of the type described in [142], learning is pretty much the *raison d'etre*. Attempts to address this issue are described in [113].

Turning to verification, axiomatic approaches suffer from two main problems. First, the temporal verification of reactive systems relies upon a simple model of concurrency, where the actions that programs perform are assumed to be atomic. We cannot make this assumption when we move from programs to agents. The actions we think of agents as performing will generally be much more coarse-grained. As a result, we need a more realistic model of concurrency. One possibility, investigated in [238], is to model agent execution cycles as intervals over the real numbers, in the style of the temporal logic of reals [10]. The second problem is the difficulty of the proof problem for agent specification languages. The theoretical complexity of proof for many of these logics is quite daunting.

Hindriks and colleagues have used Plotkin's structured operational semantics to axiomatize their 3APL language [94, 95].

With respect to model-checking approaches, the main problem, as we indicated above, is again the issue of ungrounded semantics for agent specification languages. If we cannot take an arbitrary program and say, for this program, what its beliefs, desires, and intentions are, then it is not clear how we might verify that this program satisfied a specification expressed in terms of such constructs.

A Appendix: Summary of Notation

The formal tools used in this book are loosely based on the VDM specification language: the first seven chapters of Jones [110] cover all the necessary material. However, anyone familiar with basic set notation and logic should have no difficulty.

A central idea is that of the *type*: for the purposes of this book, a type can be thought of as a (possibly infinite) set. Two "standard" types are assumed:

$$I\!N = \{0, 1, 2, \ldots\} \quad \text{the natural numbers}$$
$$I\!R \quad\quad\quad\quad\quad\quad \text{the real numbers}$$

The set of subsets of a type T (i.e., the powerset of T) is given by $\wp(T)$. Thus

$$\wp(\{1, 2, 3\}) = \{\emptyset, \{1\}, \{2\}, \{3\}, \{1, 2\}, \{1, 3\}, \{2, 3\}, \{1, 2, 3\}\}$$

The set T of all ordered n-tuples whose first element is of type T_1, second element is of type T_2, ..., n^{th} element is of type T_n, may be defined in two ways. The first is to define it as the cross product of its component types:

$$T = T_1 \times \cdots \times T_n$$

The alternative is to name the elements:

$$\langle t_1, \cdots, t_n \rangle$$

where $t_1 \in T_1, t_2 \in T_2, \ldots, t_n \in T_n$. In general, the latter method is used for large or complex types.

Functions are specified by giving their *signature*:

$$f : D_1 \times \cdots \times D_n \to R$$

This says that the function f takes n arguments, the first of type (or *from domain*) $D_1, \ldots$, the nth from domain D_n, and returns a value of type (or *from the range*) R.

The symbol

$$\hat{=}$$

should be read "is defined as." An expression of the form

$$f(x) \hat{=} e(x)$$

means that the left hand side $f(x)$ is defined as the right hand side $e(x)$. For example, consider the definition of material implication:

$$\varphi \Rightarrow \psi \;\hat{=}\; \neg\varphi \vee \psi$$

This definition tells us that a formula with the structure $\varphi \Rightarrow \psi$ should be understood as an abbreviation for $\neg\varphi \vee \psi$. It may be useful to think of such definitions as behaving like macro definitions in a programming language like C.

A useful operator on functions is to *overwrite* them. To do this, we use the dagger operator, "†." Thus by the expression $f \dagger \{x \mapsto y\}$ we mean the function that is the same as f except that it maps x to y. Thus if

$$f(2) = 3$$

and

$$g \;\hat{=}\; f \dagger \{2 \mapsto 7\}$$

then $g(2) = 7$.

Two standard operations on functions and relations are assumed: dom takes a function or relation and returns the set of elements in its domain for which it is defined; ran takes a function or relation and returns the set of elements in its range for which the corresponding elements in the domain are defined.

A *sequence* can be thought of simply as a list of objects, each of which is of the same type. We denote the set of (possibly empty) sequences over a set T by T^*.

Finally, in this book, we deal with several languages: the symbols φ, ψ, and χ are used as meta-variables, ranging over formulae of these languages.

B Appendix: Formal Foundations

In this appendix, I present an overview of the main logical tools available for reasoning about time and mental states. I assume the reader has some familiarity with propositional and first-order logic, as well as basic set notation (see appendix a).

B.1 Reasoning about Intentional Notions

Suppose one wishes to reason about belief in a logical framework. Consider the following simple statement about belief (adapted from [73, pp.210–211]):

Janine believes Cronos is the father of Zeus. (B.1)

A naive attempt to translate (B.1) into first-order logic might result in the following:

$Bel(Janine, Father(Zeus, Cronos))$ (B.2)

Unfortunately, this naive translation does not work, for at least two reasons. The first is syntactic: the second argument to the *Bel* predicate is a *formula* of first-order logic, and is not, therefore, a term. So (B.2) is not a well-formed formula of classical first-order logic. The second problem is semantic. The constants *Zeus* and *Jupiter*, by any reasonable interpretation, denote the same individual: the supreme deity of the classical world. It is therefore acceptable to write, in first-order logic:

$(Zeus = Jupiter)$. (B.3)

Given (B.2) and (B.3), the standard rules of first-order logic would allow the derivation of the following:

$Bel(Janine, Father(Jupiter, Cronos))$ (B.4)

But intuition rejects this derivation as invalid: believing that the father of Zeus is Cronos is *not* the same as believing that the father of Jupiter is Cronos.

So what is the problem? Why does first-order logic fail here? The problem is that the intentional notions — such as belief and desire — are *referentially opaque*, in that they set up *opaque contexts*, in which the standard substitution rules of first-order logic do not apply. In classical (propositional or first-order) logic, the denotation, or semantic value, of an expression is dependent solely on the denotations of its sub-expressions. For example, the denotation of the propositional logic formula $p \wedge q$ is a function of the truth-values of p and q. The operators of classical logic are thus said to be *truth functional*.

In contrast, intentional notions such as belief are *not* truth functional. It is surely not the case that the truth value of the sentence:

Janine believes p (B.5)

is dependent solely on the truth-value of p.[1] So substituting equivalents into opaque contexts is not going to preserve meaning. This is what is meant by referential opacity. The existence of referentially opaque contexts has been known since the time of Frege. He suggested a distinction between *sense* and *reference*. In ordinary formulae, the "reference" of a term/formula (i.e., its denotation) is needed, whereas in opaque contexts, the "sense" of a formula is needed (see also [204, p.3]).

Clearly, classical logics are not suitable in their standard form for reasoning about intentional notions: alternative formalisms are required. A vast enterprise has sprung up devoted to developing such formalisms.

The field of formal methods for reasoning about intentional notions is widely reckoned to have begun with the publication, in 1962, of Jaakko Hintikka's book *Knowledge and Belief* [96]. At that time, the subject was considered fairly esoteric, of interest to comparatively few researchers in logic and the philosophy of mind. Since then, however, it has become an important research area in its own right, with contributions from researchers in AI, formal philosophy, linguistics, and economics. There is now an enormous literature on the subject, and with a major biannual international conference devoted solely to theoretical aspects of reasoning about knowledge, as well as the input from numerous other, less specialized conferences, this literature is growing ever larger [54].

Despite the diversity of interests and applications, the number of basic techniques in use is quite small. Recall, from the discussion above, that there are two problems to be addressed in developing a logical formalism for intentional notions: a syntactic one, and a semantic one. It follows that any formalism can be characterized in terms of two independent attributes: its *language of formulation*, and *semantic model* [120, p.83].

---

1 Note, however, that the sentence (B.5) is itself a proposition, in that its denotation is the value "true" or "false."

There are two fundamental approaches to the syntactic problem. The first is to use a *modal* language, which contains non-truth-functional *modal operators*, which are applied to formulae. An alternative approach involves the use of a *meta-language*: a many-sorted first-order language containing terms that denote formulae of some other *object-language*. Intentional notions can be represented using a meta-language predicate, and given whatever axiomatization is deemed appropriate. Both of these approaches have their advantages and disadvantages, and will be discussed at length in what follows.

As with the syntactic problem, there are two basic approaches to the semantic problem. The first, best-known, and probably most widely used approach is to adopt a *possible worlds* semantics, where an agent's beliefs, knowledge, goals, etc. are characterized as a set of so-called *possible worlds*, with an *accessibility relation* holding between them. Possible worlds semantics have an associated *correspondence theory*, which makes them an attractive mathematical tool to work with [31]. However, they also have many associated difficulties, notably the well-known logical omniscience problem, which implies that agents are perfect reasoners. A number of minor variations on the possible worlds theme have been proposed, in an attempt to retain the correspondence theory, but without logical omniscience.

The most common alternative to the possible worlds model for belief is to use a *sentential*, or *interpreted symbolic structures* approach. In this scheme, beliefs are viewed as symbolic formulae explicitly represented in a data structure associated with an agent. An agent then believes φ if φ is present in the agent's belief structure. Despite its simplicity, the sentential model works well under certain circumstances [120].

The next part of this appendix contains detailed reviews of some of these formalisms. First, the idea of possible worlds semantics is discussed, and then a detailed analysis of normal modal logics is presented, along with some variants on the possible worlds theme. Next, some meta-language approaches are discussed, and one hybrid formalism is described. Finally, some alternative formalisms are described.

Before the detailed presentations, a note on terminology. Strictly speaking, an *epistemic logic* is a logic of knowledge, a *doxastic logic* is a logic of belief, and a *conative logic* is a logic of desires or goals. However, it is common practice to use "epistemic" as a blanket term for logics of knowledge and belief. This practice is adopted in this book; a distinction is only made where it is considered significant.

B.2   Possible Worlds Semantics

The possible worlds model for epistemic logics was originally proposed by
Hintikka [96], and is now most commonly formulated in a normal modal logic
using the techniques developed by Kripke [126].[2]

Hintikka's insight was to see that an agent's beliefs could be characterized
in terms of a set of *possible worlds*, in the following way. Consider an agent
playing the card game Gin Rummy.[3] In this game, the more one knows about
the cards possessed by one's opponents, the better one is able to play. And
yet complete knowledge of an opponent's cards is generally impossible if one
excludes cheating. The ability to play Gin Rummy well thus depends, at least
in part, on the ability to deduce what cards are held by an opponent, given
the limited information available. Now suppose our agent possessed the ace of
spades. Assuming the agent's sensory equipment was functioning normally, it
would be rational of her to believe that she possessed this card. Now suppose
she were to try to deduce what cards were held by her opponents. This could
be done by first calculating all the various different ways that the cards in the
pack could possibly have been distributed among the various players. (This
is not being proposed as an actual card-playing strategy, but for illustration!)
For argument's sake, suppose that each possible configuration is described on
a separate piece of paper. Once the process was complete, our agent can then
begin to systematically eliminate from this large pile of paper all those con-
figurations which are *not possible, given what she knows*. For example, any
configuration in which she did not possess the ace of spades could be rejected
immediately as impossible. Call each piece of paper remaining after this process a *world*. Each world represents one state of affairs considered possible,
given what she knows. Hintikka coined the term *epistemic alternatives* to describe the worlds possible given one's beliefs. Something true in *all* our agent's
epistemic alternatives could be said to be believed by the agent. For example,
it will be true in all our agent's epistemic alternatives that she has the ace of
spades.

On a first reading, this technique seems a peculiarly roundabout way
of characterizing belief, but it has two advantages. First, it remains neutral
on the subject of the cognitive structure of agents. It certainly doesn't posit

---

2 In Hintikka's original work, he used a technique based on "model sets," which is equivalent to
Kripke's formalism, though less elegant. See [101, Appendix Five, pp.351–352] for a comparison
and discussion of the two techniques.
3 This example was adapted from [88].

any internalized collection of possible worlds. It is just a convenient way of characterizing belief. Second, the mathematical theory associated with the formalization of possible worlds is extremely appealing (see below).

The next step is to show how possible worlds may be incorporated into the semantic framework of a logic. This is the subject of the next section.

Normal Modal Logics

Epistemic logics are usually formulated as *normal modal logics* using the semantics developed by Kripke [126]. Before moving on to explicitly epistemic logics, this section describes normal modal logics in general.

Modal logics were originally developed by philosophers interested in the distinction between *necessary* truths and mere *contingent* truths. Intuitively, a necessary truth is something that is true *because it could not have been otherwise*, whereas a contingent truth is something that could plausibly have been otherwise. For example, it is a fact that as I write, the Labour Party of Great Britain hold a majority in the House of Commons. But although this is true, it is *not* a necessary truth; it could quite easily have turned out that the Conservative Party won a majority at the last general election. This fact is thus only a *contingent* truth.

Contrast this with the following statement: *the square root of 2 is not a rational number*. There seems no earthly way that this could be anything *but* true, given the standard reading of the sentence. This latter fact is an example of a necessary truth. Necessary truth is usually defined as something true in *all possible worlds*. It is actually quite difficult to think of any necessary truths other than mathematical laws (those with strong religious views may well disagree).

To illustrate the principles of modal epistemic logics, a normal propositional modal logic is defined.

Syntax and Semantics

This logic is essentially classical propositional logic, extended by the addition of two operators: "$\Box$" (necessarily), and "$\Diamond$" (possibly). First, its syntax.

DEFINITION B.1: Let *Prop* = $\{p, q, \ldots\}$ be a countable set of *atomic propositions*. The syntax of normal propositional modal logic is defined by the following rules:

1. If $p \in Prop$ then p is a formula.

2. If φ, ψ are formulae, then so are:

true $\neg\varphi$ $\varphi \vee \psi$

3. If φ is a formula then so are:

$\Box\varphi$ $\Diamond\varphi$

The operators "$\neg$" (not) and "$\vee$" (or) have their standard meaning; true is a logical constant, (sometimes called *verum*), that is always true. The remaining connectives of propositional logic can be defined as abbreviations in the usual way. The formula $\Box\varphi$ is read: "necessarily φ," and the formula $\Diamond\varphi$ is read: "possibly φ." Now to the semantics of the language.

Normal modal logics are concerned with truth at worlds; models for such logics therefore contain a set of worlds, W, and a binary relation, R, on W, saying which worlds are considered possible relative to other worlds. Additionally, a valuation function π is required, saying what propositions are true at each world.

A model for a normal propositional modal logic is a triple $\langle W, R, \pi \rangle$, where W is a non-empty set of worlds, $R \subseteq W \times W$, and

$$\pi : W \rightarrow \wp(Prop)$$

is a valuation function, which says for each world $w \in W$ which atomic propositions are true in w. An alternative, equivalent technique would have been to define π as follows:

$$\pi : W \times Prop \rightarrow \{\text{true, false}\}$$

though the rules defining the semantics of the language would then have to be changed slightly.

The semantics of the language are given via the satisfaction relation, "$\models$," which holds between pairs of the form $\langle M, w \rangle$ (where M is a model, and w is a reference world), and formulae of the language. The semantic rules defining this relation are given in Figure B.1. The definition of satisfaction for atomic propositions thus captures the idea of truth in the "current" world, which appears on the left of "$\models$". The semantic rules for "true," "$\neg$," and "$\vee$" are standard. The rule for "$\Box$" captures the idea of truth in all accessible worlds, and the rule for "$\Diamond$" captures the idea of truth in at least one possible world.

$$\begin{array}{lll}
\langle M, w \rangle & \models & \text{true} \\
\langle M, w \rangle & \models & p \qquad\qquad \text{where } p \in \textit{Prop, iff } p \in \pi(w) \\
\langle M, w \rangle & \models & \neg\varphi \qquad\quad \text{iff } \langle M, w \rangle \not\models \varphi \\
\langle M, w \rangle & \models & \varphi \vee \psi \qquad \text{iff } \langle M, w \rangle \models \varphi \text{ or } \langle M, w \rangle \models \psi \\
\langle M, w \rangle & \models & \Box\varphi \qquad\quad \text{iff } \forall w' \in W \cdot \text{ if } (w, w') \in R \text{ then } \langle M, w' \rangle \models \varphi \\
\langle M, w \rangle & \models & \Diamond\varphi \qquad\quad \text{iff } \exists w' \in W \cdot (w, w') \in R \text{ and } \langle M, w' \rangle \models \varphi
\end{array}$$

Figure B.1
The semantics of normal modal logic.

Note that the two modal operators are *duals* of each other, in the sense that the universal and existential quantifiers of first-order logic are duals:

$$\Box\varphi \Leftrightarrow \neg\Diamond\neg\varphi.$$

It would thus have been possible to take either one as primitive, and introduce the other as a derived operator.

Correspondence Theory

To understand the extraordinary properties of this simple logic, it is first necessary to introduce *validity* and *satisfiability*. A formula is *satisfiable* if it is satisfied for some model/world pair, and *unsatisfiable* otherwise. A formula is *true in a model* if it is satisfied for every world in the model, and *valid in a class of models* if it true in every model in the class. Finally, a formula is valid *simpliciter* if it is true in the class of all models. If φ is valid, we write $\models \varphi$.

The two basic properties of this logic are as follows. First, the following axiom schema is valid.

$$\models \Box(\varphi \Rightarrow \psi) \Rightarrow (\Box\varphi \Rightarrow \Box\psi)$$

This axiom is called K, in honor of Kripke. The second property is as follows.

$$\text{if } \models \varphi \text{ then } \models \Box\varphi$$

Proofs of these properties are trivial, and are left as an exercise for the reader. Now, since K is valid, it will be a theorem of any complete axiomatization of normal modal logic. Similarly, the second property will appear as a rule of inference in any axiomatization of normal modal logic; it is generally called the *necessitation* rule. These two properties turn out to be the most problematic features of normal modal logics when they are used as logics of knowledge/belief (this point will be examined later).

Table B.1
Some correspondence theory.

Axiom Name	Schema	Condition on R	First-Order Characterization
T	$\Box\varphi \Rightarrow \varphi$	reflexive	$\forall w \in W \cdot (w,w) \in R$
D	$\Box\varphi \Rightarrow \Diamond\varphi$	serial	$\forall w \in W \cdot \exists w' \in W \cdot (w,w') \in R$
4	$\Box\varphi \Rightarrow \Box\Box\varphi$	transitive	$\forall w, w', w'' \in W \cdot (w,w') \in R \wedge$ $(w',w'') \in R \Rightarrow (w,w'') \in R$
5	$\Diamond\varphi \Rightarrow \Box\Diamond\varphi$	Euclidean	$\forall w, w', w'' \in W \cdot (w,w') \in R \wedge$ $(w,w'') \in R \Rightarrow (w',w'') \in R$

The most intriguing properties of normal modal logics follow from the properties of the accessibility relation, R, in models. To illustrate these properties, consider the following axiom schema.

$$\Box\varphi \Rightarrow \varphi$$

It turns out that this axiom is *characteristic* of the class of models with a *reflexive* accessibility relation. (By characteristic, we mean that it is true in all and only those models in the class.) There are a host of axioms that correspond to certain properties of R: the study of the way that properties of R correspond to axioms is called *correspondence theory*. In Table B.1, we list some axioms along with their characteristic property on R, and a first-order formula describing the property. Note that the table only lists those axioms of specific interest to this book; see [31] for others. The names of axioms follow historical tradition.

The results of correspondence theory make it straightforward to derive completeness results for a range of simple normal modal logics. These results provide a useful point of comparison for normal modal logics, and account in a large part for the popularity of this style of semantics.

A *system of logic* can be thought of as a set of formulae valid in some class of models; a member of the set is called a *theorem* of the logic (if φ is a theorem, this is usually denoted by $\vdash \varphi$). The notation $K\Sigma_1 \ldots \Sigma_n$ is often used to denote the smallest normal modal logic containing axioms $\Sigma_1, \ldots, \Sigma_n$ (any normal modal logic will contain K; cf. [81, p.25]).

For the axioms T, D, 4, and 5, it would seem that there ought to be sixteen distinct systems of logic (since $2^4 = 16$). However, some of these systems turn out to be equivalent (in that they contain the same theorems), and as a result

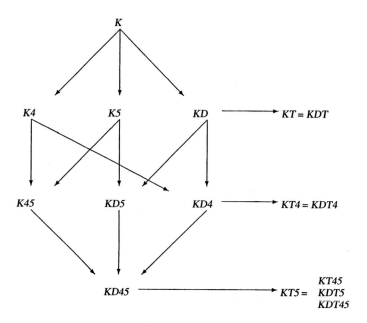

Figure B.2
The normal modal logic systems based on axioms T, D, 4, and 5.

there are only eleven distinct systems. The relationships among these systems are described in Figure B.2 (after [120, p.99], and [31, p.132]). In this diagram, an arc from *A* to *B* means that *B* is a strict superset of *A*: every theorem of *A* is a theorem of *B*, but not *vice versa*; *A* = *B* means that *A* and *B* contain precisely the same theorems.

Because some modal systems are so widely used, they have been given names:

- *KT* is known as T;
- *KT4* is known as S4;
- *KD45* is known as weak-S5; and
- *KT5* is known as S5.

Normal Modal Logics as Epistemic Logics

To use the logic developed above as an epistemic logic, the formula $\Box \varphi$ is read as: "it is known that φ." The worlds in the model are interpreted as epistemic alternatives, the accessibility relation defines what the alternatives are from any given world. The logic deals with the knowledge of a single agent. To deal with multiagent knowledge, one adds to a model structure an indexed set of accessibility relations, one for each agent. A model is then a structure:

$$\langle W, R_1, \ldots, R_n, \pi \rangle$$

where R_i is the knowledge accessibility relation of agent i. The simple language defined above is extended by replacing the single modal operator "$\Box$" by an indexed set of unary modal operators $\{K_i\}$, where $i \in \{1, \ldots, n\}$. The formula $K_i\varphi$ is read: "i knows that φ." The semantic rule for "$\Box$" is replaced by the following rule:

$$\langle M, w \rangle \models K_i\varphi \text{ iff } \forall w' \in W \cdot \text{ if } (w, w') \in R_i \text{ then } \langle M, w' \rangle \models \varphi$$

Each operator K_i thus has exactly the same properties as "$\Box$." Corresponding to each of the modal systems Σ, above, a corresponding system Σ_n is defined, for the multiagent logic. Thus K_n is the smallest multiagent epistemic logic and $S5_n$ is the largest.

The next step is to consider how well normal modal logic serves as a logic of knowledge/belief. Consider first the necessitation rule and axiom K, since any normal modal system is committed to these.

The necessitation rule tells us that an agent knows all valid formulae. Among other things, this means an agent knows all propositional tautologies. Since there are an infinite number of these, an agent will have an infinite number of items of knowledge: immediately, one is faced with a counter-intuitive property of the knowledge operator.

Now consider the axiom K, which says that an agent's knowledge is closed under implication. Suppose φ is a logical consequence of the set $\Delta = \{\varphi_1, \ldots, \varphi_n\}$, then in every world where all of Δ are true, φ must also be true, and hence

$$\varphi_1 \wedge \cdots \wedge \varphi_n \Rightarrow \varphi$$

must be valid. By necessitation, this formula will also be believed. Since an agent's beliefs are closed under implication, whenever it believes each of Δ, it must also believe φ. Hence an agent's knowledge is closed under logical consequence. This also seems counter-intuitive. For example, suppose, like every good logician, our agent knows Peano's axioms. Now Fermat's last theorem follows from Peano's axioms — but it took several hundred years, and an unthinkable amount of hard work before Andrew Wiles was able to prove it. But if our agent's beliefs are closed under logical consequence, then our agent must know it. So consequential closure, implied by necessitation and the K axiom, seems an overstrong property for resource-bounded reasoners.

The Logical Omniscience Problem

These two problems — that of knowing all valid formulae, and that of knowledge/belief being closed under logical consequence — together constitute the famous *logical omniscience* problem. This problem has some damaging corollaries.

The first concerns consistency. Human believers are rarely consistent in the logical sense of the word; they will often have beliefs φ and ψ, where $\varphi \vdash \neg\psi$, without being aware of the implicit inconsistency. However, the ideal reasoners implied by possible worlds semantics cannot have such inconsistent beliefs without believing *every* formula of the logical language (because the consequential closure of an inconsistent set of formulae is the set of all formulae). Konolige has argued that logical consistency is much too strong a property for resource-bounded reasoners: he argues that a lesser property — that of being *non-contradictory* — is the most one can reasonably demand [120]. Non-contradiction means that an agent would not simultaneously believe φ and $\neg\varphi$, although the agent might have logically inconsistent beliefs.

The second corollary is more subtle. Consider the following propositions (this example is from [120, p.88]):

1. Hamlet's favorite color is black.
2. Hamlet's favorite color is black *and* every planar map can be four colored.

The second conjunct of (2) is valid, and will thus be believed. This means that (1) and (2) are logically equivalent; (2) is true just when (1) is. Since agents are ideal reasoners, they will believe that the two propositions are logically equivalent. This is yet another counter-intuitive property implied by possible worlds semantics, as: "equivalent propositions are *not* equivalent as beliefs" [120, p.88]. Yet this is just what possible worlds semantics implies. It has been suggested that propositions are thus too *coarse-grained* to serve as the objects of belief in this way.

The logical omniscience problem is a serious one. In the words of Levesque:

Any one of these [problems] might cause one to reject a possible-world formalization as unintuitive at best and completely unrealistic at worst. [132]

Axioms for Knowledge and Belief

We now consider the appropriateness of the axioms D_n, T_n, 4_n, and 5_n for logics of knowledge/belief.

The axiom D_n says that an agent's beliefs are non-contradictory; it can be rewritten in the following form:

$$K_i\varphi \Rightarrow \neg K_i \neg \varphi$$

which is read: "if i knows φ, then i doesn't know $\neg\varphi$." This axiom seems a reasonable property of both knowledge and belief.

The axiom T_n is often called the *knowledge* axiom, since it says that what is known is true. It is usually accepted as the axiom that distinguishes knowledge from belief: it seems reasonable that one could believe something that is false, but one would hesitate to say that one could *know* something false. Knowledge is thus often defined as true belief: i knows φ if i believes φ and φ is true. So defined, knowledge satisfies T_n.

Axiom 4_n is called the *positive introspection axiom*. Introspection is the process of examining one's own beliefs, and is discussed in detail in [120, Chapter 5]. The positive introspection axiom says that an agent knows what it knows. Similarly, axiom 5_n is the *negative introspection axiom*, which says that an agent is aware of what it doesn't know. Positive and negative introspection together imply an agent has perfect knowledge about what it does and doesn't know (cf. [120, Equation (5.11), p.79]). Whether or not the two types of introspection are appropriate properties for knowledge/belief is the subject of some debate. However, it is generally accepted that positive introspection is a less demanding property than negative introspection, and is thus a more reasonable property for resource-bounded reasoners.

Given the comments above, the modal system $S5_n$ is often chosen as a logic of *knowledge*, and weak-$S5_n$ is often chosen as a logic of *belief.*

Computational Aspects

Before leaving this basic logic, it is worth commenting on its computational/proof theoretic properties. Halpern and Moses have established the following ([90]):

1. The satisfiability problem for each of the key systems K_n, T_n, $S4_n$, weak-$S5_n$, and $S5_n$ *is* decidable.

2. The satisfiability and validity problems for K_n, T_n, $S4_n$ (where $n \geq 1$), and $S5_n$, weak-$S5_n$ (where $n \geq 2$) are PSPACE complete.

The first result is encouraging, as it holds out at least some hope of automation. Unfortunately, the second result is extremely discouraging: in simple terms, it means that in the worst case, automation of these logics is not a practical proposition.

Discussion

To sum up, the basic possible worlds approach described above has the following disadvantages as a multiagent epistemic logic:

- agents believe all valid formulae;
- agents' beliefs are closed under logical consequence;
- equivalent propositions are identical beliefs;
- if agents are inconsistent, then they believe everything;
- in the worst case, automation is not feasible.

To which many people would add the following:

The ontology of possible worlds and accessibility relations ... is frankly mysterious to most practically minded people, and in particular has nothing to say about agent architecture. [204]

Despite these serious disadvantages, possible worlds are still the semantics of choice for many researchers, and a number of variations on the basic possible worlds theme have been proposed to get around some of the difficulties.

Quantified Epistemic Logics

A natural extension to the basic logic described above would be to allow quantification. In this section, we proceed (as with the propositional modal logic described above) to define a quantified modal logic and then examine its suitability as a logic for reasoning about knowledge/belief. The discussion below is adapted and expanded from [101, Part Two], [192], and [120].

The syntax of quantified modal logic is that of classical first-order logic enriched by the addition of the unary modal operators "$\Diamond$" and "$\Box$," with the same meanings as above. These operators can be applied to arbitrary formulae of the modal or first-order language. So, for example, the following are syntactically acceptable formulae of quantified modal logic:

$$\forall x \cdot \Box P(x) \Rightarrow Q(x)$$
$$P(a) \land \Box \exists x \cdot P(x)$$

It is assumed that constants of the basic first-order language belong to a set *Const*, variables to a set *Var*, and predicate symbols to a set *Pred*. A model for quantified modal logic is a structure:

$$\langle W, R, D, I, \pi \rangle$$

where W and R are a set of worlds and a binary relation on W (as before), and:

- D is a non-empty set, called the *domain*;
- I maps *Const* to D;
- π maps *Pred* $\times$ W to $\wp(D^n)$, where n is the arity of the predicate symbol, and D^n is the set of n-tuples over D; the function π gives the extension of each predicate symbol in each world.

As usual with a predicate logic, formulae can only be interpreted with respect to a variable assignment: a variable assignment V maps *Var* to D. A *term* is either a variable or a constant. It is useful to define a function $[\![\ldots]\!]_{I,V}$, which takes an arbitrary term and returns its denotation relative to I, V:

$$[\![\tau]\!]_{I,V} \hat{=} \begin{cases} I(\tau) & \text{if } \tau \in Const \\ V(\tau) & \text{otherwise.} \end{cases}$$

Reference to I and V is suppressed where these are understood.

The only semantic rule of interest is that for predicates; the remainder are essentially unchanged, except that a formula must now be interpreted with respect to a variable assignment.

$$\langle M, V, w \rangle \models P(\tau_1, \ldots, \tau_n) \text{ iff } \langle [\![\tau_1]\!], \ldots, [\![\tau_n]\!] \rangle \in \pi(P, w)$$

So, despite the added complexity of predicates and terms, the model theory for quantified modal logics remains straightforward.

Now consider such a system as an epistemic logic. The semantics can easily be extended to the multiagent case, as in propositional modal logic, by the addition of multiple accessibility relations, etc. One unfortunate property of quantified modal logics, as defined above, is that they make the *Barcan formulae* valid. The Barcan formula is:

$$\forall x \cdot \Box \varphi(x) \Rightarrow \Box \forall x \cdot \varphi(x)$$

The converse Barcan formula is the reverse implication:

$$\Box \forall x \cdot \varphi(x) \Rightarrow \forall x \cdot \Box \varphi(x)$$

(see e.g., [101, pp.142–145] for a discussion).

If "$\Box$" is interpreted as "it is known that ...," then the Barcan formula means that if it is known of all individuals independently that they have property φ, then it is known that all individuals have this property. The Barcan formula thus implies that knowers are somehow aware of the existence of all individuals, which seems to be an overstrong demand to make of resource-bounded reasoners.

The converse Barcan formula says that if an agent knows that all individuals have property φ, then it will be known that each individual has property φ. In other words, it implies that agents will perform universal instantiation wherever possible. This is a weaker property than that implied by the Barcan formula, but still seems an overstrong demand to make of resource-bounded reasoners.

If one refers back to model structures for quantified modal logics for a moment, it will be found that the domain of individuals D is fixed, for all worlds: this is called the *constant domain assumption*. If this assumption is dropped, so that the domain is indexed by worlds, and quantification is restricted to just those individuals in the domain of the reference world, then the Barcan formulae are no longer valid. As to whether this is a reasonable property for an epistemic logic, consider a semi-mythological figure such as Robin Hood, or King Arthur. An agent might reasonably be unsure as to whether these individuals ever actually existed, and so they might appear in the domain of some epistemic alternatives, but not all.

It is also worth noting that in the model structure above, constants were given a *rigid* interpretation: a constant has the same denotation in all worlds. What would it mean for this assumption to be dropped, and what would be the effect? It would be possible to drop the assumption by simply making I a map from *Const* $\times$ W to D. Consider the following formula, which is intended to express the fact that an agent believes of the individual that is Prime Minister of Britain in the actual world — the world as perceived by the author at the time of writing — that he is a cricket fan.

$$\Box CricketFan(PM)$$

Here, *PM* is a constant which in the actual world denotes the individual Tony

Blair (Prime Minister of the U.K. at the time of writing). But suppose our agent had been on a desert island since November 1990, and was somehow unaware that Margaret Thatcher was no longer Prime Minister. For this agent, the constant *PM* would denote someone entirely different to that which it denotes for us, and it is unlikely that a rational agent would believe of the individual Margaret Thatcher that she was a cricket fan. Note that the agent could still believe that the individual Tony Blair was a cricket fan, but in its ignorance, it would use a different constant for this individual. The point is that the constant *PM* has a different denotation for us and the agent, and, more generally, a different denotation in different worlds. Such constants are said to be *fluent* expressions; non-fluent expressions are called *rigid designators*.

To deal with fluent expressions, Konolige has proposed the technical device of the *bullet operator*, ("•"). Suppose a is a constant, then •a is an expression returning a constant that always denotes what a denotes for us. The use of the bullet operator is somewhat complex, and is described in detail in [120, pp.38–42 and pp.100–104].

One difficult issue in the philosophy of modal logics is *quantifying-in* to modal contexts. Consider the following English sentence:

It is known that there is a unicorn.   (B.6)

Now consider the following quantified modal logic formulae, each representing one attempt to formalize (B.6):

$$\exists x \cdot \Box Unicorn(x) \qquad\qquad\qquad (B.7)$$
$$\Box \exists x \cdot Unicorn(x) \qquad\qquad\qquad (B.8)$$

In (B.7), a *de re* reading of (B.6) is presented. The formula implies the existence of some particular individual, which the believer has a name for, which the agent believes has the property of being a unicorn. Note that *we* do not know who this individual is, or have a name for it; we simply represent the fact that the agent does.

In (B.8), a *de dicto* reading of (B.6) is presented. This reading expresses a weaker property than (B.7): namely, that the agent believes *some* individual is a unicorn. The agent does not necessarily have a name for the individual. Formulae (B.7) and (B.8) thus express quite different properties.

Meta-Languages and Syntactic Modalities

There is a school of thought — almost a cult — in mathematics, computer science, and AI, which holds that classical first-order logic is in some sense "canonical": that anything which can be done in a non-classical (e.g., modal) logic can be reduced to a problem in first-order logic. In the area of reasoning about intentional notions, this thinking manifests itself in the use of first-order meta-languages to represent and reason about beliefs, goals, etc.

The basic idea of a meta-language is quite simple. Recall the naive attempt to formalize the statement "Janine believes Cronos is the father of Zeus" presented earlier:

$$Bel(Janine, Father(Zeus, Cronos)) \qquad (B.9)$$

The syntactic problem with this formalization is that $Father(Zeus, Cronos)$ is a formula of first-order logic, not a term, so the whole formula is ill-formed. Now suppose the domain of the first-order language (hereafter called the meta-language) contains formulae of another language (hereafter called the object-language). Suppose also that the meta-language contains terms which denote object-language formulae. Then it would be possible to write a meta-language formula capturing the sense of (B.9).

To make meta-language formulae readable, it is useful to employ a *quoting convention*. Suppose that φ is an object-language formula, then it is usual to let $\ulcorner \varphi \urcorner$ be an abbreviation for a meta-language term standing for φ. A formulation of the above sentence might then be:

$$Bel(Janine, \ulcorner Father(Zeus, Cronos) \urcorner) \qquad (B.10)$$

Since $\ulcorner Father(Zeus, Cronos) \urcorner$ is a meta-language term, (B.10) is a syntactically acceptable formula of the meta-language. Using this approach, belief, knowledge, etc. can be axiomatized using the first-order meta-language and given whatever properties are deemed appropriate. One obvious difficulty seems to be that it is not possible to quantify over object-language terms. This difficulty can be overcome by using an *un-quoting convention*: see [73, pp.241–242] for a discussion of this point.

The quote marks, $\ulcorner \ldots \urcorner$, are sometimes called *Frege quotes*, or *sense quotes*. The process of making formulae into objects in a meta-language domain is sometimes called *arithmetization*, after Gödel, who used a meta-language technique in his proof of the incompleteness of arithmetic; the names given to object-language formulae are sometimes called Gödel numbers.

It is often claimed that meta-language approaches enjoy the following advantages over modal languages:

1. *Expressive power.*
The following meta-language formulae have no quantified modal logic counterparts:

$\exists x \cdot Bel(i, x)$ "*i* believes something"

$\forall x \cdot Bel(i, x) \Rightarrow Bel(j, x)$ "*i* believes everything *j* believes"

2. *Computational tractability.*
Meta-languages are just many-sorted first-order languages, for which automated theorem provers exist. It should therefore be possible — in principle at least — to use existing theorem provers for meta-languages. However, this claim has yet to be satisfactorily demonstrated.

The key difficulty with meta-language approaches is that many naive attempts to treat meta-language predicates as *syntactic modalities* run into inconsistency. These difficulties arise, for the large part, from the issue of *self reference.*[4]

Suppose one wished to use a meta-language approach to represent and reason about knowledge and belief. Following "standard" practice, knowledge may be defined as true belief. One might begin by setting object-language = meta-language, so that the object- and meta-language are the same; in such circumstances, the meta-language is said to be *self-referential*, since it may contain terms that refer to its own formulae. A *truth predicate* can then be defined.

$$True(\ulcorner \varphi \urcorner) \Leftrightarrow \varphi \tag{B.11}$$

Knowledge may then be defined as a composite concept.

$$Know(\ulcorner \varphi \urcorner) \Leftrightarrow Bel(\ulcorner \varphi \urcorner) \wedge True(\ulcorner \varphi \urcorner) \tag{B.12}$$

The *Bel* predicate can then be given whatever axiomatization is deemed appropriate. This approach seems simple, intuitive, and satisfactory. Unfortunately, in general, any first-order meta-language theory containing axiom (B.11) turns out to be inconsistent. This problem was first recognized by Tarski; the difficulty is with the possibility of formulae asserting their own falsity (as in the famous "liar" paradox).

---

4 A good discussion of these issues may be found in [173]; the issue of self reference is examined in detail in [171] and [172].

Several proposals have been put forward to remedy the problem. One possibility is to define *True* and *False* predicates, such that for some formulae φ, neither $True(\ulcorner\varphi\urcorner)$ nor $False(\ulcorner\varphi\urcorner)$ hold; in effect, one axiomatizes a system in which the law of the excluded middle does not hold. This solution is unintuitive, however, and seems rather *ad hoc*.

Another solution, due to Perlis [171], is to replace (B.11) with an axiom of the form:

$$True(\ulcorner\varphi\urcorner) \Leftrightarrow \varphi^* \tag{B.13}$$

where φ^* is the formula obtained from φ by replacing every occurrence of $\neg True(\ulcorner\psi\urcorner)$ in φ by $True(\ulcorner\neg\psi\urcorner)$. This simple expedient prevents inconsistency (see [171, pp.312–315] for proof). This proposal has been criticized by Konolige, on a number of grounds, however: see [120, p.116] for details.

A problem not alleviated by Perlis' schema was first recognized by Montague [155]. Consider the following axiom:

$$Bel(\ulcorner\varphi\urcorner) \Rightarrow \varphi$$

and the following inference rule:

From $\vdash \varphi$ infer $\vdash Bel(\ulcorner\varphi\urcorner)$

(cf. the modal system *KT*). Montague showed that any moderately sophisticated first-order theory (and in particular, basic arithmetic) containing the above axiom and inference rule is inconsistent. This result appears to be devastating, and for a long time dampened down research into first-order meta-languages. A similar result by Thomason ([229]) is also discouraging.

However, des Rivieres and Levesque have recently shown that, while Montague's results are technically correct, a careful reworking, with slightly different assumptions, leads back to consistency [45].[5] Also, Perlis has shown how a similar technique to that proposed by him for recovering from Tarski's result can be used to recover from Montague's results [172].

If nothing else, the above discussion illustrates that the whole issue of self-referential languages is a difficult one. It is hardly surprising, therefore, that some researchers have rejected self reference entirely. One critic is Konolige, who suggests that an observer of a system of agents can hardly have any use for a self-referential language. He argues that the logical puzzles caused by

---

5 In fact, they showed that it was a naive translation from a modal to meta-language that was causing difficulties.

self-reference are just that: puzzles, which an agent will never usually need to consider (unless she is a philosophy or logic student) [120, p.115].

One "standard" alternative to self-referential languages is to use an *hierarchical* language structure. Consider a "tower" of languages:

$$L_0 - L_1 - L_2 - \cdots - L_k - \cdots$$

Let language L_0 be a non-self-referential "base" language; standard first-order logic, for example. Then let each of the languages L_k, where $k > 0$, be a meta-language containing terms referring only to formulae of languages lower down in the hierarchy. Thus no language in the hierarchy is self-referential. It is possible to write formulae such as (B.10) in any of the languages L_k, where $k > 0$, but the paradoxes of self-reference will not arise.

The hierarchical approach has problems of its own, however. Consider the following scenario, adapted from [231]. There are two agents, A and B, each with equal expressive powers of belief: anything A can believe, B can believe, and *vice versa*. Consider the following statement.

A believes that everything B believes is true.   (B.14)

How might this statement be represented, using the hierarchical approach? It obviously cannot be represented in L_0. One obvious solution is to write:

$Bel(A, ^\ulcorner \forall x \cdot Bel(B, x) \Rightarrow True(x)^\urcorner)$.

Suppose that the inner *Bel* predicate belongs to language L_k, where $k > 0$. The variable x in this formula ranges over all formulae of languages L_j, where $j < k$. It does *not*, therefore, range over the language of B's beliefs, but over some language lower in the hierarchy. Moving to a language farther up the hierarchy does not solve the problem:

No matter how far we climb up the object/meta-language hierarchy, we will not be able to capture the intuitive content of [(B.14)]. [231, pp.7–8]

Other objections to the hierarchical approach have been raised. For example, Morgenstern points out that the truth predicate paradox is only resolved by positing an infinite number of truth predicates, one for each language in the hierarchy. She argues that this is not a satisfactory solution, for two reasons:

In the first place, it is implausible that people are consciously aware of using different truth predicates when they speak. Secondly, we often do not know which truth predicate to use when we utter a particular statement. Finally, it is impossible ... to construct a pair of sentences, each of which refers to the other, although such sentences may make perfect sense. [160, p.104]

So both self-referential and hierarchical languages have their difficulties. One problem common to both is that meta-languages are, in general, notationally cumbersome, unintuitive, and complex: see [120, p.111] for a discussion of this point. However, the difficulties described above have not prevented the development of some ingenious and useful meta-language formulations of intentional notions. Examples include [119, 41].

B.3 Temporal Logics

There seem to be almost as many different temporal logics as there are people using temporal logics to reason about programs. In this section, we briefly describe some important developments in temporal logics.

The earliest temporal logic studied in detail was the modal logic K_t, corresponding to a modal system with two basic modal operators (often written "[P]" or "H" — "heretofore," or "always past," and "[F]" or "G" — "henceforth," or "always") [182]. The semantics of these operators are given via two ordering relations R_P and R_F on the set of worlds, such that the two relations are the inverse of each other. The usual "was" and "sometime" operators (written "$\langle P \rangle$" or "P" and "$\langle F \rangle$" or "F") are defined as the duals of these operators. This logic is discussed at length in [81, Chapter 6].

Although such a system *can* be used to crudely reason about programs, it cannot describe the "fine structure" of the state sequences generated by executing programs (see below). For this reason, a "next time" operator was used by Pnueli in his original proposal [176]. Also, the standard heretofore/always combination of operators was discovered to be inadequate for expressing many properties, and so the basic temporal logic was augmented by the *since* and *until* operators (written "S" and "U"). In his 1968 doctoral thesis, Kamp demonstrated that the logic with since and until operators was *expressively complete* over continuous linear orders [115].[6]

The "standard" linear discrete temporal logic is based on until/since and next/last [144, 145]. In the propositional case, this logic is decidable (though the problem is PSPACE complete — see [219]), and is generally regarded as expressive enough to capture many interesting properties of reactive systems. Gough has developed tableaux-based decision procedures for this logic [82]; Fisher has developed resolution methods [62].

---

6 The since/until operators are assumed to be *strict*: the since operator refers strictly to the past, the until operator refers strictly to the future.

In the first-order case, temporal logics containing these operators are not decidable, but this should come as no surprise! Perhaps more worrying is that first-order temporal logic is not finitely axiomatizable [1].

A temporal logic based solely on these operators does have its limitations, however. Sistla et al. showed that it could not be used to describe an unbounded FIFO buffer [221].

Many variations on this basic temporal logic theme exist. For example, the use of *fixpoint* operators has been discussed. Banieqbal and Barringer describe a logic that keeps the next operator as basic, but then defines two fixpoint operators from which the other standard operators of linear discrete temporal logic can be derived [7]. Wolper has described a logic ETL, which extends the standard temporal logic with a set of *grammar operators* [235]. Yet another variation is to add a *chop* operator, C, which "composes" two finite sequences [9].

All of the logics mentioned above have assumed the model of time is *discrete* (i.e., that for any time point, there exists a time such that no other time point occurs between them) and *linear* (i.e., that each point in time has at most one successor). But these assumptions are not essential: a temporal logic of reals (where the worlds are isomorphic with the real numbers) has been developed; however, such logics are complex and uncommon.

Much more common are *branching time* logics. Briefly, a branching time structure is one where each time point may have a number of "successor" times, each one intuitively corresponding to one way things *could* turn out. The repertoire of operators in linear temporal logic is not sufficient to express all the properties of such structures (despite Lamport's claims in his famous 1980 paper [129]).

The earliest branching time logic to be studied at length was UB (unified system of branching time) [12]. This logic extended linear time temporal logic by the addition of two operators, "A" ("on all paths ...") and "E" ("on some path ..."), called *path quantifiers*, which could be prefixed to any formula containing at most one occurrence of the usual linear time temporal operators. This introduces an obvious restriction on the expressibility of UB.

UB does not contain an "until" operator; this omission was rectified in a logic CTL (computation tree logic). However, CTL is still not expressive enough to capture many interesting properties of branching time structures. The most expressive branching time logic so far studied in any detail is called CTL* [50]. This logic allows path quantifiers to be prefixed to arbitrary formulae of the language: intermixing of path quantifiers and standard temporal logic operators is freely allowed, resulting in a highly expressive logic. In the propositional case, all of these branching time logics are known to be decidable. A good general review of branching time logics is provided in [51]. CTL* forms the basis of $\mathcal{LORA}$, the logic used in the main text of this book.

References

[1] M. Abadi. *Temporal Logic Theorem Proving*. PhD thesis, Computer Science Department, Stanford University, Stanford, CA 94305, 1987.

[2] J. F. Allen, J. Hendler, and A. Tate, editors. *Readings in Planning*. Morgan Kaufmann Publishers: San Mateo, CA, 1990.

[3] D. E. Appelt. Planning natural language utterances. In *Proceedings of the Second National Conference on Artificial Intelligence (AAAI-82)*, pages 59–62, Pittsburgh, PA, 1982.

[4] D. E. Appelt. *Planning English Sentences*. Cambridge University Press: Cambridge, England, 1985.

[5] D. E. Appelt and K. Konolige. A nonmonotonic logic for reasoning about speech acts and belief revision. In M. Reinfrank, J. de Kleer, M. L. Ginsberg, and E. Sandewall, editors, *Non-Monotonic Reasoning — Proceedings of the Second International Workshop (LNAI Volume 346)*, pages 164–175. Springer-Verlag: Berlin, Germany, 1988.

[6] J. L. Austin. *How to Do Things With Words*. Oxford University Press: Oxford, England, 1962.

[7] B. Banieqbal and H. Barringer. A study of an extended temporal language and a temporal fixed point calculus. Technical Report UMCS–86–10–2, Department of Computer Science, Manchester University, Oxford Rd., Manchester M13 9PL, UK, 1986.

[8] H. Barringer, M. Fisher, D. Gabbay, G. Gough, and R. Owens. METATEM: A framework for programming in temporal logic. In *REX Workshop on Stepwise Refinement of Distributed Systems: Models, Formalisms, Correctness (LNCS Volume 430)*, pages 94–129. Springer-Verlag: Berlin, Germany, June 1989.

[9] H. Barringer, R. Kuiper, and A. Pnueli. Now you may compose temporal logic specifications. In *Proceedings of the Sixteenth ACM Symposium on the Theory of Computing*, pages 51–63, 1984.

[10] H. Barringer, R. Kuiper, and A. Pnueli. A really abstract concurrent model and its temporal logic. In *Proceedings of the Thirteenth ACM Symposium on the Principles of Programming Languages*, pages 173–183, 1986.

[11] M. Ben-Ari. *Principles of Concurrent and Distributed Programming*. Prentice Hall, 1990.

[12] M. Ben-Ari, Z. Manna, and A. Pnueli. The temporal logic of branching time. In *Proceedings of the Eighth ACM Symposium on the Principles of Programming Languages (POPL)*, pages 164–176, 1981.

[13] M. Benerecetti, F. Giunchiglia, and L. Serafini. A model checking algorithm for multiagent systems. In J. P. Müller, M. P. Singh, and A. S. Rao, editors, *Intelligent Agents V (LNAI Volume 1555)*. Springer-Verlag: Berlin, Germany, 1999.

[14] K. Binmore. *Fun and Games: A Text on Game Theory*. D. C. Heath and Company: Lexington, MA, 1992.

[15] L. Birnbaum. Rigor mortis. In D. Kirsh, editor, *Foundations of Artificial Intelligence*, pages 57–78. The MIT Press: Cambridge, MA, 1992.

[16] J. Blythe. An overview of planning under uncertainty. In M. Wooldridge and M. Veloso, editors, *Artificial Intelligence Today (LNAI 1600)*, pages 85–110. Springer-Verlag: Berlin, Germany, 1999.

[17] R. P. Bonasso, D. Kortenkamp, D. P. Miller, and M. Slack. Experiences with an architecture for intelligent, reactive agents. In M. Wooldridge, J. P. Müller, and M. Tambe, editors, *Intelligent Agents II (LNAI Volume 1037)*, pages 187–202. Springer-Verlag: Berlin, Germany, 1996.

[18] A. H. Bond and L. Gasser, editors. *Readings in Distributed Artificial Intelligence*. Morgan Kaufmann Publishers: San Mateo, CA, 1988.

[19] G. Booch. *Object-Oriented Analysis and Design (second edition)*. Addison-Wesley: Reading, MA, 1994.

[20] M. E. Bratman. *Intention, Plans, and Practical Reason*. Harvard University Press: Cambridge, MA, 1987.

[21] M. E. Bratman. What is intention? In P. R. Cohen, J. L. Morgan, and M. E. Pollack, editors, *Intentions in Communication*, pages 15–32. The MIT Press: Cambridge, MA, 1990.

[22] M. E. Bratman, D. J. Israel, and M. E. Pollack. Plans and resource-bounded practical reasoning. *Computational Intelligence*, 4:349–355, 1988.

[23] P. Bretier and D. Sadek. A rational agent as the kernel of a cooperative spoken dialogue system: Implementing a logical theory of interaction. In J. P. Müller, M. Wooldridge, and N. R. Jennings, editors, *Intelligent Agents III (LNAI Volume 1193)*, pages 189–204. Springer-Verlag: Berlin, Germany, 1997.

[24] R. A. Brooks. *Cambrian Intelligence*. The MIT Press: Cambridge, MA, 1999.

[25] M. A. Brown. On the logic of ability. *Journal of Philosophical Logic*, 17:1–26, 1988.

[26] P. Busetta, N. Howden, R. Ronnquist, and A. Hodgson. Structuring BDI agents in functional clusters. In N.R. Jennings and Y. Lespérance, editors, *Intelligent Agents VI — Proceedings of the Sixth International Workshop on Agent Theories, Architectures, and Languages (ATAL-99)*, Lecture Notes in Artificial Intelligence, pages 277–289. Springer-Verlag, Berlin, 2000.

[27] C. Castelfranchi. Social power. In Y. Demazeau and J.-P. Müller, editors, *Decentralized AI — Proceedings of the First European Workshop on Modelling Autonomous Agents in a Multi-Agent World (MAAMAW-89)*, pages 49–62. Elsevier Science Publishers B.V.: Amsterdam, The Netherlands, 1990.

[28] C. Castelfranchi. Guarantees for autonomy in cognitive agent architecture. In M. Wooldridge and N. R. Jennings, editors, *Intelligent Agents: Theories, Architectures, and Languages (LNAI Volume 890)*, pages 56–70. Springer-Verlag: Berlin, Germany, January 1995.

[29] L. Catach. Normal multimodal logics. In *Proceedings of the Seventh National Conference on Artificial Intelligence (AAAI-88)*, pages 491–495, St. Paul, MN, 1988.

[30] L. Catach. TABLEAUX: A general theorem prover for modal logics. *Journal of Automated Reasoning*, 7:489–510, 1991.

[31] B. Chellas. *Modal Logic: An Introduction*. Cambridge University Press: Cambridge, England, 1980.

[32] E. M. Clarke and E. A. Emerson. Design and synthesis of synchronization skeletons using branching time temporal logic. In D. Kozen, editor, *Logics of Programs — Proceedings 1981 (LNCS Volume 131)*, pages 52–71. Springer-Verlag: Berlin, Germany, 1981.

[33] E. M. Clarke, O. Grumberg, and D. A. Peled. *Model Checking*. The MIT Press: Cambridge, MA, 2000.

[34] W. F. Clocksin and C. S. Mellish. *Programming in Prolog*. Springer-Verlag: Berlin, Germany, 1981.

[35] P. R. Cohen and H. J. Levesque. Intention is choice with commitment. *Artificial Intelligence*, 42:213–261, 1990.

[36] P. R. Cohen and H. J. Levesque. Rational interaction as the basis for communication. In P. R. Cohen, J. Morgan, and M. E. Pollack, editors, *Intentions in Communication*, pages 221–256. The MIT Press: Cambridge, MA, 1990.

[37] P. R. Cohen and H. J. Levesque. Teamwork. *Nous*, 25(4):487–512, 1991.

[38] P. R. Cohen and H. J. Levesque. Communicative actions for artificial agents. In *Proceedings of the First International Conference on Multi-Agent Systems (ICMAS-95)*, pages 65–72, San Francisco, CA, June 1995.

[39] P. R. Cohen and C. R. Perrault. Elements of a plan based theory of speech acts. *Cognitive Science*, 3:177–212, 1979.

[40] D. Connah and P. Wavish. An experiment in cooperation. In Y. Demazeau and J.-P. Müller, editors, *Decentralized AI — Proceedings of the First European Workshop on Modelling Autonomous Agents in a Multi-Agent World (MAAMAW-89)*, pages 197–214. Elsevier Science Publishers B.V.: Amsterdam, The Netherlands, 1990.

[41] N. J. Davies. A first-order theory of truth, knowledge and belief. In *Logics in AI — Proceedings of the European Workshop JELIA-90 (LNAI Volume 478)*, pages 170–179. Springer-Verlag: Berlin, Germany, 1991.

[42] D. C. Dennett. *Brainstorms*. The MIT Press: Cambridge, MA, 1978.

[43] D. C. Dennett. *The Intentional Stance*. The MIT Press: Cambridge, MA, 1987.

[44] D. C. Dennett. *Kinds of Minds*. London: Phoenix, 1996.

[45] J. des Rivieres and H. J. Levesque. The consistency of syntactical treatments of knowledge. In J. Y. Halpern, editor, *Proceedings of the 1986 Conference on Theoretical Aspects of Reasoning About Knowledge*, pages 115–130. Morgan Kaufmann Publishers: San Mateo, CA, 1986.

[46] M. d'Inverno, D. Kinny, M. Luck, and M. Wooldridge. A formal specification of dMARS. In M. P. Singh, A. Rao, and M. J. Wooldridge, editors, *Intelligent Agents IV (LNAI Volume 1365)*, pages 155–176. Springer-Verlag: Berlin, Germany, 1997.

[47] C. Dixon, M. Fisher, and M. Wooldridge. Resolution for temporal logics of knowledge. *Journal of Logic and Computation*, 8(3):345–372, 1998.

[48] C. Eliasmith. Dictionary of the philosophy of mind. Online at http://www.artsci.wustl.edu/~philos/MindDict/, 1999.

[49] E. A. Emerson. Temporal and modal logic. In J. van Leeuwen, editor, *Handbook of Theoretical Computer Science Volume B: Formal Models and Semantics*, pages 996–1072. Elsevier Science Publishers B.V.: Amsterdam, The Netherlands, 1990.

[50] E. A. Emerson and J. Y. Halpern. 'Sometimes' and 'not never' revisited: on branching time versus linear time temporal logic. *Journal of the ACM*, 33(1):151–178, 1986.

[51] E. A. Emerson and J. Srinivasan. Branching time logic. In J. W. de Bakker, W.-P. de Roever, and G. Rozenberg, editors, *REX School-Workshop on Linear Time, Branching Time and Parial Order in Logics and Models for Concurrency (LNCS Volume 354)*, pages 123–172. Springer-Verlag: Berlin, Germany, 1988.

[52] H. B. Enderton. *A Mathematical Introduction to Logic*. The Academic Press: London, England, 1972.

[53] O. Etzioni. Intelligence without robots. *AI Magazine*, 14(4), December 1993.

[54] R. Fagin, J. Y. Halpern, Y. Moses, and M. Y. Vardi. *Reasoning About Knowledge*. The MIT Press: Cambridge, MA, 1995.

[55] R. Fagin, J. Y. Halpern, Y. Moses, and M. Y. Vardi. Knowledge-based programs. *Distributed Computing*, 10(4):199–225, 1997.

[56] J. Ferber. *Multi-Agent Systems*. Addison-Wesley: Reading, MA, 1999.

[57] I. A. Ferguson. Towards an architecture for adaptive, rational, mobile agents. In E. Werner and Y. Demazeau, editors, *Decentralized AI 3 — Proceedings of the Third European Workshop on Modelling Autonomous Agents in a Multi-Agent World (MAAMAW-91)*, pages 249–262. Elsevier Science Publishers B.V.: Amsterdam, The Netherlands, 1992.

[58] I. A. Ferguson. Integrated control and coordinated behaviour: A case for agent models. In M. Wooldridge and N. R. Jennings, editors, *Intelligent Agents: Theories, Architectures, and Languages (LNAI Volume 890)*, pages 203–218. Springer-Verlag: Berlin, Germany, January 1995.

[59] R. E. Fikes and N. Nilsson. STRIPS: A new approach to the application of theorem proving to problem solving. *Artificial Intelligence*, 5(2):189–208, 1971.

[60] FIPA. Specification part 2 — Agent communication language, 1999. The text refers to the specification dated 16 April 1999.

[61] K. Fischer, J. P. Müller, and M. Pischel. A pragmatic BDI architecture. In M. Wooldridge, J. P. Müller, and M. Tambe, editors, *Intelligent Agents II (LNAI Volume 1037)*, pages 203–218. Springer-Verlag: Berlin, Germany, 1996.

[62] M. Fisher. A resolution method for temporal logic. In *Proceedings of the Twelfth International Joint Conference on Artificial Intelligence (IJCAI-91)*, Sydney, Australia, August 1991.

[63] M. Fisher. A survey of Concurrent METATEM — the language and its applications. In D. M. Gabbay and H. J. Ohlbach, editors, *Temporal Logic — Proceedings of the First International Conference (LNAI Volume 827)*, pages 480–505. Springer-Verlag: Berlin, Germany, July 1994.

[64] M. Fisher. An introduction to executable temporal logic. *The Knowledge Engineering Review*, 11(1):43–56, 1996.

[65] M. Fisher and M. Wooldridge. Executable temporal logic for distributed A.I. In *Proceedings of the Twelfth International Workshop on Distributed Artificial Intelligence (IWDAI-93)*, pages 131–142, Hidden Valley, PA, May 1993.

[66] M. Fitting. *Proof Methods for Modal and Intuitionistic Logics*. D. Reidel Publishing Company: Dordrecht, The Netherlands, 1983. (Synthese library volume 169).

[67] The Foundation for Intelligent Physical Agents. See http://www.fipa.org/.

[68] J. R. Galliers. *A Theoretical Framework for Computer Models of Cooperative Dialogue, Acknowledging Multi-Agent Conflict*. PhD thesis, Open University, UK, 1988.

[69] J. R. Galliers. Cooperative interaction as strategic belief revision. In S. M. Deen, editor, *CKBS-90 — Proceedings of the International Working Conference on Cooperating Knowledge Based Systems*, pages 148–163. Springer-Verlag: Berlin, Germany, 1991.

[70] A. Galton. Temporal logic and computer science: An overview. In A. Galton, editor, *Temporal Logics and their Applications*, pages 1–52. The Academic Press: London, England, 1987.

[71] P. Gärdenfors. *Knowledge in Flux*. The MIT Press: Cambridge, MA, 1988.

[72] C. Geissler and K. Konolige. A resolution method for quantified modal logics of knowledge and belief. In J. Y. Halpern, editor, *Proceedings of the 1986 Conference on Theoretical Aspects of Reasoning About Knowledge*, pages 309–324. Morgan Kaufmann Publishers: San Mateo, CA, 1986.

[73] M. R. Genesereth and N. Nilsson. *Logical Foundations of Artificial Intelligence*. Morgan Kaufmann Publishers: San Mateo, CA, 1987.

[74] M. Georgeff, B. Pell, M. Pollack, M. Tambe, and M. Wooldridge. The belief-desire-intention model of agency. In J. P. Müller, M. P. Singh, and A. S. Rao, editors, *Intelligent Agents V (LNAI Volume 1555)*, pages 1–10. Springer-Verlag: Berlin, Germany, 1999.

[75] M. P. Georgeff. Communication and interaction in multi-agent planning. In *Proceedings of the Third National Conference on Artificial Intelligence (AAAI-83)*, Washington, D.C., 1983.

[76] M. P. Georgeff. A theory of action for multi-agent planning. In *Proceedings of the Fourth National Conference on Artificial Intelligence (AAAI-84)*, Austin, TX, 1984.

[77] M. P. Georgeff and F. F. Ingrand. Decision-making in an embedded reasoning system. In *Proceedings of the Eleventh International Joint Conference on Artificial Intelligence (IJCAI-89)*, pages 972–978, Detroit, MI, 1989.

[78] M. P. Georgeff and A. L. Lansky. Reactive reasoning and planning. In *Proceedings of the Sixth National Conference on Artificial Intelligence (AAAI-87)*, pages 677–682, Seattle, WA, 1987.

[79] M. P. Georgeff and A. S. Rao. The semantics of intention maintenance for rational agents. In *Proceedings of the Fourteenth International Joint Conference on Artificial Intelligence (IJCAI-95)*, pages 704–710, Montréal, Québec, Canada, August 1995.

[80] M. P. Georgeff and A. S. Rao. A profile of the Australian AI Institute. *IEEE Expert*, 11(6):89–92, December 1996.

[81] R. Goldblatt. *Logics of Time and Computation (CSLI Lecture Notes Number 7)*. Center for the Study of Language and Information, Ventura Hall, Stanford, CA 94305, 1987. (Distributed by Chicago University Press).

[82] G. D. Gough. Decision procedures for temporal logic. Master's thesis, Department of Computer Science, Manchester University, Oxford Rd., Manchester M13 9PL, UK, October 1984.

[83] M. Greaves and J. Bradshaw, editors. *Specifying and Implementing Conversation Policies — Proceedings of the Autonomous Agents 2000 Workshop*. Seattle, WA, May 1999.

[84] B. J. Grosz and S. Kraus. Collaborative plans for complex group action. *Artificial Intelligence*, 86(2):269–357, 1996.

[85] B. J. Grosz and S. Kraus. The evolution of SharedPlans. In M. Wooldridge and A. Rao, editors, *Foundations of Rational Agency*, pages 227–262. Kluwer Academic Publishers: Boston, MA, 1999.

[86] A. Haddadi. Towards a pragmatic theory of interactions. In *Proceedings of the First International Conference on Multi-Agent Systems (ICMAS-95)*, pages 133–139, San Francisco, CA, June 1995.

[87] A. Haddadi. *Communication and Cooperation in Agent Systems (LNAI Volume 1056)*. Springer-Verlag: Berlin, Germany, 1996.

[88] J. Y. Halpern. Using reasoning about knowledge to analyze distributed systems. *Annual Review of Computer Science*, 2:37–68, 1987.

[89] J. Y. Halpern. Knowledge and common knowledge in a distributed environment. *Journal of the ACM*, 37(3), 1990.

[90] J. Y. Halpern and Y. Moses. A guide to completeness and complexity for modal logics of knowledge and belief. *Artificial Intelligence*, 54:319–379, 1992.

[91] J. Y. Halpern and M. Y. Vardi. The complexity of reasoning about knowledge and time. I. Lower bounds. *Journal of Computer and System Sciences*, 38:195–237, 1989.

[92] J. Y. Halpern and M. Y. Vardi. Model checking versus theorem proving: A manifesto. In V. Lifschitz, editor, *AI and Mathematical Theory of Computation — Papers in Honor of John McCarthy*, pages 151–176. The Academic Press: London, England, 1991.

[93] D. Harel. Dynamic logic. In D. Gabbay and F. Guenther, editors, *Handbook of Philosophical Logic Volume II — Extensions of Classical Logic*, pages 497–604. D. Reidel Publishing Company: Dordrecht, The Netherlands, 1984. (Synthese library Volume 164).

[94] K. V. Hindriks, F. S. de Boer, W. van der Hoek, and J.-J. Ch. Meyer. Formal semantics for an abstract agent programming language. In M. P. Singh, A. Rao, and M. J. Wooldridge, editors, *Intelligent Agents IV (LNAI Volume 1365)*, pages 215–230. Springer-Verlag: Berlin, Germany, 1998.

[95] K. V. Hindriks, F. S. de Boer, W. van der Hoek, and J.-J. Ch. Meyer. Control structures of rule-based agent languages. In J. P. Müller, M. P. Singh, and A. S. Rao, editors, *Intelligent Agents V (LNAI Volume 1555)*. Springer-Verlag: Berlin, Germany, 1999.

[96] J. Hintikka. *Knowledge and Belief*. Cornell University Press: Ithaca, NY, 1962.

[97] C. A. R. Hoare. An axiomatic basis for computer programming. *Communications of the ACM*, 12(10):576–583, 1969.

[98] C. A. R. Hoare. Communicating sequential processes. *Communications of the ACM*, 21:666–677, 1978.

[99] W. van der Hoek, B. van Linder, and J.-J. Ch. Meyer. An integrated modal approach to rational agents. In M. Wooldridge and A. Rao, editors, *Foundations of Rational Agency*, pages 133–168. Kluwer Academic Publishers: Boston, MA, 1999.

[100] M. Huber. JAM: A BDI-theoretic mobile agent architecture. In *Proceedings of the Third International Conference on Autonomous Agents (Agents 99)*, pages 236–243, Seattle, WA, 1999.

[101] G. E. Hughes and M. J. Cresswell. *Introduction to Modal Logic*. Methuen and Co., Ltd., 1968.

[102] M. Huhns and M. P. Singh, editors. *Readings in Agents*. Morgan Kaufmann Publishers: San Mateo, CA, 1998.

[103] D. J. Israel. The role(s) of logic in artificial intelligence. In D. M. Gabbay, C. J. Hogger, and J. A. Robinson, editors, *Handbook of Logic in Artificial Intelligence and Logic Programming*, pages 1–29. Oxford University Press: Oxford, England, 1993.

[104] N. R. Jennings. On being responsible. In E. Werner and Y. Demazeau, editors, *Decentralized AI 3 — Proceedings of the Third European Workshop on Modelling Autonomous Agents in a Multi-Agent World (MAAMAW-91)*, pages 93–102. Elsevier Science Publishers B.V.: Amsterdam, The Netherlands, 1992.

[105] N. R. Jennings. Commitments and conventions: The foundation of coordination in multi-agent systems. *The Knowledge Engineering Review*, 8(3):223–250, 1993.

[106] N. R. Jennings. Controlling cooperative problem solving in industrial multi-agent systems using joint intentions. *Artificial Intelligence*, 74(2), 1995.

[107] N. R. Jennings. Agent-based computing: Promise and perils. In *Proceedings of the Sixteenth International Joint Conference on Artificial Intelligence (IJCAI-99)*, pages 1429–1436, Stockholm, Sweden, 1999.

[108] N. R. Jennings, K. Sycara, and M. Wooldridge. A roadmap of agent research and development. *Autonomous Agents and Multi-Agent Systems*, 1(1):7–38, 1998.

[109] N. R. Jennings and M. Wooldridge, editors. *Agent Technology: Foundations, Applications and Markets*. Springer-Verlag: Berlin, Germany, 1998.

[110] C. B. Jones. *Systematic Software Development using VDM (second edition)*. Prentice Hall, 1990.

[111] C. G. Jung. Emergent mental attitudes in layered agents. In J. P. Müller, M. P. Singh, and A. S. Rao, editors, *Intelligent Agents V (LNAI Volume 1555)*. Springer-Verlag: Berlin, Germany, 1999.

[112] L. P. Kaelbling. An architecture for intelligent reactive systems. In M. P. Georgeff and A. L. Lansky, editors, *Reasoning About Actions & Plans — Proceedings of the 1986 Workshop*, pages 395–410. Morgan Kaufmann Publishers: San Mateo, CA, 1986.

[113] L. P. Kaelbling. *Learning in Embedded Systems*. The MIT Press: Cambridge, MA, 1993.

[114] L. P. Kaelbling and S. J. Rosenschein. Action and planning in embedded agents. In P. Maes, editor, *Designing Autonomous Agents*, pages 35–48. The MIT Press: Cambridge, MA, 1990.

[115] J. A. W. Kamp. *Tense Logic and the Theory of Linear Order*. PhD thesis, University of California, 1968.

[116] D. Kinny and M. Georgeff. Commitment and effectiveness of situated agents. In *Proceedings of the Twelfth International Joint Conference on Artificial Intelligence (IJCAI-91)*, pages 82–88, Sydney, Australia, 1991.

[117] D. Kinny, M. Georgeff, and A. Rao. A methodology and modelling technique for systems of BDI agents. In W. Van de Velde and J. W. Perram, editors, *Agents Breaking Away: Proceedings of the Seventh European Workshop on Modelling Autonomous Agents in a Multi-Agent World, (LNAI Volume 1038)*, pages 56–71. Springer-Verlag: Berlin, Germany, 1996.

[118] D. Kinny, M. Ljungberg, A. S. Rao, E. Sonenberg, G. Tidhar, and E. Werner. Planned team activity. In C. Castelfranchi and E. Werner, editors, *Artificial Social Systems — Selected Papers from the Fourth European Workshop on Modelling Autonomous Agents in a Multi-Agent World, MAAMAW-92 (LNAI Volume 830)*, pages 226–256. Springer-Verlag: Berlin, Germany, 1992.

[119] K. Konolige. A first-order formalization of knowledge and action for a multi-agent planning system. In J. E. Hayes, D. Michie, and Y. Pao, editors, *Machine Intelligence 10*, pages 41–72. Ellis Horwood: Chichester, England, 1982.

[120] K. Konolige. *A Deduction Model of Belief.* Pitman Publishing: London and Morgan Kaufmann: San Mateo, CA, 1986.

[121] K. Konolige. Hierarchic autoepistemic theories for nonmonotonic reasoning: Preliminary report. In M. Reinfrank, J. de Kleer, M. L. Ginsberg, and E. Sandewall, editors, *Nonmonotonic Reasoning — Proceedings of the Second International Workshop (LNAI Volume 346)*, pages 42–59. Springer-Verlag: Berlin, Germany, 1988.

[122] D. Kozen and J. Tiuryn. Logics of programs. In J. van Leeuwen, editor, *Handbook of Theoretical Computer Science Volume B: Formal Models and Semantics*, pages 789–840. Elsevier Science Publishers B.V.: Amsterdam, The Netherlands, 1990.

[123] S. Kraus. Negotiation and cooperation in multi-agent environments. *Artificial Intelligence*, 94(1-2):79–98, July 1997.

[124] S. Kraus, M. Nirke, and K. Sycara. Reaching agreements through argumentation: A logical model. In *Proceedings of the Twelfth International Workshop on Distributed Artificial Intelligence (IWDAI-93)*, pages 233–247, Hidden Valley, PA, May 1993.

[125] S. Kraus, K. Sycara, and A. Evenchik. Reaching agreements through argumentation: a logical model and implementation. *Artificial Intelligence*, 104:1–69, 1998.

[126] S. Kripke. Semantical analysis of modal logic. *Zeitschrift für Mathematische Logik und Grundlagen der Mathematik*, 9:67–96, 1963.

[127] Y. Labrou and T. Finin. Semantics and conversations for an agent communication language. In *Proceedings of the Fifteenth International Joint Conference on Artificial Intelligence (IJCAI-97)*, pages 584–591, Nagoya, Japan, 1997.

[128] Y. Labrou and T. Finin. Agent communication languages: The current landscape. *IEEE Intelligent Systems*, 14(2):45–52, 1999.

[129] L. Lamport. Sometimes is sometimes not never — but not always. In *Proceedings of the Seventh ACM Symposium on the Principles of Programming Languages (POPL)*, 1980.

[130] Y. Lésperance, H. J. Levesque, F. Lin, D. Marcu, R. Reiter, and R. B. Scherl. Foundations of a logical approach to agent programming. In M. Wooldridge, J. P. Müller, and M. Tambe, editors, *Intelligent Agents II (LNAI Volume 1037)*, pages 331–346. Springer-Verlag: Berlin, Germany, 1996.

[131] H. Levesque, R. Reiter, Y. Lespérance, F. Lin, and R. Scherl. Golog: A logic programming language for dynamic domains. *Journal of Logic Programming*, 31:59–84, 1996.

[132] H. J. Levesque. A logic of implicit and explicit belief. In *Proceedings of the Fourth National Conference on Artificial Intelligence (AAAI-84)*, pages 198–202, Austin, TX, 1984.

[133] H. J. Levesque, P. R. Cohen, and J. H. T. Nunes. On acting together. In *Proceedings of the Eighth National Conference on Artificial Intelligence (AAAI-90)*, pages 94–99, Boston, MA, 1990.

[134] O. Lichtenstein and A. Pnueli. Checking that finite state concurrent programs satisfy their linear specification. In *Proceedings of the Eleventh ACM Symposium on the Principles of Programming Languages*, pages 97–107, 1984.

[135] O. Lichtenstein and A. Pnueli. Propositional temporal logics: Decidability and completeness. *Logic Journal of the IGPL*, 8(1):55–85, 2000.

[136] V. Lifschitz. On the semantics of STRIPS. In M. P. Georgeff and A. L. Lansky, editors, *Reasoning About Actions & Plans — Proceedings of the 1986 Workshop*, pages 1–10. Morgan Kaufmann Publishers: San Mateo, CA, 1986.

[137] B. van Linder, W. van der Hoek, and J.-J. Ch. Meyer. How to motivate your agents. In M. Wooldridge, J. P. Müller, and M. Tambe, editors, *Intelligent Agents II (LNAI Volume 1037)*, pages 17–32. Springer-Verlag: Berlin, Germany, 1996.

[138] M. Ljunberg and A. Lucas. The OASIS air traffic management system. In *Proceedings of the Second Pacific Rim International Conference on AI (PRICAI-92)*, Seoul, Korea, 1992.

[139] A. Lomuscio. *Knowledge Sharing among Ideal Agents*. PhD thesis, School of Computer Science, University of Birmingham, Birmingham, UK, June 1999.

[140] A. Lomuscio and M. Ryan. A spectrum of modes of knowledge sharing between agents. In N.R. Jennings and Y. Lespérance, editors, *Intelligent Agents VI — Proceedings of the Sixth International Workshop on Agent Theories, Architectures, and Languages (ATAL-99)*, Lecture Notes in Artificial Intelligence. Springer-Verlag, Berlin, 2000.

[141] M. Luck, N. Griffiths, and M. d'Inverno. From agent theory to agent construction: A case study. In J. P. Müller, M. Wooldridge, and N. R. Jennings, editors, *Intelligent Agents III (LNAI Volume 1193)*, pages 49–64. Springer-Verlag: Berlin, Germany, 1997.

[142] P. Maes. Agents that reduce work and information overload. *Communications of the ACM*, 37(7):31–40, July 1994.

[143] Z. Manna and A. Pnueli. Verification of concurrent programs: The temporal framework. In R. S. Boyer and J. S. Moore, editors, *The Correctness Problem in Computer Science*, pages 215–273. The Academic Press: London, England, 1981.

[144] Z. Manna and A. Pnueli. *The Temporal Logic of Reactive and Concurrent Systems*. Springer-Verlag: Berlin, Germany, 1992.

[145] Z. Manna and A. Pnueli. *Temporal Verification of Reactive Systems — Safety*. Springer-Verlag: Berlin, Germany, 1995.

[146] Z. Manna and P. Wolper. Synthesis of communicating processes from temporal logic specifications. *ACM Transactions on Programming Languages and Systems*, 6(1):68–93, January 1984.

[147] J. Mayfield, Y. Labrou, and T. Finin. Evaluating KQML as an agent communication language. In M. Wooldridge, J. P. Müller, and M. Tambe, editors, *Intelligent Agents II (LNAI Volume 1037)*, pages 347–360. Springer-Verlag: Berlin, Germany, 1996.

[148] J. McCarthy. Ascribing mental qualities to machines. Technical report, Stanford University AI Lab., Stanford, CA 94305, 1978.

[149] J. McCarthy. *Formalization of common sense: papers by John McCarthy*. Ablex Publishing Corp., 1990.

[150] J. McCarthy. Modality, Si! Modal logic, No! *Studia Logica*, 59:29–32, 1997.

[151] J. McCarthy and P. J. Hayes. Some philosophical problems from the standpoint of artificial intelligence. In B. Meltzer and D. Michie, editors, *Machine Intelligence 4*. Edinburgh University Press, 1969.

[152] J.-J. Ch. Meyer and W. van der Hoek. *Epistemic Logic for AI and Computer Science*. Cambridge University Press: Cambridge, England, 1995.

[153] J.-J. Ch. Meyer, W. van der Hoek, and B. van Linder. A logical approach to the dynamics of commitments. *Artificial Intelligence*, 113:1–40, 1999.

[154] R. Milner. *Communication and Concurrency*. Prentice Hall, 1989.

[155] R. Montague. Syntactical treatments of modality, with corollaries on reflexion principles and finite axiomatizations. *Acta Philosophica Fennica*, 16:153–167, 1963.

[156] R. C. Moore. Reasoning about knowledge and action. In *Proceedings of the Fifth International Joint Conference on Artificial Intelligence (IJCAI-77)*, Cambridge, MA, 1977.

[157] R. C. Moore. A formal theory of knowledge and action. In J. F. Allen, J. Hendler, and A. Tate, editors, *Readings in Planning*, pages 480–519. Morgan Kaufmann Publishers: San Mateo, CA, 1990.

[158] M. Móra, J. G. Lopes, R. Viccari, and H. Coelho. BDI models and systems: reducing the gap. In J. P. Müller, M. P. Singh, and A. S. Rao, editors, *Intelligent Agents V (LNAI Volume 1555)*. Springer-Verlag: Berlin, Germany, 1999.

[159] C. Morgan. *Programming from Specifications (second edition)*. Prentice Hall International: Hemel Hempstead, England, 1994.

[160] L. Morgenstern. A first-order theory of planning, knowledge, and action. In J. Y. Halpern, editor, *Proceedings of the 1986 Conference on Theoretical Aspects of Reasoning About Knowledge*, pages 99–114. Morgan Kaufmann Publishers: San Mateo, CA, 1986.

[161] L. Morgenstern. Knowledge preconditions for actions and plans. In *Proceedings of the Tenth International Joint Conference on Artificial Intelligence (IJCAI-87)*, pages 867–874, Milan, Italy, 1987.

[162] J. P. Müller. *The Design of Intelligent Agents (LNAI Volume 1177)*. Springer-Verlag: Berlin, Germany, 1997.

[163] J. P. Müller, M. Pischel, and M. Thiel. Modelling reactive behaviour in vertically layered agent architectures. In M. Wooldridge and N. R. Jennings, editors, *Intelligent Agents: Theories, Architectures, and Languages (LNAI Volume 890)*, pages 261–276. Springer-Verlag: Berlin, Germany, January 1995.

[164] J. P. Müller, M. Wooldridge, and N. R. Jennings, editors. *Intelligent Agents III (LNAI Volume 1193)*. Springer-Verlag: Berlin, Germany, 1997.

[165] N. Muscettola, P. Pandurang Nayak, B. Pell, and B. C. Williams. Remote agents: To boldly go where no AI system has gone before. *Artificial Intelligence*, 103:5–47, 1998.

[166] A. Newell. The knowledge level. *Artificial Intelligence*, 18(1):87–127, 1982.

[167] N. J. Nilsson. Towards agent programs with circuit semantics. Technical Report STAN–CS–92–1412, Computer Science Department, Stanford University, Stanford, CA 94305, January 1992.

[168] P. Noriega and C. Sierra, editors. *Agent Mediated Electronic Commerce (LNAI Volume 1571)*. Springer-Verlag: Berlin, Germany, 1999.

[169] S. Parsons, C. A. Sierra, and N. R. Jennings. Agents that reason and negotiate by arguing. *Journal of Logic and Computation*, 8(3):261–292, 1998.

[170] R. S. Patil, R. E. Fikes, P. F. Patel-Schneider, D. McKay, T. Finin, T. Gruber, and R. Neches. The DARPA knowledge sharing effort: Progress report. In C. Rich, W. Swartout, and B. Nebel, editors, *Proceedings of Knowledge Representation and Reasoning (KR&R-92)*, pages 777–788, 1992.

[171] D. Perlis. Languages with self reference I: Foundations. *Artificial Intelligence*, 25:301–322, 1985.

[172] D. Perlis. Languages with self reference II: Knowledge, belief, and modality. *Artificial Intelligence*, 34:179–212, 1988.

[173] D. Perlis. Meta in logic. In P. Maes and D. Nardi, editors, *Meta-Level Architectures and Reflection*, pages 37–49. Elsevier Science Publishers B.V.: Amsterdam, The Netherlands, 1988.

[174] C. R. Perrault. An application of default logic to speech acts theory. In P. R. Cohen, J. Morgan, and M. E. Pollack, editors, *Intentions in Communication*, pages 161–186. The MIT Press: Cambridge, MA, 1990.

[175] J. Pitt and E. H. Mamdani. A protocol-based semantics for an agent communication language. In *Proceedings of the Sixteenth International Joint Conference on Artificial Intelligence (IJCAI-99)*, Stockholm, Sweden, August 1999.

[176] A. Pnueli. The temporal logic of programs. In *Proceedings of the Eighteenth IEEE Symposium on the Foundations of Computer Science*, pages 46–57, 1977.

[177] A. Pnueli. Specification and development of reactive systems. In *Information Processing 86*. Elsevier Science Publishers B.V.: Amsterdam, The Netherlands, 1986.

[178] A. Pnueli and R. Rosner. On the synthesis of a reactive module. In *Proceedings of the Sixteenth ACM Symposium on the Principles of Programming Languages (POPL)*, pages 179–190, January 1989.

[179] M. E. Pollack. Plans as complex mental attitudes. In P. R. Cohen, J. Morgan, and M. E. Pollack, editors, *Intentions in Communication*, pages 77–104. The MIT Press: Cambridge, MA, 1990.

[180] M. E. Pollack. The uses of plans. *Artificial Intelligence*, 57(1):43–68, September 1992.

[181] R. Power. Mutual intention. *Journal for the Theory of Social Behaviour*, 14:85–102, March 1984.

[182] A. Prior. *Past, Present and Future*. Oxford University Press: Oxford, England, 1967.

[183] A. S. Rao. AgentSpeak(L): BDI agents speak out in a logical computable language. In W. Van de Velde and J. W. Perram, editors, *Agents Breaking Away: Proceedings of the Seventh European Workshop on Modelling Autonomous Agents in a Multi-Agent World, (LNAI Volume 1038)*, pages 42–55. Springer-Verlag: Berlin, Germany, 1996.

[184] A. S. Rao. Decision procedures for propositional linear-time Belief-Desire-Intention logics. In M. Wooldridge, J. P. Müller, and M. Tambe, editors, *Intelligent Agents II (LNAI Volume 1037)*, pages 33–48. Springer-Verlag: Berlin, Germany, 1996.

[185] A. S. Rao and M. Georgeff. Decision procedures for BDI logics. *Journal of Logic and Computation*, 8(3):293–344, 1998.

[186] A. S. Rao and M. P. Georgeff. Asymmetry thesis and side-effect problems in linear time and branching time intention logics. In *Proceedings of the Twelfth International Joint Conference on Artificial Intelligence (IJCAI-91)*, pages 498–504, Sydney, Australia, 1991.

[187] A. S. Rao and M. P. Georgeff. Modeling rational agents within a BDI-architecture. In R. Fikes and E. Sandewall, editors, *Proceedings of Knowledge Representation and Reasoning (KR&R-91)*, pages 473–484. Morgan Kaufmann Publishers: San Mateo, CA, April 1991.

[188] A. S. Rao and M. P. Georgeff. An abstract architecture for rational agents. In C. Rich, W. Swartout, and B. Nebel, editors, *Proceedings of Knowledge Representation and Reasoning (KR&R-92)*, pages 439–449, 1992.

[189] A. S. Rao and M. P. Georgeff. A model-theoretic approach to the verification of situated reasoning systems. In *Proceedings of the Thirteenth International Joint Conference on Artificial Intelligence (IJCAI-93)*, pages 318–324, Chambéry, France, 1993.

[190] A. S. Rao, M. P. Georgeff, and E. A. Sonenberg. Social plans: A preliminary report. In E. Werner and Y. Demazeau, editors, *Decentralized AI 3 — Proceedings of the Third European Workshop on Modelling Autonomous Agents in a Multi-Agent World (MAAMAW-91)*, pages 57–76. Elsevier Science Publishers B.V.: Amsterdam, The Netherlands, 1992.

[191] H. Reichgelt. A comparison of first-order and modal logics of time. In P. Jackson, H. Reichgelt, and F. van Harmelen, editors, *Logic Based Knowledge Representation*, pages 143–176. The MIT Press: Cambridge, MA, 1989.

[192] H. Reichgelt. Logics for reasoning about knowledge and belief. *The Knowledge Engineering Review*, 4(2):119–139, 1989.

[193] R. Reiter. A logic for default reasoning. *Artificial Intelligence*, 13:81–132, 1980.

[194] J. S. Rosenschein. Synchronisation of multi-agent plans. In *Proceedings of the Second National Conference on Artificial Intelligence (AAAI-82)*, Pittsburgh, PA, 1982.

[195] J. S. Rosenschein and G. Zlotkin. *Rules of Encounter: Designing Conventions for Automated Negotiation among Computers*. The MIT Press: Cambridge, MA, 1994.

[196] S. Rosenschein and L. P. Kaelbling. The synthesis of digital machines with provable epistemic properties. In J. Y. Halpern, editor, *Proceedings of the 1986 Conference on Theoretical Aspects of Reasoning About Knowledge*, pages 83–98. Morgan Kaufmann Publishers: San Mateo, CA, 1986.

[197] S. J. Rosenschein and L. P. Kaelbling. A situated view of representation and control. In P. E. Agre and S. J. Rosenschein, editors, *Computational Theories of Interaction and Agency*, pages 515–540. The MIT Press: Cambridge, MA, 1996.

[198] S. Russell and P. Norvig. *Artificial Intelligence: A Modern Approach*. Prentice-Hall, 1995.

[199] T. Sandholm. Distributed rational decision making. In G. Weiß, editor, *Multiagent Systems*, pages 201–258. The MIT Press: Cambridge, MA, 1999.

[200] K. Schild. On the relationship between BDI logics and standard logics of concurrency. In J. P. Müller, M. P. Singh, and A. S. Rao, editors, *Intelligent Agents V (LNAI Volume 1555)*. Springer-Verlag: Berlin, Germany, 1999.

[201] M. J. Schoppers. Universal plans for reactive robots in unpredictable environments. In *Proceedings of the Tenth International Joint Conference on Artificial Intelligence (IJCAI-87)*, pages 1039–1046, Milan, Italy, 1987.

[202] J. R. Searle. *Speech Acts: An Essay in the Philosophy of Language*. Cambridge University Press: Cambridge, England, 1969.

[203] J. R. Searle. Collective intentions and actions. In P. R. Cohen, J. Morgan, and M. E. Pollack, editors, *Intentions in Communication*, pages 401–416. The MIT Press: Cambridge, MA, 1990.

[204] N. Seel. *Agent Theories and Architectures*. PhD thesis, Surrey University, Guildford, UK, 1989.

[205] Y. Shoham. Agent-oriented programming. Technical Report STAN–CS–1335–90, Computer Science Department, Stanford University, Stanford, CA 94305, 1990.

[206] Y. Shoham. Agent-oriented programming. *Artificial Intelligence*, 60(1):51–92, 1993.

[207] Carles Sierra, Nick R. Jennings, Pablo Noriega, and Simon Parsons. A framework for argumentation-based negotiation. In M. P. Singh, A. Rao, and M. J. Wooldridge, editors, *Intelligent Agents IV (LNAI Volume 1365)*, pages 177–192. Springer-Verlag: Berlin, Germany, 1998.

[208] H. A. Simon. *The Sciences of the Artificial (second edition)*. The MIT Press: Cambridge, MA, 1981.

[209] M. Singh. Agent communication languages: Rethinking the principles. *IEEE Computer*, pages 40–47, December 1998.

[210] M. P. Singh. Group intentions. In *Proceedings of the Tenth International Workshop on Distributed Artificial Intelligence (IWDAI-90)*, 1990.

[211] M. P. Singh. Towards a theory of situated know-how. In *Proceedings of the Ninth European Conference on Artificial Intelligence (ECAI-90)*, pages 604–609, Stockholm, Sweden, 1990.

[212] M. P. Singh. Group ability and structure. In Y. Demazeau and J.-P. Müller, editors, *Decentralized AI 2 — Proceedings of the Second European Workshop on Modelling Autonomous Agents in a Multi-Agent World (MAAMAW-90)*, pages 127–146. Elsevier Science Publishers B.V.: Amsterdam, The Netherlands, 1991.

[213] M. P. Singh. Social and psychological commitments in multiagent systems. In *AAAI Fall Symposium on Knowledge and Action at Social and Organizational Levels*, 1991.

[214] M. P. Singh. Towards a formal theory of communication for multi-agent systems. In *Proceedings of the Twelfth International Joint Conference on Artificial Intelligence (IJCAI-91)*, pages 69–74, Sydney, Australia, 1991.

[215] M. P. Singh. A semantics for speech acts. *Annals of Mathematics and Artificial Intelligence*, 8(I-II):47–71, 1993.

[216] M. P. Singh. *Multiagent Systems: A Theoretical Framework for Intentions, Know-How, and Communications (LNAI Volume 799)*. Springer-Verlag: Berlin, Germany, 1994.

[217] M. P. Singh. The intentions of teams: Team structure, endodeixis, and exodeixis. In *Proceedings of the Thirteenth European Conference on Artificial Intelligence (ECAI-98)*, pages 303–307, Brighton, United Kingdom, 1998.

[218] M. P. Singh and N. M. Asher. Towards a formal theory of intentions. In J. van Eijck, editor, *Logics in AI — Proceedings of the European Workshop JELIA-90 (LNAI Volume 478)*, pages 472–486. Springer-Verlag: Berlin, Germany, 1991.

[219] A. Sistla. Theoretical issues in the design and verification of distributed systems. Technical Report CMU-CS-83-146, School of Computer Science, Carnegie-Mellon University, Pittsburgh, PA, 1983.

[220] A. P. Sistla and E. M. Clarke. The complexity of propositional linear temporal logics. *Journal of the ACM*, 32(3):733–749, 1985.

[221] A. P. Sistla, E. M. Clarke, N. Francez, and A. R. Meyer. Can message buffers be axiomatized in temporal logic? *Information and Control*, 63(1/2):88–112, 1985.

[222] R. G. Smith. *A Framework for Distributed Problem Solving*. UMI Research Press, 1980.

[223] R. M. Smullyan. *First-Order Logic*. Springer-Verlag: Berlin, Germany, 1968.

[224] M. Spivey. *The Z Notation (second edition)*. Prentice Hall International: Hemel Hempstead, England, 1992.

[225] L. Steels. Cooperation between distributed agents through self organization. In Y. Demazeau and J.-P. Müller, editors, *Decentralized AI — Proceedings of the First European Workshop on Modelling Autonomous Agents in a Multi-Agent World (MAAMAW-89)*, pages 175–196. Elsevier Science Publishers B.V.: Amsterdam, The Netherlands, 1990.

[226] S. P. Stich. *From Folk Psychology to Cognitive Science*. The MIT Press: Cambridge, MA, 1983.

[227] C. Stirling. Completeness results for full branching time logic. In *REX School-Workshop on Linear Time, Branching Time, and Partial Order in Logics and Models for Concurrency*, Noordwijkerhout, Netherlands, 1988.

[228] K. P. Sycara. Multiagent compromise via negotiation. In L. Gasser and M. Huhns, editors, *Distributed Artificial Intelligence Volume II*, pages 119–138. Pitman Publishing: London and Morgan Kaufmann: San Mateo, CA, 1989.

[229] R. Thomason. A note on syntactical treatments of modality. *Synthese*, 44:391–395, 1980.

[230] R. Tuomela and K. Miller. We-intentions. *Philosophical Studies*, 53:367–389, 1988.

[231] R. Turner. *Truth and Modality for Knowledge Representation*. Pitman Publishing: London, 1990.

[232] M. Y. Vardi and P. Wolper. Reasoning about infinite computations. *Information and Computation*, 115(1):1–37, 1994.

[233] G. Weiß, editor. *Multi-Agent Systems*. The MIT Press: Cambridge, MA, 1999.

[234] E. Werner. What can agents do together: A semantics of co-operative ability. In *Proceedings of the Ninth European Conference on Artificial Intelligence (ECAI-90)*, pages 694–701, Stockholm, Sweden, 1990.

[235] P. Wolper. Temporal logic can be more expressive. *Information and Control*, 56, 1983.

[236] P. Wolper. The tableau method for temporal logic: An overview. *Logique et Analyse*, 110–111, 1985.

[237] M. Wooldridge. *The Logical Modelling of Computational Multi-Agent Systems*. PhD thesis, Department of Computation, UMIST, Manchester, UK, October 1992.

[238] M. Wooldridge. This is MYWORLD: The logic of an agent-oriented testbed for DAI. In M. Wooldridge and N. R. Jennings, editors, *Intelligent Agents: Theories, Architectures, and Languages (LNAI Volume 890)*, pages 160–178. Springer-Verlag: Berlin, Germany, January 1995.

[239] M. Wooldridge. Practical reasoning with procedural knowledge: A logic of BDI agents with know-how. In D. M. Gabbay and H.-J. Ohlbach, editors, *Practical Reasoning — Proceedings of the International Conference on Formal and Applied Practical Reasoning, FAPR-96 (LNAI Volume 1085)*, pages 663–678. Springer-Verlag: Berlin, Germany, June 1996.

[240] M. Wooldridge. Agent-based software engineering. *IEE Proceedings on Software Engineering*, 144(1):26–37, February 1997.

[241] M. Wooldridge. Verifiable semantics for agent communication languages. In *Proceedings of the Third International Conference on Multi-Agent Systems (ICMAS-98)*, pages 349–365, Paris, France, 1998.

[242] M. Wooldridge. Intelligent agents. In G. Weiß, editor, *Multiagent Systems*, pages 27–78. The MIT Press: Cambridge, MA, 1999.

[243] M. Wooldridge. Verifying that agents implement a communication language. In *Proceedings of the Sixteenth National Conference on Artificial Intelligence (AAAI-99)*, pages 52–57, Orlando, FL, July 1999.

[244] M. Wooldridge, C. Dixon, and M. Fisher. A tableau-based proof method for temporal logics of knowledge and belief. *Journal of Applied Non-Classical Logics*, 8(3):225–258, 1998.

[245] M. Wooldridge and M. Fisher. A first-order branching time logic of multi-agent systems. In *Proceedings of the Tenth European Conference on Artificial Intelligence (ECAI-92)*, pages 234–238, Vienna, Austria, 1992.

[246] M. Wooldridge and M. Fisher. A decision procedure for a temporal belief logic. In D. M. Gabbay and H. J. Ohlbach, editors, *Temporal Logic — Proceedings of the First International Conference (LNAI Volume 827)*, pages 317–331. Springer-Verlag: Berlin, Germany, July 1994.

[247] M. Wooldridge and N. R. Jennings. Formalizing the cooperative problem solving process. In *Proceedings of the Thirteenth International Workshop on Distributed Artificial Intelligence (IWDAI-94)*, pages 403–417, Lake Quinalt, WA, July 1994. Reprinted in [102].

[248] M. Wooldridge and N. R. Jennings. Towards a theory of cooperative problem solving. In *Proceedings of the Sixth European Workshop on Modelling Autonomous Agents and Multi-Agent Worlds (MAAMAW-94)*, pages 15–26, August 1994.

[249] M. Wooldridge and N. R. Jennings. Intelligent agents: Theory and practice. *The Knowledge Engineering Review*, 10(2):115–152, 1995.

[250] M. Wooldridge and N. R. Jennings. Cooperative problem solving. *Journal of Logic and Computation*, 9(4):563–594, 1999.

[251] M. Wooldridge and S. D. Parsons. Intention reconsideration reconsidered. In J. P. Müller, M. P. Singh, and A. S. Rao, editors, *Intelligent Agents V (LNAI Volume 1555)*, pages 63–80. Springer-Verlag: Berlin, Germany, 1999.

Index